WAYFARING
STRANGER

Also by Emma John

Following On: A Memoir of Teenage
Obsession and Terrible Cricket

WAYFARING STRANGER

A Musical Journey
in the American South

EMMA JOHN

WEIDENFELD & NICOLSON

First published in Great Britain in 2019 by Weidenfeld & Nicolson
an imprint of The Orion Publishing Group Ltd
Carmelite House, 50 Victoria Embankment
London EC4Y 0DZ

An Hachette UK Company

1 3 5 7 9 10 8 6 4 2

A CIP catalogue record for this book
is available from the British Library.

ISBN (hardback) 978 1 4746 0684 4
ISBN (ebook) 978 1 4746 0686 8

Typeset at The Spartan Press Ltd,
Lymington, Hants

Printed and bound by
CPI Group (UK) Ltd, Croydon, CR0 4YY

www.orionbooks.co.uk

To Kate, Justin
and Isabella

Any good history of bluegrass begins with Bill Monroe.

We'll get to him later.

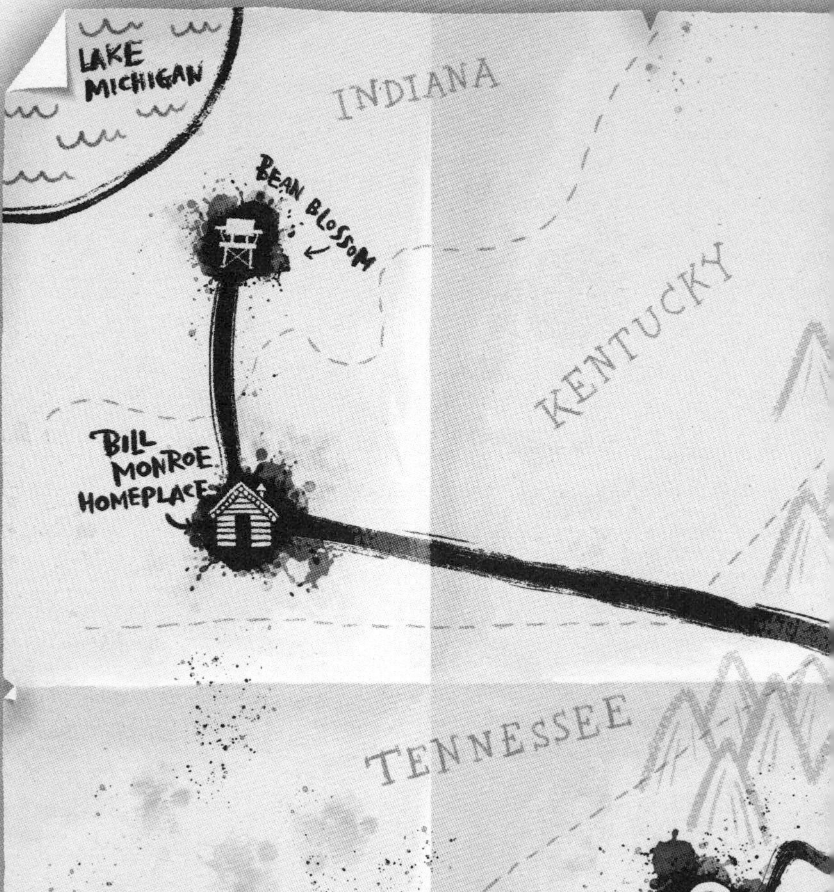
LAKE MICHIGAN
INDIANA
BEAN BLOSSOM
KENTUCKY
BILL MONROE HOMEPLACE
TENNESSEE
ASHEVILLE
NASHVILLE
N
NORTH

WEST VIRGINIA
VIRGINIA
STANLEY BROTHERS HOMEPLACE
RIP
GALAX
WEST JEFFERSON
MT AIRY
BOONE
THOMASVILLE & RALEIGH
HAPPY VALLEY
TAYLORSVILLE
CAROLINA
CHARLOTTE

CHAPTER 1

It wasn't a town so much as a crossroads. A hardware store squatted on the corner, the sole building in sight, pickup trucks collected outside at careless angles, sun a half-hour gone. The only street lighting strayed weakly from its grimy windows; from its timber boards escaped the sound of jaunty string music. Sometimes a voice, too, seeped through the cracks: a simple melody with a keening edge and a lyric about an unfaithful woman. The song pooled onto the pavement, colouring it with nostalgia.

Inside, we sat on folding metal chairs pulled into a rough circle, showing our backs to shelves of weedkiller and bug spray. Tin signs on the walls advertised products from fishing rods to Cherry Coke; at the back, near a bathroom, hung the head of an eight-point buck. There was sawdust on the concrete floor. A nip of engine oil in the air. From the ceiling, slow wooden fans nudged the still summer heat across a dozen balding heads.

I was the only woman in the room, and most of my fellow musicians were well past middle age. But I had long stopped noticing the obvious. Most of the guys who still had hair wore it white or grey; one had his in a military flat-top so sharp he resembled a box hedge. Next to General Flat-Top sat a young boy, apparently his grandson, wearing a camo shirt and khaki shorts and a baseball cap advertising John Deere tractors. Everyone else in the room wore check, or plaid, or flannel.

Our haphazard assembly of instruments produced a thick cloud of sound, from which emerged snatches of tune. The notes themselves seemed to move around our group like a swarm, settling for a short while on a banjo, next buzzing gently in the strings of a mandolin. I gripped the neck of my violin and willed them not to come my way. The music was flighty, cheerful, virtuosic; a thin, spectacled bassist kept the pace high. There were no chord sheets or pages of lyrics; everyone here knew the song, or at least knew how to follow along. Everyone except me.

I married me a wife, she gave me trouble all my life
Left me out in the cold rain and snow...

At the end of each chorus, the singer's voice receded and the tune passed to the instrumentalists, who bounced it between them through a combination of inscrutable glances and flat-out telepathy. When it was their turn to solo, each player - or picker, as they preferred to call themselves - struck up a blaze of outrageous bravado, fingers scampering up and down their fretboards, strings shooting out semiquavers like a semi-automatic.

Bluegrass music was the sound of an America of long ago: of railroads and prison gangs, of church revival and illegal liquor. Once you'd heard it, and loved it, you could never mistake it for anything else. Country music sounded slow, languid, doleful by comparison; folk seemed simplistic. Only jazz could compare to its orgy of invention, and to be played well, it had to be touched by genius. This was some of the best I'd ever witnessed.

I've done all I can do, to try and get along with you
And I ain't gonna be treated this a way

The problem was, I couldn't really watch it. Because if I looked up at the wrong moment, or made the mistake of smiling in wonder, they might misunderstand my intention, and the tune would suddenly be thrown to me. And I knew exactly what would happen next. My fingers would stab blindly at the far end of my fiddle. The bow in my right hand would shuffle timidly and out of time. And into the complex synchronicity and melodic flow of this fast-paced musical machine, I would hurl a random assortment of junk. If I was lucky, the machine would simply crush it under its tracks; if not, I would bring everyone to a screeching, shuddering halt.

I had hoped to watch from a distance, to learn simply by listening. I'd stood near the door clutching my violin case to my chest like a riot shield, until an ancient figure in a Stetson hat, who presided over the session, refused to let me sit out. 'If you're gonna bring a fiddle,' he growled, 'y'all had better play it.'

Embarrassed and terrified, I had taken a seat. As someone who grew up in the prodigiously polite Home Counties of England, my middle-class reserve was trumped by my equally middle-class inclination to never make a fuss, leading to the *very* middle-class mortification at the situation I had got myself in. Sitting in the round left nowhere to hide. Jamming was a pretty democratic process; everyone received their moment to shine.

The only way to avoid disaster, I decided, was to avoid eye contact with everyone in the circle. My techniques included taking regular sips from a water bottle, suddenly catching sight of my shoes (hi, shoes!), and pretending to be so enraptured by the music that I had to play with my eyes closed.

3

We were already an hour into the session, and I had barely looked at a soul.

She came into the room, where she met her final doom
And I ain't gonna be treated this a way

The song ended. A new one kicked off, a tale of a rambling man with two loves: whisky, and the girl he'd left back home. It was a pretty common theme in bluegrass music, where being a man was far preferable to being a woman. Most women in these songs were either patiently waiting for their wandering sweethearts, or getting killed by them.

I'd got used to being the only female in the room. I had taken my violin to jams all over this part of the Appalachian Mountains, where North Carolina met Virginia met Tennessee. The two of us had shown up to sessions in threshing barns and barber's shops, dive bars and strangers' basements. But the music – and the machismo – wasn't getting any less intimidating.

The music hurried on, an antique hybrid blending Celtic and country sounds with blues, jazz, gospel. I joined in the only way I knew how. It was, sadly, impossible to mime with the other players so close by. But there was an alternative, a trick I'd learned years ago, in my first encounter with this music. I'd noticed that when they weren't playing clever fills and trills, bluegrass fiddlers frequently hacked at their strings in a rhythmic fashion, their bows chopping down so hard that the actual notes barely registered, only a wooden, percussive smack. *Mm-chop! Mm-chop!*

It was a good way to look like I was playing along, when all I was doing was beating my poor violin like a drum. Here in the hardware store, I repeated that steady drumbeat. *Mm-chop! Mm-chop!* Occasionally, fuelled by adrenaline, I would try to

4

expand and play a note or two of the tune, but it was usually hopeless. Trying to get involved in the melody was like snatching at a fish in a tank - just when I had grasped the tail-end, it darted on to a different chord and left me floundering.

A large part of the humiliation I felt came from the knowledge that I was not a novice musician. I was actually a good one. Or, more accurately, I had *been* a good one. As a kid, I was the nerd who practised hard and passed music exams, whose evenings disappeared in a timetable of extracurricular lessons and rehearsals. In my late teens I'd been on track for a career in the classical world. I'd performed concertos and led orchestras. But twenty years later, my once-familiar instrument now felt like a lump of useless driftwood in my hands. I could no more jump on board these breakneck rhythms than I could a speeding train.

The banjo player next to me was a mean-looking forty-something. He had a goatee and a black ponytail and tattoos that reached down to his wrists and, every so often, an utterly incongruous grin. When he played, the little metal picks on his right hand would alight on the strings, descending momentarily, then hastening away, like a highly trained fleet of butterflies. The rest of him never moved, and he gazed into the middle distance as if engaged in nothing more taxing than drinking iced tea. My face, meanwhile, was rigid with concentration. At one stage, he leaned over to me and asked, 'Are you OK? You're looking a-skeered.'

I gave him a short smile. He seemed nice enough, but I was wound as tightly as a barracuda and his Zen banjo playing just emphasised the gulf between us. I listened as the men spoke to each other in guttering drawls and idioms I could rarely comprehend. 'He don't give a hoo-hickey!' I heard General Flat-Top say to another player. 'Ain't gonna do nothing but dance and split wood!' 'Yeah,' replied his friend, 'but he holds down bluegrass like a bluetick hound...'

Some of the men wore bib overalls – denim dungarees that signified a daily routine working outside or in their sheds. They all looked at home surrounded by power tools, gardening equipment, rows of apparatus and tins of solvents I couldn't have named if you'd given me a catalogue and a page number. Before I left my job, earlier in the year, I had spent eight hours a day encased in a glass-walled office in central London. The only dexterity required was the mental kind needed to persuade co-workers to perform tasks they didn't feel inclined to. The only manual labour I understood was typing a couple of thousand words to deadline.

Gazing around our makeshift arena, my eyes fell on the one crossover I recognised between our worlds: the tray of doughnuts on a nearby table, readied for breaktime. They sat next to a jug of dun-coloured sweet tea, and a couple of thermos flasks that I knew, without tasting their contents, would contain aggressively nasty coffee. I could also predict the conversation that would go with it, the moment I opened my mouth and people heard my British accent.

The first person to notice it was bound to say:

'Y'all ain't from around here, are you?'

And the second person, making what they believed to be an original joke, and not one I'd heard in countless iterations, would add:

'No, she's from eastern Kentucky!'

Then the room would laugh, and someone would ask me what I was doing out here, in the boondocks, in a county even Southerners struggled to locate on a map. And I would reply that I was here to learn bluegrass. And if I could have found a bookmaker to take a wager on the next words past their lips, I would have beaten the odds every single time. Because the reply was always - *always* - the same.

'Well, I guess you've come to the right place.'

And I had. If I ever wanted to master the sound and speed of this seemingly impossible music, I needed to spend as much time as I could in hardware stores, with men called Frank and Dale and Bobby. I needed to immerse myself in the alien world of bib overalls and shotguns and saying grace before eating snacks. I needed to understand the rural roots of the music, and the social mores of playing it.

But right now, as I sat under an advert for snake repellent, inhaling dust and paint thinner, my foreignness had never seemed more acute. When I'd begun my journey, I had felt like an adventuress; now I felt like a fraud. A committed city girl, a lover of creature comforts and liberal politics, learning songs whose evocation of humble country living meant nothing to me, whose corniness and attitudes to women made my modern sensibilities cringe. Bluegrass music was suffused with its love of home, of mountain mamas and cabins in the woods - a sentimentality I couldn't share, for a place I'd never lived. In a style I couldn't even play.

As the music hustled on and I stumbled behind, catching at its coat-tails, all I felt was the vast distance between me and everything it represented. And I wondered: why did I ever think this was a good idea?

CHAPTER 2

I blamed the woman on the plane.

A few years earlier, I had taken my first ever trip to the American South. The flight to Charlotte, North Carolina, was full and I was trapped in the middle seat. The woman who had the aisle was in her seventies, and so keen to talk that she was starting conversations with her luggage.

You would think that a single woman like me, travelling alone to a place I'd never visited before, might have welcomed the chance for some company. But I'm British. When faced with a shared public space, it is the inclination of my people to keep our heads down and pretend that no one else exists.

The woman in the aisle seat made several attempts to draw me in - remarking on the quality of the in-flight magazine, fussing with her armrest, leaning back and drawing the kind of big sigh that suggested, boy, did she have a tale to tell. I gave her no quarter and stuck in my earphones. Then, half-way through the flight, a steward appeared suddenly with a drinks trolley.

This was such an unexpected show of largesse - this airline charged for luggage, after all - that my brain froze. Unable to name a single soft beverage, I pointed at the can of fizzy pop in front of my chatty neighbour and yelped, 'I'll have what she's having!' It was a breach, and she knew it. Over the course of the next hour I learned a great deal about Diane, her daughter, her grandchildren, and her house on the lake.

Once we'd exhausted Diane's story, she asked why I was heading to Charlotte.

'You going to visit with family there, honey?'

'No,' I said, 'I'm on vacation.'

'Oh,' she replied, doubtfully. 'Do you ... often travel on your own?'

It was, in fact, my first time. Although it was almost a surprise that I hadn't run out of willing travel companions before this. My trips were usually intensive affairs; I exhausted friends and family with my determination to wring a place dry. Restaurant bookings, theatre tickets, walking tours: I liked to know that there would be no wasted moment.

Now a quirk of scheduling at the newspaper I worked for had left me with a considerable accrual of unused holiday. I had no boyfriend, and my friends were all otherwise engaged (at least, that's what they told me). A more balanced human being might have seen this as an opportunity to take time off at home - to enjoy a rest. I didn't even consider the idea.

I had moved to London a decade ago, in my early twenties, and I hadn't taken my foot off the gas since. I loved to be busy. If I wasn't filling my spare time with dinners, shows, social activities and weekend trips, then I honestly couldn't have told you the point of it. A long vacation had to be made the most of. Somewhere abroad. Something to *do*. Something with a bit of purpose.

The bizarre decision I made next, I can only attribute to the sporadically popular folk-rockers Mumford & Sons. Their debut album had been dominating the airwaves for a year. Unless you locked yourself in a soundproof vault and filled your ears with cement, you couldn't avoid their ecstatic anthems, wistful lyrics and wild instrumentals, which reached out of every car radio, store PA and TV advert. At no point prior to this had I ever heard someone claim to enjoy the sound of the banjo. Now there was a band that had had a bestselling record with one.

My relationship with popular music was estranged to non-existent, but Marcus Mumford and his associates were now playing my neural network several times a day – and I didn't hate the sensation. Some people had referred to their style as 'bluegrass', and since their appearance on the scene the word seemed to be dropped all over, like a crumb trail for the musical zeitgeist. I'd only come across it once before – when the Coen brothers' movie *O Brother, Where Art Thou?* had come out, with its highly musical comedy about convicts who become accidental radio stars. But London loves a trend, and soon the city was full of office employees swapping their fixie bikes for ukuleles, and bands that looked like nineteenth-century farmers in their Sunday best.

Many of the groups had a fiddle player somewhere in the background, emerging at intervals to put the rest of the instruments to shame with melodic riffs and jaunty solos. And the strange, Americana-inspired sound intrigued me. I had never heard a violin played like that before: fast and furious, in unpredictable and impenetrable patterns. This wasn't music you could imitate, it was a secret code, its cleverness so complete that, without the key, all efforts were in vain. All the while its playfulness, its cocky swagger, tantalised the listener. Even the most explosive technical fireworks were handled with outrageous nonchalance. I'd never seen a violin player look so *cool*. And it tempted me, for the first time in a long time, to pick up my instrument again.

I didn't tell Diane all this. I didn't explain that I'd made one of the most impulsive travel decisions of my life based on a bizarre British pop trend. I didn't reveal that I would rather fly two thousand miles to resurrect my teenage violin playing than relax quietly with my own thoughts for a couple of weeks. I didn't admit that my destination was based on nothing more than a quick google of the word 'bluegrass', or that I'd picked North Carolina over the other Southern states because it was the one that had voted for Obama.

I just said: 'I'm interested in bluegrass music.'

Diane's eyes lit up.

'*Ah* know someone who plays bluegrass!' she exclaimed. 'Ah'll introduce you! Ah'll call him when we get off the plane!'

And then, as an afterthought: 'Ah haven't talked to him any in *fifteen* years!'

It transpired that this someone, Fred, was a friend of Diane's late husband, who had died a decade and a half previously. She didn't even have Fred's number any more, but the plane had barely hit the tarmac before she was putting in calls to track him down. I thanked Diane for her efforts, and silently wondered how interested *I'd* be if a voice from my past unexpectedly rang to tell me that they'd sat next to someone on a plane. Her lift arrived to pick her up from the airport before she could find a contact for him. We swapped email addresses at the luggage carousel, and I assumed that was the end of it.

A day later, I was sitting on Fred's porch drinking lemonade.

A week later, I was still there.

Fred and his wife, Doris, lived on a suburban street in a small town in the south of the state, not far from the city of Charlotte. Mailboxes stretched languorously down the road and each house nestled comfortably on a large apron-front of immaculately groomed, discreetly watered lawn. Doris, grey-haired and a full head shorter than me, had greeted me at the

11

door like a relative she'd not seen in years. Fred spoke with the formality of the old-fashioned man of business, and wore a collared shirt and capacious beige trousers. He had white hair in a soft side-parting, and deep bifocals that seemed to take up much of his generous face. Eighty-three years old, he had been born the year before the Wall Street Crash.

They had offered me a place to stay, before we'd even met, on the basis of a voicemail Diane had left on their phone. I tried to imagine the same scenario in London. What would an Englishman do if a friend he hadn't heard from in over a decade called him up, said she'd met a tourist on a plane, and could he help? What would *I* do? Send a taut little email, perhaps, offering advice on nearby hotels.

But Southern hospitality had its own rules. And, anyway, Fred didn't turn up a chance to evangelise about bluegrass. He had been a fanatic of the music since his college years, performing on banjo and guitar all over the South, when he wasn't working at his law firm. These days, though, a gig was a catalogue of stresses. His banjo was getting too heavy to lift and he struggled to communicate with the other players on stage, being deaf in one ear, and 'not hearing too good out of the other'. But the music was still there – in his fingers, in his soul, in his constantly tapping feet – and he was thrilled to have someone to introduce it to.

Fred had never heard of Mumford & Sons. This seemed fair enough. But it was a bit of a shock when the music he played me bore no relation to theirs at all. The sound that came out of his speakers was like nothing I had ever heard before: raw and rhythmic, bald and ballsy, unapologetically traditional, and outrageously energetic. It was the sound of the past, being enjoyed with all the verve and vivacity of the present.

I realised that I had left England with even less of an understanding of bluegrass than I had thought – in other words, none whatsoever. But I liked what I heard, and I was eager to be educated. The band I was listening to, said Fred, was Flatt and Scruggs and the Foggy Mountain Boys; his collection was full of their recordings.

'Now this is the one I want y'all to hear,' he said as the next track came up. 'This here's one of my favourites.'

I listened carefully. A guitar kept up a fast-paced rhythm, *boom-chuck boom-chuck*. A fiddle provided background texture, the long notes sounding sticky on the strings. Sometimes there was just one singer - 'Lester Flatt,' said Fred -

Standing on a corner with the lowdown blues
Great big hole in the bottom of my shoes

And then suddenly the song would break out in three-part harmony, as if two more guys had leapt out of a secret door, to plead -

Honey let me be your salty dog!

The lyrics baffled me. I interrupted the song to ask Fred what a salty dog was. He looked at me very professionally. 'I believe, ma'am, it's a term for a sexual partner.'

The instrument you really couldn't avoid, the one that seemed to direct the music's entire course, was the banjo. In the background, it formed a taut weave of rolling chords, like tank tracks propelling the whole operation relentlessly forward. When it took the spotlight, it was a second voice to Flatt's, mirroring the singer's lines back at him, sometimes melodic and gentle, sometimes in a brief, ironic spurt - the musical equivalent of a wink and a grin.

It was played by the very man who had inspired Fred to take up bluegrass half a century ago. When Fred had first heard Earl Scruggs, on his room-mate's gramophone, he was still a law student on the GI Bill. 'No one had ever played the instrument the way he did,' said Fred. 'He invented what we call the banjo roll, using three fingers to pick the strings instead of two.'

I listened hard, trying to appreciate what Earl was doing. At times his banjo helped out the bassline; at others it sat above the vocals so high you wondered if he'd quietly put it down and moved on to a glockenspiel. Often his banjo didn't sound like a banjo at all – at least, not the twanging irritant that banjo-haters imagine, that sets their ears on edge as soon as they hear the word. A delicate line of melody could sound like the plink of a right hand upon a piano. Harmonics could sound like a gentle breath eased over a bottletop. A tremolo could sound like a steel drum.

In his instrumental pieces, though, there was no hiding it. 'Foggy Mountain Breakdown' – Earl's most famous tune, aka the music that played on the *Bonnie and Clyde* soundtrack whenever Warren Beatty and Faye Dunaway were making a run for it – was all banjo, all the time. Earl could play twice as many notes as the players who came before him, explained Fred. 'And when he first went on the *Grand Ole Opry* radio programme and played that hard-driving banjo – faster than anyone had picked it before – well, that was the beginning of bluegrass right there. The next week, everyone and his uncle wanted to play like Earl.'

The place where Earl grew up wasn't far from where we were now, Fred told me. Earl had been born in Cleveland County, a forty-five-minute drive west of Charlotte, and worked in the textile mills, Fred said, to avoid the draft. By the early 1960s, he was number one in the country music hit parade. He ended up a mighty-rich man with a mansion in Nashville and a star on the Hollywood Walk of Fame. Fred said all this with a personal pride, as if Earl's success reflected well on everyone, including himself.

I found myself happily absorbed in Fred's stories, never sure *quite* how true any of them were. Most were about the roguish pioneers of bluegrass, although not all; some were of flying transport planes in Japan after the Second World War, or arguing in court to keep his wayward bandmates out of jail. Fred treated me like a surrogate granddaughter and I succumbed to the role without demur. My own grandfathers had both died before I was born, and I liked the feeling of tranquillity as we sat and chatted about times gone by. I never got the gnawing sense, as I often did at home, that I ought to be somewhere else.

The longer I stayed with Fred and Doris, the less I wanted to leave. I took walks and drives in the North Carolina countryside; I joined in with the routines of their small-town life. The change of pace was an unexpected relief; my usual restlessness fell away; I embraced my unproductivity. Some days I got no further than the porch. In the still, heavy heat, the backyard throbbed with colour - purple coneflowers, tangerine lilies - and an occasional breeze stirred up the scent of honeysuckle.

Beyond the flowerbeds extended a large, lush lawn, but there was no barbecue, no folding chairs - no sign, in fact, that anyone but a gardener had ever trodden the virgin grass. Gardens in the South, I discovered, were for show, not use. The summer was too humid, the mosquitoes too vicious, to dare go further than the reach of the overhead fans and the insect screen.

So we would sit on the wooden decking and watch the birds, its only visitors: red cardinals swooping between tall pines on parabolic curves; goldfinches chivvying each other from the bird tables; and, closest to us, where Doris had hung water feeders, hummingbirds descending through the air, wings fizzing, nosing out the best way to approach the water.

Encouraged by Fred, I'd sometimes even take my fiddle out and join in as he sang. He still picked a little guitar, although his fingers didn't move as swiftly these days and - due to a dodgy knee, and being rather round about the middle - he had to play sitting down. To see him getting in and out of the chair on his porch engendered a thrill of danger, like watching a recently repatched frigate creak out of its runners and back into the water.

It was the first time I had enjoyed playing my fiddle in two decades; I got a kick every time I managed to replicate something Fred showed me. The challenge of the music appealed to me; it was full of brio and technical wizardry, aspects of violin playing I'd particularly enjoyed when I was young. It was music that showed off; it scratched an exhibitionist itch. Sometimes we even ventured out together to local jams where the standard of musicianship was extraordinary; I felt like an anthropologist, stumbling across an uncontacted civilisation. 'Ah, this ain't nothing,' Fred would tell me. 'Y'all should go to the Appalachian Mountains sometime.'

This music felt like a portal to another world. It wasn't just that life around me was different; I was different. Was it possible to feel nostalgia for something you had never experienced? Time had warped since I'd arrived in North Carolina, and I'd glimpsed a version of myself from a parallel universe, one where I didn't need the trappings or endless stimuli of city life, one where I moved slower and didn't mind it.

I had always thought I knew exactly where I belonged - the idea that I was suited to anywhere but London had never occurred to me. But this brief adventure felt less like a break from reality than an introduction to a new one. The songs, stories, and kindness of strangers had given me a taste of an alternative existence I'd never imagined for myself.

When I eventually returned home to Britain, it was tough to describe the experience to friends in a way that wouldn't make them worry for my sanity. I had travelled to a nowhere-town and stayed with a couple of eighty-year-old strangers; I had come back infatuated with a music I'd known no longer than the span of a holiday fling. As it was, normality swiftly re-established itself. Back on the city's busy schedule and escalators, the person I'd been in North Carolina was consumed by the one I knew how to be at home: busy, anxious, a touch self-absorbed. My violin returned to its case, and rarely saw the light.

Life rolled on. I fell in love, and out of it again. I was promoted at work, then lost the best boss I'd ever had. Friends got engaged - got married - got kids - got distant - got out of the city. I stayed. I reasoned that, if I worked hard enough, I'd enjoy my job again; if I made enough effort to meet guys, I'd find one to settle down with. But neither happened. I had plenty of fun times with my friends, but living alone in the city was finally beginning to feel lonely.

I emailed Fred often. I had never shaken the memory of that curious holiday, or my fascination with bluegrass, and, fixed at my desk, I would daydream about returning to North Carolina. Not to Fred and Doris - Fred's mobility issues had got the better of him, and they had moved into a nursing home - but to the music, and the life of the South, and the parallel me I'd encountered there. I remembered how relaxed I'd felt on the other side of the Atlantic, and how kind and generous the people I'd met in the South had been. How even I had felt a little less superficial, a little more - dare I think it? - myself.

Admittedly, in these daydreams I also pictured myself

becoming a brilliant bluegrass fiddler, and the vast sense of achievement it would give me. Wouldn't it be nice to discover, even this late in life, something I was *really* good at?

The worse I felt about life in London, the more romantic my fantasy bluegrass life appeared. Until one day, I decided I was done with my job. And I was going to go back to the States to turn myself into a bona fide fiddler.

I figured it would only take six months.

A brief and incomplete history of bluegrass, part I

Once upon a time – the 1930s, to be precise – there were two brothers. They had grown up on a farm in Kentucky, and learned to play music from their mother, who loved to sing and dance and play the accordion. They came from a large family, and when their parents died the siblings had to make their own way in the world. That's how Charlie and Bill wound up steam-cleaning oil barrels on the shores of Lake Michigan, and making extra cash in the evenings, playing for dances in local bars.

The young men had talent. Charlie, the older brother, was a charismatic guitar player, and Bill could pick a mandolin as well as anyone alive. Their voices went well together. Charlie sang lead and Bill sang harmonies. Since Charlie had a naturally high range, Bill had to sing even higher – almost like a girl. Somehow, it worked.

The Monroe Brothers, as their act became known, were offered a radio show. It was sponsored by a laxative company. They toured the Midwest and the South. They were given a recording contract. Their girlfriends became their wives – in Bill's case, because he knocked her up.

Life as a musician was still tough. But it was worse, Bill decided, when your big brother called all the shots. Charlie could be a bully – he was once fired for punching a co-worker. And Bill was stubborn. They argued and fought and, two years after their first hit single, they couldn't bring themselves to look at each other. Even on stage.

Tired of being bossed around, Bill left Charlie and started his own band. He sang many of the same songs he'd performed with his brother. He booked the same gigs. Charlie was furious. But Bill wasn't going to back down. If anything, their rivalry made his music better. Sharper. More ambitious.

And then Charlie decided to audition for America's most popular country radio show – the *Grand Ole Opry*, out of Nashville. It was supposed to be his big break. But Bill had had the same idea, and his band got to Nashville first. Once they'd got the gig, the producer wasn't interested in a second Monroe brother.

Charlie and Bill didn't speak for a long while.

CHAPTER 3

We were the leftovers. Fifteen minutes ago, the hall had groaned with the metallic, atonal clatter of amateur musicians on their first day of camp. Eighty different instruments being nervously handled, inexpertly tuned and infuriatingly noodled. And a painful percentage of them were banjos. When I'd decided on my full-immersion baptism into bluegrass, I hadn't considered how torturously noisy it might be.

Then the camp director, Pete, had appeared, a Hawaiian shirt attempting to camouflage his belly, a round face supporting a tonsure of grey curls. He called out names above the din, calving the musical morass into individual bands and sending them out with words of advice and a mutual sense of purpose. When the winnowing was complete, Pete looked at the misfit assortment that remained – two guitars, a banjo, three fiddles and something that looked like a table-top harp, which its owner referred to as a dulcimer. 'And ... um ... you guys!' he said, enthusiastically.

Pete Wernick advertised his week-long instructional camps as a safe space for beginners. I needed a grounding in the basics of bluegrass, so I'd come here straight from the plane. Pete was messianic about his teaching methods – he could, he said, help even the tone-deaf to sing – and his chief strategy was to give his students no hiding place.

'If you're gonna learn bluegrass, you don't start in the closet,' was Pete's mantra. He was adamant that this was not a musical style that could be learned at home by yourself: 'The *only* way you'll get better is playing with other people.'

The other people, in this case, were a mixture of retirees indulging an old or new hobby, and schoolkids with more talent than their parents could handle. Our little group pulled up chairs in the vast dining hall of the YMCA camp, which appeared to be built of sauna cladding. Perky Bible verses beamed down at us from the walls. We introduced ourselves like strangers at an AA meeting.

'Hi, my name's Tommy . . .'

'Hi, Tommy.'

'. . . and I've been playing banjo for two years.'

Gentle applause. Tommy's baseball cap bore a picture of a rattlesnake, and underneath, the words 'Don't Tread on Me'. I didn't know what it meant, but I knew I wouldn't be messing with Tommy.

We went round the circle, taking turns to sing songs. The circle is the foundational geometry of bluegrass: it's where the music begins - a group of players, maybe friends, maybe strangers, facing each other and sharing the tunes they know by heart. As in a board game, each player has their go, leading the others in a song or a common instrumental tune; as in a board game, there are rules. Unfortunately, no one leaves you instructions on the back of the box lid or tells you what pieces you'll need to play.

The bluegrass jam might seem like a come-as-you-are kind of affair - its dress code inclines to a checked shirt and a baseball cap - but it carries a surprisingly strict set of terms and conditions. If you don't observe its unique etiquette, you're likely to find yourself frozen out of the circle and never asked back. Here is a beginner's guide to the rules of jamming:

1. Bluegrass music uses specific instruments: in its strictest definition, a bluegrass band is one that contains some combination of a guitar, a banjo, a mandolin, a fiddle and a bass. Dobros and harmonicas are welcome, spoons and washboards are considered gauche. Don't ask me what the dulcimer was doing in our class.

2. Bluegrass is acoustic music. You can't start shredding on a Stratocaster and expect people to take you seriously. (However, plenty of performers have pushed boundaries by plugging in their mandolins or adding wah-wah pedal to their banjo. Including our camp director, Pete.)

3. Bluegrass has an offbeat 'groove'. Stressing the second and fourth beats rather than the first and third gives the music its rhythmic drive. It is every musician's responsibility to help create this groove. Without it, you're just playing some pretty string music. And no one here wants that.

4. The lead singer takes the melody; a couple of additional singers will add the tenor (higher) and baritone (lower) harmonies during the chorus. In other words, this isn't a mass sing-along. The rest of the instruments provide back-up - rhythm, riffs, the occasional ear-catching fill. It's considered very bad form to drown out the singer with too much flashy playing.

5. You leave that to the solos, which are improvised, usually in between the verses of the song. If you get the nod from the lead singer, who acts like a sort of low-key conductor, this is your chance to show off. If you don't get the nod, you shut up and keep playing back-up.

My first morning of camp confirmed a hunch I had long held: the songs weren't difficult in themselves. Most of the melodies were relatively simple. Many of them only used three chords, which meant that even a novice could bash them out on a guitar.

Think of songs like 'When the Saints Go Marching In', or 'She'll Be Coming Round the Mountain When She Comes', or even 'Jingle Bells'. They all use the same three chords as a lot of traditional bluegrass, based on the first, fourth and fifth notes of the major scale (bluegrassers call them the 'one', 'four' and 'five' chords, although they have other more technical names too). And their progressions - in other words, the way the tune moves from one chord to the next - are instinctive enough that even if you're a non-musician, you can sense where the song is going. Whether you know music theory or not, you've been able to follow those kind of musical patterns since you were first taught nursery rhymes.

There is one problem with songs that have limited chord structures and basic melodies, and that's that they can start to sound quite similar. It might have been easier to tell the songs apart - and therefore play the notes in the right order - if they hadn't, many of them, had such similar names, or covered such similar ground. For instance, there wasn't just one song about someone 'going down the road feeling bad'. There were dozens. Every other song seemed to be a hard-luck story about a man who'd worn out the soles of his shoes, and had no money to buy a new pair. Within a couple of hours, I had compassion fatigue.

And why did a single musical genre require songs about a 'Little Cabin Home on the Hill', a 'Blue Ridge Cabin Home', and a 'Cabin in Caroline'? Why did it need to pay tribute to both a John Hardy and a John Henry? Why did it choose to confuse its instrumentalists with a 'Foggy Mountain Special' *and* a 'Foggy Mountain Breakdown'? There weren't even lyrics to help you tell those last two apart. At one stage I mistook one for the other and caused the musical equivalent of a ten-car pile-up.

By the end of the first day, my head was swimming and my body was a twisted torque of tension. My shoulders stung, my jaw was clenched, and my left hand kept threatening to close up like a frightened clam. My back ached. My hands ached. Even, for some unknown reason, my buttocks ached.

The camp took place in North Carolina's Piedmont region, the state's central plateau, linking the Appalachian Mountains in the west with the coastal plains to the east - a lush patchwork of valleys and foothills. With great consideration for his fellow ear-possessing humans, Pete had gathered us on an isolated campground surrounded by miles of barely populated farmland.

Not fancying a week in its dormitory-style chalets, I had found a place to stay in nearby Taylorsville - a rural town which had proved its progressive mindset just the year before by voting to allow the sale of alcohol in the town for the first time since the nineteenth century. The margin in the referendum was 598 for, 319 against (malt beverage), and 600 for, 317 against (mixed beverage). In other words, two residents voted for cocktails but against beer.

Where this new-flowing booze was available was not obvious. It would be no exaggeration to say that Taylorsville offered more places to pray than places to eat and drink. I had passed a half-dozen Baptist churches before I reached the KFC, the Taco Bell, and the Scotz BBQ and Diner (closed from 8 p.m.). The only other signs of industry were the flurry of orchards at the edges of town. The rest was a silent swathe of desolation - empty storefronts with dejected windows, the paint on their 'To Lease' signs fading pessimistically.

25

I ate breakfast at the Coffee House, a waffle shop on the outskirts of town. It was the only joint whose parking lot ever attracted vehicles; the booths inside were populated with white-haired regulars eating a variety of white-coloured foodstuffs – grits, gravy and watery eggs – that disappeared against their plates.

The first morning, I asked for a couple of pancakes with a side of cooked apples, the closest thing to a vegetable on the menu (unless you counted the hash browns, which you wouldn't if you'd seen them). The waitress, a happy woman with an unapologetic moustache, scribbled my order on a notepad; I noticed the wallet had the words 'Oh brother Scott' written in biro on the reverse side, and asked who Scott was. 'He's my relation,' she beamed. 'He's been in the jail these twenty years, and he's just got out on parole.'

Taylorsville used to be a furniture town, she told me, but the manufacturing plants and the textile mills had mostly moved out or shut down. There wasn't much work here now. Still, it wasn't a bad place to live. They had the Apple Festival in the fall, and the mayor had started an Apple Blossom Festival in the spring too, and up the road in the next town along there was the Apple Butter Festival. If you liked apples, there was plenty for you here.

At camp, the songs became more familiar. It helped that I heard them numerous times a day, echoed back from neighbouring jam groups. One catchy ditty called 'Sitting on Top of the World' was so popular that it would sweep across the campsite like a contagion. From the moment it got played at the furthest end of the grounds, you knew you had only twenty minutes before it overtook you and your buddies. No one ever developed immunity, and the very next day, it would be back, infecting everyone all over again.

When people weren't playing their favourite songs, they were talking about them. It was another unwritten rule of the jam session: you didn't just bring tunes, you brought stories about their originators. 'That's an old Jimmy Martin number,' someone in a checked shirt and baseball cap would nod sagely, before launching into a tale of the time Martin, a notorious rogue, had started a fight outside a gig, or peed from his bus window. I scribbled down the names to look up later, although I was never completely confident of what I'd heard. *Reno and something-that-sounds-like Smiley. A brother-sister duet called Jim and Jessie?*

A lot of the stories were about Bill Monroe, which was only natural, since Monroe was to bluegrass what Picasso was to Cubism. One of the oldest students in camp, Alan, had just turned eighty; in 1947, when Bill Monroe and the Blue Grass Boys blew through Alan's hometown of Charlestown, West Virginia, he had been a sixteen-year-old usher at the movie theatre. Nearly a decade after splitting up with his brother Charlie, after constant experimentation with his band, Bill had found his signature line-up, featuring Lester Flatt, Earl Scruggs, Chubby Wise and Cedric Rainwater. 'They played two days and two nights, and I didn't usher no one,' said Alan, lifting his shoulders to his ears in an endearing, what-you-gonna-do-about-it shrug. 'I reported for work and then I found a place to sit and hide from the boss. I saw every show.'

Monroe was thirty-six; he and his band wore suits and Stetsons and approached the stage as if it were their office. 'There was very little theatre in what they were doing,' said Alan. 'It was all about the music.' No one had played mandolin the way Monroe did, he said, but then, heck, no one sang like Lester, or played banjo like Earl – the world had never heard *anything* like their sound before. Even Pete looked envious at Alan's story. The so-called 'classic' band, with Flatt and

Scruggs, only lasted two years. Seeing them live made Alan one of the knights of the bluegrass grail.

What was surprising about people's Bill Monroe stories wasn't that they were such common currency – it was that most of them made him look bad. A sour seam ran through them like spinach in a turkey sandwich; a high percentage involved him stitching up other musicians. There were stories of how he employed his bandmates to work his farm, but paid them peanuts; how he claimed the credit for their musical creations; how he used his influence to keep his rivals out of work. He didn't even come out of his romances well. I found a moment of feminist cheer in the discovery that he'd employed his girlfriend, Bess, as a bass player, until someone pointed out he had a wife at home at the time.

The fact that the author and perfecter of the bluegrass faith was an ill-tempered, miserly philanderer didn't dim anyone's reverence for him. This wasn't just a shrugging acceptance that you could be a great artist and a bad person, either. Bill's single-mindedness and machismo were part of the bluegrass myth; you could even say they were woven into the fabric of the music, in its obsessive drive and its show-off speed.

His competitive nature had left an imprint of one-upman-ship on the bluegrass formula, in which the players passed around the tune, taking successive instrumental breaks. These solos were based on the Annie Oakley principle: anything you can do, I can do better. Each player tried to outdo the last, using the basic outline of the song (or instrumental tune) as a sort of skeleton around which to construct their layers of improvisation. Underneath, the chords remained the same, but each player took the intrinsic melody and refashioned it in endless kaleidoscopic style. The only limit was their own imagination.

Those showy breaks had been a big part of what had drawn

me to bluegrass; like a mountain range on the horizon, their outlines had exerted a long-range fascination and inspired me with awe. Now that I finally stood at their base - and was expected to take them on myself - the rockface proved overwhelming and impenetrable.

None of the musical skills I possessed from my classical training gave me any purchase; in fact they seemed almost redundant. My ability to read music, for instance, was of no use in a tradition where everything was learned by ear, either passed on from person to person or by listening to recordings. Even more problematic was the fact I was used to playing pieces note for note, with no deviation whatsoever from the script provided by the composer. I had never improvised before. I didn't even know how.

For a classical musician, improvising is a bit like your dad taking the stabilisers off your bike - then replacing your bike with an imaginary spaceship. Instead of a book of meticulously inked blobs telling you where to lay every finger every fraction of a second, there's just a big long stretch of nothing. Sure, there's a background structure of chords and scales and abstract rules, but those theoreticals aren't going to fill the next sixteen bars of silence when the singer's stepped away from the microphone and called your name.

Unsure where to start, I asked some of the camp teachers for advice. Their replies ranged from the dogmatic ('Always play the melody!') to the obvious ('Be in time and in tune!'). Some advice was obtuse ('Watch the guitar player's left hand!'), some philosophical ('Just let yourself go!'). One teacher offered to show me some hot licks, which sounded deeply inappropriate until he explained that this was a term for short musical phrases that you could drop into your playing to make it sound cool.

It was only after I'd spent a couple of hours copying and

learning these licks that I realised the problem: I had no idea where to put them. It was as if I'd gone to the hardware store and asked for a bag of 10 x 100 countersunk screws and a couple of shield anchor projecting bolts. I still didn't know how to use them, and mere possession was not going to turn me into a master craftsman.

The jams became a sort of Sisyphean torture. I sat there holding an instrument I knew I could play, yet I was utterly unable to summon out of it the sounds that everyone else was making. One day, Pete moved me into a group with some of the talented teenagers; when they played, they held their banjos and guitars to their chests as if they were halfway assimilated into their bodies. Their hands ran over them with the surety of a touch typist. I reminded myself that there was no need to feel intimidated, because they, unlike me, had been brought up with this music. 'How long have you been playing?' I asked the tall, blond youth next to me, picturing him being handed a guitar pick on his first birthday. 'A couple of years,' he said. I tried not to want to punch him.

His name was Eliot, and he was eighteen; he and his friend Tray sat quietly as we jammed together, and seemed at first a little shy. It turned out they were unused to having to sing; in the band they were in, singing was the preserve of a boy called Liam. I had seen Liam around – a short kid with arty hair who looked like he could be a member of One Direction. Eliot had been learning a new instrument every six months, he told me, because Liam was always changing his mind about what he wanted to play. Tray would have liked to play guitar more often, but Liam told him he had to stick to banjo. I decided Liam sounded well suited to life as a lead singer already.

Their band, called Cane Mill Road, was based out of Boone, a town in the Blue Ridge Mountains, an hour west of where we were. Tray, the only black student at our camp, was going to college in the fall to study music, while Eliot was apprenticing to be a violin maker. He'd already made his first two violins, and had one with him; he handed me an elegant-looking instrument of a sandy hue. I picked a couple of fiddle tunes on it, then, feeling expansive, gave it a blast of Mozart. The sweet, bright opening of *Eine Kleine Nachtmusik* bounced out of its belly and resonated around the room. Eliot looked thrilled. No one had played classical on it before, he said.

With a heavy rain turning the campsite into a mudscape, we stayed indoors and kept picking. Tray expressed himself much faster in his music than he did in his leisurely sentences. He gazed at his left hand as he played, as if curious to see what it would do next. Sometimes he would look up with a puzzled frown, or an expression of disbelief. It took me a long while to realise that these had nothing to do with my own playing, or, in fact, anyone else's. They were just the facial muscles his brain tweaked at random while his fingers were so busily employed.

Pete wandered by a couple of times to listen to us. He always showed a special interest in Tray, who, I discovered, had a scholarship to the camp. While Tray was a good banjo player now, said Pete, he had the potential to be a great one. And Pete knew what he was talking about. Pete, it turned out, was kind of a big deal himself.

I didn't know the band Hot Rize; being one of the biggest bluegrass bands of the eighties doesn't mean much in Britain, and by much, I mean anything. Early on in the week, one of the retirees, horrified that I hadn't heard of Pete before, had pulled up a video on his phone over lunch. The footage presented four rather low-resolution men wearing beige suits that seemed to exactly match their skin tone, although that

31

may have been the lighting; they were in a studio, in front of a TV audience.

The bass player had David Hasselhoff's *Knight Rider* hair. The mandolin player sang about a woman called Nellie from behind a pair of wire-rimmed spectacles and was a dead ringer for Napoleon Dynamite. After each chorus, the mandolin and banjo inserted a catchy riff; attached to the banjo was a surprisingly slim Pete Wernick. He had a rich head of hair, although occasionally, when he turned his head from the camera, a small patch on the crown winked at his future.

Hot Rize still toured, forty years later, and nearly twenty after they lost their original guitar player to leukaemia. Wernick was now one of the senior statesmen of bluegrass. He'd earned the title 'Dr Banjo' in reference both to his bestselling instructional books and his PhD in sociology from Cornell University. Clearly, none of this had made him rich – I'd seen his car – and even with his elevated profile, his teaching programmes weren't reaching as many people as he'd like. 'Our target market is people who are just starting to play,' he told me, 'but how do you advertise to those people? They don't read "Would-be Jammers Weekly", or "I Jammed Once and I'd Like to Again Magazine".'

Pete's pupils were mostly middle-class suburbanites. The micro-universe in which bluegrass existed was fairly geographically and ethnically constrained – its heartlands were Virginia, West Virginia, North Carolina, Kentucky and Tennessee, and it thrived in the stretch of Appalachian Mountains where their state lines came together. 'It's not really a picture of America,' said Pete, who had been a demographer before his musical career took off. 'Because there are still hardly any African Americans or Hispanics or Native Americans. We're always a little late in mirroring society – it's a socially conservative crowd.

'Of course, back in the day they were all farmers. That's why Flatt and Scruggs had a radio show at five thirty in the morning - that's when their audience was up. They did another at noon because that's when folk were coming in from the fields for lunch. It used to be that all the bluegrass acts grew up on farms, or in mining towns.'

That explained why there were so many song titles about chickens and weevils and pigs in pens. I sat and learned them alongside men who had run their own businesses, or worked for multinationals; had run for office, built second homes, put their kids through a cripplingly expensive education system. And I wondered - for the first but not the last time - who bluegrass music was really for. Was it just an exercise in nostalgic make-believe, for old white dudes, their grandkids, and voyeurs like me? Was I helping to preserve an endangered music, or just to maintain a shared cultural delusion?

That question hadn't even occurred to me on my first North Carolina visit. But things had changed dramatically in America since then. Whatever liberal fantasies I'd had about living in the USA under its first female president had been punctured shortly before I bought my plane ticket. Donald Trump had now been president for three months and acrimony was pouring out of the White House daily.

Still, no one spoke of it at camp. The tumultuous politics and divisive national mood went largely unmentioned, until Pete announced that we would all be playing a song together at the end-of-camp concert. He had chosen 'This Land Is Your Land', because he felt it was especially timely, and 'a good way to stop people yelling at each other, however briefly'. He invited people to write alternative lyrics for the concert, but most were heartily vetoed by the group, including a nice little rhyming couplet:

We used to live in an age of reason
Now we've entered danger season

which was deemed too controversial for public consumption.

Perhaps the camp was considered a no man's land, a place of musical truce. Or perhaps everyone here had voted for Trump and was perfectly happy with their choice. As long as Tommy was wearing that rattlesnake hat, I wasn't going to be the one to bring it up.

Instead, I concentrated on learning how to kick off a song, and how to follow a bassline, and what to do to signal the end of a tune, which involved lifting one leg and waving it in the air like I was doing the Hokey Cokey. Towards the end of the week, Tray and Eliot asked me where I was headed next, when camp was over. I had to admit that I didn't have a plan.

Fred's words - 'Y'all should go to the mountains' - had stayed with me. But Google Maps showed the Appalachians covering pretty much the entire eastern seaboard, and the thought that I might need to scour a 2,000-mile-long stretch of densely forested mountain range for banjo players made my stomach churn with anxiety. Even the heartland that Pete had talked about - from the Blue Ridge in Virginia down to the Smokies in Tennessee - was too vast to contemplate. I felt lost already.

'Well, we've got music in Boone,' said Eliot. 'You could always start there.'

CHAPTER 4

I got my first sight of the mountains just after sunset. The road from Taylorsville had distracted me with out-of-town furniture stores and surprise strip malls; occasionally, a stand-alone restaurant tried to bait me with 99-cent burgers or all-you-could-eat BBQ. The sun stared me down through the windshield, making it impossible to see where, exactly, I was headed. Under my wheels, though, the road began to rise and fall in soft parabolas, like a Disneyland ride for the under-eights.

There was no warning shot from the horizon. A forest rushed up alongside and ambushed me as the road began to curve and climb, accommodating its guests with a polite camber. The larger the enclosing hillsides grew, the smaller the passing cars began to look. Then a sign told me that I had crossed the county line into Watauga, and, as if by some municipal agreement, the wooded surrounds dropped away. To my left, a continuous range of tree-covered peaks revealed themselves in a vast panorama.

I had no special yen for mountains. However impressive the size and scale of, for instance, the Alps, their rocky grandeur was too austere for me: distant, harsh, off-putting. Maybe it was my own insecurity – they did make me feel puny – but I never felt like we had much in common.

35

This, though, was different. These weren't the craggy faces of grumpy granite gods. These were the kind of mountains you could make friends with. Each soft nub of a peak was covered to its very tip in dense green forest. They looked no more threatening than a head of broccoli.

They also looked strangely homey. Some slopes carried finger-shaped declivities, as if a large hand had reached down and squeezed them when they were still damp. In a few places, a shaved patch of lighter green where the trees had been cleared indicated a farmer still willing to battle gravity. They rolled away from me in soft waves, their green turning to lilac, lavender and indigo as they reached the horizon.

Above them, the hidden sun had left behind a sky riven with colour. Bland yellow gave way to Bunsen-burner orange, while creeping peaches and pinks began their own invasion. For twenty twilit minutes, the highway carried me beneath the painterly sky, its palette deepening and modernising from Michelangelo ceiling to Warhol silkscreen. Broad strokes of cloud finished in Elvis quiffs, or a Nike swoosh; a three-quarter moon peered over my left shoulder, and winked in my rear mirror.

It was impossible to drive safely under these circumstances, and a couple of times my rented Hyundai Elantra veered carelessly towards the dividing line as I turned my head to the view. Then dusk came, and the road dipped down towards the town of Boone, and the magical mountainscape disappeared behind a parade of red neon advertising Toyota dealerships and Advance Autoparts and something called Bojangles.

At camp, there had been unspecific, undecipherable allusions to legendary musicians who lived 'up in the hills', cut off from civilisation, making some of the best music you'd never heard. I'd have loved to track them down but no one ever seemed to have co-ordinates. Eliot had, however, been able to tell me about a weekly Wednesday jam at a pub called Murphy's. According to Facebook, Boone also held a 'Red White and Bluegrass jam' on Tuesday nights. It was now Tuesday night, and my GPS had told me to pull off the four-lane highway. It deposited me in an after-hours parking lot, where the only business showing any sign of life was a bowling alley.

The empty lanes were being hosed with eighties rock. No, the teenage shoe monitor said, this wasn't where the bluegrass happened. She pointed at the silent, unlit building next door. I quavered. The journey here had kept me occupied, but the reality of what I was doing began to sink in. It was one thing playing at a camp awash with mutual goodwill, run by teachers whose job was to welcome and encourage newbies. Turning up in a strange town and attempting to join in with music I'd been learning for exactly one week now seemed ambitious to the point of foolhardy. Just the act of walking a dozen yards along a dark pavement to push at an unmarked door made me want to give up and run home to the people I loved and the life I knew.

But home was a long way away and Boone didn't look big enough to have its own airport. I went through the door, down a corridor, and emerged into a modern hall with hundreds of chairs set out in rows, and a stage that looked thirty foot wide. A full-scale lighting rig illuminated it in purple and blue; a half-dozen microphones stood to attention. Around them, a male posse was busy running cables and emptying instrument cases.

I felt a wash of relief. I must have arrived on the wrong day: this was clearly a band preparing for a show. Slinking to the side of the room, I tried to hold my fiddle as casually as if I always carried it around with me. One of the men, whose glasses and close-cropped beard half-hid a much younger face, wandered over.

'Y'all here for the jam?' he asked.

I nodded, but didn't speak.

'Well, howdy!' he said. 'C'mon over and join us, I'm Isaac, and this all's Tim...'

Isaac led me up some stairs onto the stage, where Tim - a shaven-headed man in his thirties - was tweaking the pegs of his banjo. He gave me a grin and a large bulge appeared beneath his lower lip. I tried not to stare at it. It would be a few days before I learned about dipping tobacco.

'...And this is JM.' In front of me was an upright bass, held by a man who seemed to match its dimensions exactly. I shook his hand, and found some words.

'So you jam... on stage?'

'Yes, ma'am, and there's plenty of mics, so you just step right on up whenever you want to play.' JM's voice was a basso profundo; in other circumstances, I'd have found it comforting. But right now I was looking at the microphones and wondering how quietly I'd have to play to make sure I wasn't picked up by them. What had happened to the god-damn circle?

A sizeable audience began to gather, each paying five dollars on the door. An anticipatory shame was already working its way from my chest to my fingers. Taking the stage in front of a hundred or more people was sheer madness. I'd left Pete's camp with only a rough memory of the songs and tunes we'd played, and I *still* hadn't figured out how to improvise. This was clearly a public performance. I had no place here.

I retreated to the back of the stage, where a hazard of empty cases gaped open like hungry hippos, and busied myself with my violin. A muffled, dissonant chord sounded as I unwrapped the instrument from its duster, and fixed the small rubbery claws of the shoulder rest to its sides. The case emitted a sticky, slightly sickly smell of rosin. I dragged a hard little puck of the stuff across my bow, willing it to imbue that lifeless stick with some instant magic.

Isaac stood up to the microphone. I braced myself for the first song, but instead the audience rose with him, and turned towards a video screen I'd not noticed before. Up came an American flag, moving with a romantic ripple against a blue sky.

'I pledge allegiance to my Flag...'

Everyone's hands were on their heart.

'...and to the Republic for which it stands...'

I froze. I'd never been in a room where people did this before. Did it look rude not to hold my hand to my chest?

'...one nation under God...'

I wasn't even sure where I stood on flag-pledging. This much patriotism didn't feel comfortable to me. Could they tell? Oh God, should I be moving my lips so I didn't look like a stony-faced dissident?

'...and justice for all.'

Too late. Isaac moved on to a prayer. I dutifully bowed my head. Then he picked up his fiddle and kicked off a song.

I backed away from the microphones and tucked myself behind the largest guitar player I could find, as the musicians moved swiftly from one number to the next. Isaac's fiddling was of the kind I had heard on Flatt and Scruggs's records, an unstoppable train of notes coupled to a smooth, swift bow. I felt marooned on stage, an obvious spare part, a glaring incompetent. I tried to play back-up, making sounds that I hoped couldn't be traced back to me, and wished myself invisible.

Just as I thought I had made it through the evening without

39

drawing any attention, a voice shouted from the floor: 'How about some twin fiddle, son?'

I'd learned about twin fiddling at camp: two violins, playing a tune in harmony, the way singers would harmonise a chorus. But I'd never tried it with anyone. Isaac looked round to see me skulking at the back.

'How about it?' he asked. 'You got a fiddle tune you play?'

I had memorised a handful so far, jaunty little affairs with names like 'Cherokee Shuffle', 'Whiskey Before Breakfast', 'Blackberry Blossom'. With the spotlights, and what felt like two hundred sets of eyes, on me, I didn't dare try any of them. I thought of the slowest, easiest tune I knew.

'Um... "Tennessee Waltz"?' I said.

I had no idea why bluegrass, with its emphasis on speed and virtuosity, occasionally threw on the brakes, slipped down to second gear, and tootled languidly along in 3/4 time. As I understood, bluegrass wasn't a music you danced to, so why it should suddenly quit its rowdy ways to offer up a waltz was unclear. But right now, I was in favour. The artless melodies and ambulatory tempo were like a gasp of air to a drowning woman. They must also, I figured, be easy for a man as talented as Isaac to lay a harmony on.

I was right. The notes were simple, and thanks to my classical background I knew how to make them sound good with smooth phrasing and rich vibrato. Together the two of us moved sweetly through the piece, as if we were dancing in hold ourselves. The audience applauded, and Isaac asked my name, so he could introduce me to them. Something about the way he spoke - a combination of bouncy Southern iambs and a relentlessly positive energy - reminded me of those early Looney Tunes cartoons.

'This is *Ay*-ma, everybody! Where y'all from, Emma?'

He nudged me towards the microphone, and I explained that I was from London.

'London, England? You – *flew* – from England?'

A sound of appreciation rustled through the room. This was the first time a real live English person had been seen in this part of town. I explained to the barrage of follow-up questions from the floor how I'd come to learn about bluegrass music. Yes, I was here alone. No, I wasn't married. Yes, it was my first visit to the South. No, I didn't own a gun.

Soon, our informal Q&A had become a full audience-participation session. There were concerns that I was travelling alone, and offers of places to stay, and endless compliments on my fiddle playing. This unprecedented explosion of interest in my life settled on me like confetti; overwhelmed by their kindness and praise, I felt like a celebrity and a con woman all at once. The musicians, at least, must have seen through me: I couldn't have spent two hours wasting space on their stage without their knowing it.

Isaac asked to see my violin, and I handed it to him. The colour of the wood was a matte, chocolate brown, far darker than the rich, almost orange-y tones you might associate with violins, and there were narrow striations running like pinstripes along its front. Years of build-up and dirt had rendered the central area between the fingerboard and the bridge virtually black; its tailpiece, pegs and chinrest were all made of a swirling ebony. The strings, steel with a core of catgut, were a little worn.

Isaac played a few notes on it and gave a whistle of appreciation. 'You play classical?'

'I used to,' I said.

'How old's this thing?'

'Nearly three hundred years.'

'Lord, that's older than our country,' someone said.

'You know the difference between a violin and a fiddle?' piped up another voice.

'No,' I said, grateful for any tips I could get.

'A violin has strings. And a fiddle has *straaaangs*.' The room hooted with laughter.

'I can tell this here's a fine instrument,' said Isaac. I thanked him. I'd had it a long time, I said. You could, perhaps, describe it as an old friend. But the feelings I bore towards this inanimate, hollow piece of wood were more complicated than that.

A short history of my violin

In the second half of the seventeenth century, a German craftsman called Matthias Kloz travelled to Cremona, Italy, home of the great Amati violin makers, including Stradivarius himself. Kloz learned what skills he could, then returned to Bavaria, where he set up a violin-making workshop in the market town of Mittenwald. His instruments weren't masterpieces, but he made such good money selling them that soon the entire community had picked up his trade. Matthias became a founding father of German violin-making.

My violin was born in 1737. If you look through the f-holes, those squiggly slots that appear on either side of the strings, you can see the label bearing, in Gothic script, the name of Matthias Kloz, and the words: *Lautenmacher in Mittenvaldt, Anno 1737.* My parents bought it from a dealer in London when I was twelve and ready to graduate to a full-size instrument. I don't know who owned it before me.

I did say this was a short history.

I can tell you what has happened to the violin since. Throughout my teenage years, it was my constant companion – there was barely a day when we were out of each other's company. Entrusting a fragile item older than the American constitution to an adolescent cannot have been an easy decision for my mum and dad: I was known for extreme clumsiness, not to mention forgetfulness, which regularly resulted in the loss of clothing, schoolbooks and other essentials. I once managed to drop my violin from shoulder height and, on another occasion, left it on a train bound for Brighton.

It survived those indignities, and in return I practised it every day. On Saturdays it travelled with me to London to spend the day at music college, where it tried, and mostly failed, to please my martinet of a violin teacher.

I'd begun violin lessons when I was four, and by the time I went to secondary school, music was less of a hobby, more of a part-time occupation. The college where I spent my Saturdays was a proving ground for classical musicians, and we were considered professionals in training; my spare time disappeared in rehearsals, recitals and orchestral concerts. My teacher was a terrifying Serb whose high standards and refusal to mince words often had his pupils in tears. He taught me that playing music wasn't necessarily supposed to be fun, but it would always be hard work.

Thanks to the rigours of the system, and a lack of imagination on my part, classical music was almost all I absorbed from a young age. By my early teens, when I should by rights have been bopping along to Cyndi Lauper, and known the right place to 'woop!' in every Michael Jackson song, I owned vastly more sheet music than I did cassettes or CDs. I couldn't tell you the name of Aerosmith's frontman, or why Chesney Hawkes was the one and only, but I could sing you Tchaikovsky's Serenade for Strings from start to finish, all four movements.

I don't remember exactly when music stopped feeling like a pleasure. It crept up on me, the necrotising sense that I'd never be good enough, no matter how much time I put in. I grew weary not of the practices and rehearsals but of the constant judgement, both from my teachers and from myself. I'd never been the best student, and the further I progressed, the more talented my peers became. Instead of getting enjoyment from the music I made, I could only hear how poor it sounded by comparison with everyone around me. It began to dawn on me that I didn't belong. Every time I played, it felt like failure.

I decided I was never going to make it as a professional musician: and with that realisation, something snapped. By the time I was twenty-one, I had given up violin and was suddenly, profoundly uninterested in music at all. A decade of discipline abandoned me and never returned. The idea that I might play 'just for fun' was completely alien to everything I'd known. At the august age of two hundred and sixty-two, and still in the prime of its life, my violin found itself put out to pasture.

For the next ten years, it had sat in the corner of my bedroom, hidden in its long rectangular case, propped rakishly between a chest of drawers and a wall. The tough, blue canvas of the case was covered in dust, which formed a greyish veil and settled into the zip that ran like a tramline around the case. Holding the case together was a metal hasp that sat in the centre like a single corroded tooth, its silver colour browning at the edges. Hidden in its accidental alcove, rarely out of shadow, my violin could go months without me noticing it at all.

It emerged occasionally to cameo at a friend's wedding, playing the tiniest of bit parts in my life. But reunions with this particular childhood companion were abject affairs. Initially, thrilled with the novelty of each other's company, the violin would make excitable noises and I'd congratulate myself on how well I could do on so little practice. Within half an hour things would start to sour and the effect sounded more like grumbling. A little longer and the violin would be screeching at me. We'd both remember how the other one was such hard work, and shouldn't we just avoid each other from now on?

Its only champion had been my mother, who often concluded our phone conversations by asking, 'Have you practised your violin lately?' I was always too ashamed to give the honest answer, so I couched my reply in excuses. 'I've been *so* busy,' I'd whimper. 'Maybe I'll get some time this weekend...' 'I just need to find some other people to play with...'

Why we went through the charade was a mystery. I was busy with my job, and my social life didn't need any help from a musical instrument. It made no discernible difference to me whether I played or not, and the need to account for my last practice belonged to the era of homework, pleated skirts and plaited hair. But my mother still asked the question, and my cheeks still burned when she did. My guilt was doused in the frustration that comes with knowing that you once were good at something, and now you're not, and it's nobody's fault but your own.

This had been my relationship with my violin for the past two decades. Until Mumford & Sons. Until Fred and Doris. Until now.

CHAPTER 5

I stayed overnight in Taylorsville, and returned to Boone the next afternoon. In the daytime, it revealed itself as a small town where a large university had sprouted. Nestled within a bowl in the mountains – which played havoc with the car radio – the diminutive downtown was peered on by college buildings built of brick and houses stacked upon the hillside. A football stadium was elevated, grandly, above the rest.

Compared to Taylorsville, Boone's modest main street was a fury of commerce. There were several neat-looking cafés, a couple of bars, an ice creamery. A row of shops sold a bamboozling mix of fishing tackle and waders and yoga gear and tie-dye. Jumbled between them were unexpected treasures – a post office with its own flower garden; a fire station whose open doors allowed the better admiration of its three gleaming trucks.

I tried to build a picture in my mind of the Boone resident, who caught trout on weekends and volunteered for the fire department while sporting a tattoo of Buddha on their ankle. Even as I was pondering this improbability, I came across a store whose window displayed beard oil and bags of posh coffee. It was called Cornbread Tactical and the scent of hipsterdom drew me in like a moth to a bergamot-and-quince-candle flame.

It took a while for my brain to catch up with the various items displayed on the cool white shelves. A stack of khaki T-shirts with a trendy logo. An overly expensive enamel mug. Coasters. Corkscrews. A flight of raw honey in a test-tube set. Hunting knives. Bigger hunting knives. A machete. A... samurai sword?

I knew I looked nervous, because a handsome guy behind the counter stepped out to meet me with a reassuring smile. 'Do you need any help, ma'am?' He had a serious torso contained in a body-hugging T-shirt. Everything he wore was black. He looked like an Agent of S.H.I.E.L.D.

'I'm just browsing,' I said, hopelessly. I was fooling no one. What would *I* be browsing for, here?

'Would you like to see the guns?' he asked. Just like that.

'Yes, please,' I said, as if people asked me that every day.

He led me through to the back room, where a glass-topped jewellery cabinet proffered a dozen choice handguns like so many Tiffany bracelets. The wall opposite groaned with larger firearms. I needed to come clean.

'I have to tell you something,' I said. 'I'm...' I blushed. 'I'm European.'

He nodded sympathetically. 'We've had a few of y'all in here before,' he said. 'I understand you're scared by this stuff. But, you know, there's really nothing to be afraid of.' He pointed at a large automatic weapon that looked like the ones with which Arnie unleashed hell on his human, alien, and time-travelling robot enemies. 'Even that AK-47 still only fires a tiny bullet,' he said, in a comforting tone.

Kevin, it turned out, was a soldier who had done two tours of Afghanistan, and helped out at the store while he was studying for his degree. I found it hard, faced with his experience and expertise, to articulate my queasiness at the sight of these - well - death machines. Kevin just seemed so much more worldly than me. He showed me the make and model of handgun he'd just given his grandma, because she lived out of town on her own, and who else was going to protect her if a bad guy showed up? 'It's different here,' he said. 'We're a lot more isolated, and the cops aren't going to reach you in time.'

Faced with his smooth reasonableness, and a little in thrall to the commando look, I struggled to remember my deeply felt arguments against the Second Amendment. I saw Kevin reach for a semi-automatic - 'You know, if you just *hold* one . . .' - and sensed that I was about to lose too many of my principles in a single encounter. So I made a solemn promise to do so next time I was in the store, shook Kevin's hand, and left.

Murphy's, where the Wednesday-night jam was held, was at the fire-truck end of the street, next to a firm whose sign read 'Eggers, Eggers, Eggers & Eggers, Attorneys at Law'. It had two entrances; one took you into a dingy dive bar with flyers laminating the walls and the clackety-clack of pool playing; the other deposited you in a more family-friendly establishment with booths and sensible lighting and the smell of French fries. Eliot had told me to get there early, when there was free pizza for the musicians, and emerging from one of the booths I could already see his and Tray's heads bent intently over a plate of pepperoni.

In the middle of the room, the tables had been removed to accommodate a large circle of chairs. I recognised some of the tutors from the camp, including Zeb and Julie, a couple in their twenties who had taught mandolin and fiddle respectively. Also there was Liam, the Harry-Styles-a-like, and Eliot's grandfather John - a jolly, kindly man who had found the perfect outlet for his self-confessed limited guitar skills by playing comic novelty songs with a twinkling grin.

49

The jam was a far less intimidating prospect than the one the night before. Rather than prayers and a patriotic oath, this one began (and continued) with beers. Several of the players, like me, were still novices, and each of our tentative, flawed attempts to take a solo made the rest feel less out of place. The circle itself created a protective barrier from the world around us – we were playing for each other, rather than the audience of diners – and even if the music we produced wasn't always that beautiful to the ear, the experts, like Julie and Zeb, held everyone together and kept us on the beat.

There was no sign of Isaac, or Tim, or JM; and it seemed strange that such a small town as this would hold two bluegrass jams, on subsequent nights, with a completely different cast. The song choices at Murphy's were also notably different. At the Red, White and Bluegrass jam, even the tunes I didn't know had all had the patina of tradition: Flatt and Scruggs, Jimmy Martin, Bill Monroe. Here people sang numbers by Dolly Parton and Alison Krauss – 'Jolene', 'Steel Rails' – and the chords weren't just the simple ones any more, the 'one', 'four' and 'five' chords of 'Jingle Bells' and the rest. There were 'twos' and 'threes' thrown in as well, and exotic-sounding minor sixths.

As he riffed riotously around the jazzier numbers, Liam's teenage proto-stardom was undeniable. He was able to tear up any instrument he was handed. I'd convinced myself that, with all that talent, he *must* be an annoying little punk; then he came over to ask me, in the most courteous manner, how I had enjoyed my stay in America so far. 'I hope you'll be staying in Boone longer,' he added sweetly, before excusing himself; 'Well, it's been good talking to you.' I wouldn't pretend to know much about fourteen-year-old boys, but I was sure that most of them didn't have manners as nice as this. I told myself I would never again be prejudiced against someone on the basis of trendy hair.

And I *did* want to stay in Boone longer. It was quirky, and welcoming, and John, Eliot's grandfather, knew where I could rent a spare room.

The night I arrived at Andrew and Carrie's home, we sat on their porch, watching a thunderstorm play out over the town and drinking Old Fashioneds. I was in love with the pair of them by the time my ice cube had melted.

Andrew was John's son and Eliot's uncle. All I knew about him before I moved in was that he was in his forties, worked with his dad in insurance, and had a penchant for board games and horror movies; and that his partner, Carrie, was writing a PhD. All they knew about me was that I was English.

I knew we were going to be friends the moment I saw their DVD shelves, and everything Joss Whedon had ever made was on them. The fact that they also had a *Buffy*-inspired sampler that read 'Hellmouth, Sweet Hellmouth' just sealed the deal. And when we'd finished discussing the fictional town of Sunnydale, the conversation turned to their own town, and its own strange undercurrents.

The way Andrew and Carrie described it, living in Boone was like slipping in and out of a wormhole. On one side, there were families who had inhabited these mountains for over a century, worshipping at their local church, hunting and fishing in the forests and the rivers. Andrew's people, for instance, had lived in Watauga County for seven or eight generations and there was a family legend that one of their ancestors had traded with Daniel Boone himself, the pioneer after whom the town was named. Andrew and his dad still liked to shoot, although they didn't go to church. 'If your grandfather wasn't born here,' said Andrew, 'you can't really say you're "from" Boone.'

On the other side were those attached to the university, like Carrie - students, tutors, and the many graduates who enjoyed the town so much they'd decided to make it their home. The college had been imprinting its progressive ideas on its surroundings since the seventies, and now the population of Watauga County was split almost equally down conservative and liberal lines - it had voted for Barack Obama in 2008, and Mitt Romney in 2012. In the 2016 election, Donald Trump had beaten Hillary Clinton by a 2 per cent margin.

Andrew and Carrie had been devastated by Trump's shock win. But while they railed against the new world order in private, they had to be careful what they said outside their walls: it caused too much aggravation, not least with other members of their families who thought Trump was doing a fine job. They knew folk who hadn't gone home for Thanksgiving or Christmas last year, because the strain was too much. 'You don't talk politics here,' Carrie warned me. 'Not unless you're sure you're in like-minded company.'

I bore that in mind when I next saw Tim, JM and Isaac. Tim had a recording studio in his yard, and he'd invited me over to pick with them there. The Red, White and Bluegrass jam only happened every two weeks, he said, but those guys would play every day if they could.

'What about the jam at Murphy's?' I'd asked. 'Don't you go to that one?'

'Where's Murphy's?' said Tim.

They were gathered to work on a CD of old classics they were making. The studio crouched opposite Tim's house, a windowless building that might have been a workshop if it hadn't been so large. Past a green room - sofas, a mini fridge, multiple instrument cases – was a control booth, where Tim sat at a console, talking to someone who wasn't there. He reached for his mouse, and a glut of music instantly filled the room.

'One more time!' said a disembodied voice, drowned in reverb. A few seconds later, a swirl of fiddle joined the pre-existing sounds.

JM stood at the back, next to a guy called Bryan who I recognised as the guitar player I'd hidden behind at the jam. Bryan wasn't as tall as JM, but his overalls made the same par-enthetical shape. They showed me down a narrow corridor to the individual recording booths, one for each instrument in a five-piece band. Isaac was in the last one, ensconced in headphones. The equipment looked state-of-the-art, the soundproofing – rows of egg boxes and squares of thick, scooped foam stapled to the walls – distinctly DIY. Tim had built the place himself ten years ago, said JM. Before that, they used to record in his living room.

'I flipped out first time I ever heard myself sing,' remem-bered Bryan. 'Dang! About made me gonna quit.'

One of Isaac's fills erupted in the air around us, and Tim whooped with delight. 'D'ya hear that? Yes, *sir!*'

'Man, he burns that up,' said Bryan. '*Lord* have mercy!'

I sat in an armchair and listened as Tim faced his one-man mission control, interacting with the wiggly lines that traced their way across two giant computer monitors. There were towers of hardware on either side of the room; perhaps he was running a side project to launch a banjo player into deep space. When Tim turned his head, I could see the same bulge beneath his lower lip that indicated the little hamster-pouch of tobacco he usually kept there; after a while, he leaned over the side of his desk and disgorged it into a trash can.

'Help yourself to a drink,' he said. 'We've got Pepsi and

53

water and tea.' I was a little surprised to discover there were no beers in a man cave like this, but it turned out that JM and Isaac were Baptists, and Tim was a Pentecostal. That explained why they didn't know about the Murphy's jam.

This was Bryan's last day in Boone for some time; the next morning, he was headed to Wyoming to join the trucking company he drove for every summer. Even though he gigged most weekends, there wasn't enough work to make money as a musician here. 'Lord, no. Wish you could, but you cain't.'

'Here, there's so many people play, there's people who don't even get on stage that are awesome musicians,' said JM. He told me that Isaac had given up life as a touring musician when he got married, because he couldn't support a family and still spend time with them. 'The only way you can make money is go up north - New York, Indiana, Pennsylvania. My dad played in a band for years, they'd book stuff they had no business playing - two thousand, three thousand dollars a gig.'

'We're getting fifty dollars a gig,' snorted Bryan.

'And this ain't a cheap place to live,' said JM. 'North Carolina's the worst for tax. Inbound freight, outbound freight, they tax your property, each vehicle you own. They'll tax you to death.'

'I wish they'd cut some of that crap out of here,' said Bryan. 'You don't make no money! The government's getting rich and we're getting poor.'

I recalled Carrie's words and kept my opinions on taxes to myself. Instead, I listened to them talk about the instruments they'd buy if they had the money (D-28s, J-45s, dreadnoughts, flat-tops - why guitar models all sounded like nuclear missiles I didn't know). And I took in the photos on the walls: their picking buddies, their wives, the cover shots of albums they'd made together.

I hadn't figured their ages, but in the pictures it was apparent that Isaac and Bryan were a fair bit younger than the other two. Isaac had been playing with them since he was at school, and was completely self-taught. I was amazed by this – how had he mastered fiddle without lessons? If you can play guitar, it's not such a leap to pick up something else you strum and pluck, like mandolin or banjo; but violin is an entirely different skill set. 'That's why there aren't so many fiddlers,' said JM. 'You play fiddle some, you're welcome wherever you go. You play the fiddle *and* you sing, that's a gold mine right there.'

Bryan and JM began debating the relative merits of the greatest bluegrass fiddlers, names like Chubby Wise and Bobby Hicks and Benny Martin and Vassar Clements and Kenny Baker. I jotted the names in my notebook, determined to track down some old recordings.

'You know what I like in this old stuff?' said Bryan. 'The roughness in it. I hate the new crap. It's not my style.'

I asked what counted as new crap.

'Anything since the late eighties.'

'Anything past the fifties is modern to me,' said Isaac, who had finished laying down his track and emerged from his cubby.

'Isaac's like me,' chuckled Tim. 'He likes the Flatt and Scruggs stuff. Ain't nobody can touch them. 'Cept maybe Monroe in the fifties when he had Jimmy Martin playing the *gee*-tar.'

'What about the Stanley Brothers?' said Bryan. 'Their music was serious business.'

'Serious killin',' agreed JM. 'Serious lovin'.'

Isaac nodded. He was a big fan. He usually went to Ralph Stanley's festival, the one held on the family's farm, deep in the mountains of southwest Virginia; but it was happening this weekend, and he had to work. 'I hate to miss it,' said Isaac, 'since Ralph passed last year. This'll be the first time they have the festival without him.'

'Do you know about the Stanley Brothers?' asked JM.

Of course I didn't.

A brief and incomplete history of bluegrass, part 2

Once upon a time - the 1930s, in fact - there were two brothers. They grew up on a farm in southwestern Virginia and learned to play music from their mother; she owned a banjo, and their father had a good singing voice. When he left them all for another woman, the teenagers had to make their own way in the world. That's how they wound up running moonshine for their uncle.

When they weren't flouting the law, they made extra cash playing gigs at local schoolhouses. Carter was a gregarious guitar player who made a natural frontman. Ralph, shy and two years younger, was happy picking banjo in Carter's shadow. His high tenor sounded good paired with Carter's mellifluous lead singing.

The Stanley Brothers, as their act was known, played regularly on the radio. The gig didn't pay, but it created free advertising for their shows. Ralph and Carter were fervent fans of the Blue Grass Boys - Bill Monroe was their hero. They would tune in to the band's programme and recreate their set the next day on their own show. Unfortunately, Bill did not find this flattering. In fact, it made him pretty mad.

Ralph and Carter continued what they considered their loving homage. It was so popular that one of their first records, in 1948, was a copy of a song called 'Molly and Tenbrooks' that Bill and his band liked to play, and had, as it happened, recorded in their own studio sessions.

The Stanleys' recording came out before Bill's. He was furious.

Bill didn't speak to the Stanley Brothers for a long while.

CHAPTER 6

I know it sounds implausible, but it had not occurred to me, while preparing for my trip, that there might be camping involved. Going to festivals wasn't any part of my experience and, whenever I pictured them, I saw daytime activities: drinking, sitting out in the sun, drinking, listening to live bands, drinking, eating burgers from vans, and drinking. At no stage had I considered where I'd sleep, or in what.

There were plenty of culture shocks waiting for me at the 'Hills of Home' - the Ralph Stanley Festival, in southwest Virginia, that Isaac had told me about. But the realisation that I was about to spend a couple of nights in a field that was 90 per cent slurry was the first unpleasant bolt. It was 8 p.m., it had been raining for twelve hours, and the plots set aside for tents were empty, save for one doubtful-looking couple, testing their guy lines and wearing black bin bags. My new friends in Boone had generously provided me with a borrowed tent and sleeping bag and roll mat; I took one look at that desolate terrain and knew that I'd be sleeping in my car.

A hundred or so trailers, caravans and RVs were parked in close formation across the site, so I knew there must be at least a hundred people at the festival, but I couldn't see a single one. I pulled my plastic poncho over my head, sploshed along a small stream that had once been a footpath, and arrived at the centre of operations. A wooden pavilion sheltered a couple of dozen rows of camp chairs and a stage that could have belonged to a boy-scout jamboree. The four-piece band were singing a miserable-sounding song to a three-quarter-empty venue. At least they weren't bringing too many people down.

I flung myself into the nearest seat and wondered how soon I would leave. It seemed ridiculous, right now, that I'd travelled four hours to be here, through the action sequences of Noah's Flood, along viciously winding mountain roads. Ralph Stanley's old homeplace was in the Clinch Mountains, northwest of Boone; he'd grown up in one of the 'deep hollers' that bluegrass songs liked to refer to. These hollows were tiny, isolated, and barely liveable gaps in the mountains, with enough workable land for a little subsistence farming. It was like living in the centre of a maze.

Isaac had warned me about the journey; he'd tried it in a pickup once, he said, and thought the switchbacks were going to break his truck in half. I liked an interesting drive, I told him. But by the third hour of dragging my steering wheel around the switchbacks – some of them, somehow, *more* than 180 degrees – both my arms and my brain were jelly. And the Ralph Stanley CD I had brought as the soundtrack to my journey hadn't helped my mental state.

It had seemed smart to familiarise myself with the songs that made Ralph and his brother, Carter, famous and the two-disc set I'd found at a second-hand store promised to deliver all the greatest hits, both the ones that they had performed as the Stanley Brothers, and Ralph's later work with the Clinch Mountain Boys. The titles should have warned me that this was not going to be a happy affair. 'Short Life of Trouble'. 'Motherless Children'. 'The Fields Have Turned Brown'.

There was a considerable amount of death packaged into

my two-disc set. I had already begun to notice bluegrass's fascination with fatalities, particularly violent ones – the murder ballad, where some poor girl was nastily killed because her lover didn't trust her, was a staple of the genre. And then there were the gospel numbers, which viewed life as a mere stepping stone en route to eternal glory (or, possibly, damnation), and looked forward to the day when it was all over.

The Stanleys, however, were especially interested in heart-tugging, almost Dickensian deaths – as in 'The Orphan Girl', who dies at the door of the rich man who has refused to shelter her. Or 'The Drunken Driver', who runs down two children, only to discover, as they lie dying, that they're his own. Possibly the greatest pathos was reserved for the poor mother who died repeatedly in their lyrics, often forgotten by or separated from her son. A title like 'Memories of Mother', for instance, sounded heart-warming enough, until you put it in the context of the others: 'Mother No Longer Awaits Me at Home', 'A Mother's Prayer', 'Mother's Only Sleeping'. Most of these were written by Carter. Clearly, someone had Mummy issues.

Ralph Stanley's tenor was perfectly calibrated to wring every maudlin, Little-Nell-is-Dead tear out of his subject matter. There was a reason the Coen brothers chose him to sing 'O Death' over the lynching scene in *O Brother, Where Art Thou?* Nothing could conjure the same level of doom-laden mournfulness as his plaintive-oboe of a voice. And the further I reached into the cold, wet, lonely mountains where he had grown up, in a holler so remote even modern transport couldn't smooth over the journey, the more that voice made sense to me.

I sat, pathetically, in a campground with no campfires, and listened to the four-piece band pay tribute to their lost chief. Then I bought a bag of doughnuts, ate half, and squelched back to my car.

Next morning I woke in a deep sweat; the returning sun had converted my vehicle into a mobile sauna. I had only just finished my breakfast (the rest of the doughnuts) when a golf cart pulled up next to my car and its two occupants – men of indeterminate age, but approximately a hundred years between them – introduced themselves as Bill and Burley. Burley was well named: tall and broad, he wore his shirt unbuttoned almost to the waist, revealing a belly that suggested his pursuit of the alternative kind of six-pack. 'But everyone calls me Taters,' he said. I asked why. 'Because I like taters,' he replied.

Bill was shorter, older, and wore a ball cap that announced him as a US Marine Corps Veteran. 'You're not from around these parts,' he told me. 'Is this your first time?' I nodded, and he jabbed his thumb to his chest. 'This is my forty-fifth time here,' he declared. 'Jump on! We'll show you around. Have y'all seen the cemetery yet?'

The cart whined and wobbled over the rutted ground as Bill and Taters gave me their credentials. 'Everyone knows that's my spot,' said Bill, waving his hand at a small trailer as we passed. 'Ralph used to tell 'em all: this is Bill's place, you can't park here.' He had been at the inaugural festival here in 1970, and had only missed two since; he spoke of Ralph and the Stanley family with a proprietorial love and pride that was both heartfelt and seemingly excessive.

'My wife knows this weekend is sacred to me,' said Bill, explaining why she wasn't here. His granddaughter was equally understanding, he said, of why he was not at her graduation right now. 'Have you seen Too-ie before?' Taters asked me. I was so baffled by this gnomic utterance that I simply shook my head. 'You'll have a treat later!' said Bill.

The motorhomes ran out at the bottom of a small hill; at

the top was a metal gate welcoming you to the Hills of Home, and a cedar surrounded by gravestones. Past the tree, and the older-looking stones which rose and fell with the slope of the ground, emerged two solid marble vaults, their bulk reflected in the polished slate floor before them. One was big enough to hold three bodies, the other two; the name 'STANLEY' was stamped on each, as well as on the trio of marble benches that crouched nearby for contemplation. The Stars and Stripes flew over the scene, with an eagle, wings spread, at the top of the flagpole.

'There's where we buried Ralph last year,' said Bill, nodding his head at the larger vault. There were two other names next to Ralph's: Lucy Jane and Jimmi. Lucy Jane was his mother, said Bill, the one who taught Ralph to play the banjo, and kept her boys alive on the vegetables she grew in their garden after their father walked out. 'And this one's for his wife, Jimmi. She's still living. She'll be right there.'

There was a sniffling sound behind me, and I turned round, surprised to see Taters's red-rimmed eyes. 'It's sad,' he said, shaking his big head. 'This is the first time I've been up here since the funeral.'

'That was something else,' remembered Bill. 'Me and Taters stood over yonder' – he pointed at a corner of the slate floor – 'and Jimmi was on her knees in front of the vault until they opened it up and put him in.' There were hundreds of mourners, he told me; country stars like Vince Gill and Ricky Skaggs and Patty Loveless flew in to sing at Ralph's graveside. I marvelled that Bill and Taters had snagged such prime positions. 'I told you, they treat us like family here,' said Bill. 'C'm over here and look at brother Carter's.'

The two-person vault commemorated Carter and his wife, Mary. 'He died in '66, same year my dad did,' said Bill. 'He was only forty-one.'

I noticed that his mother, Lucy Jane, had outlived him. Which made all those dolorous refrains about dead mothers even weirder.

'Him and my dad drunk together a lot,' said Taters. 'He'd come to the house and make music, and, Lord, I'd watch 'em.'

'Ralph told me that Carter could take a pint of bourbon and it just made one drink,' said Bill. 'That's how bad it was. The war had pickled his brain.'

Carter drank with a lot more people than just Taters's dad, it seemed. The Stanley Brothers' frontman possessed a voice so supple and sympathetic that even Monroe, not given to compliments, once called him the best lead singer in bluegrass. But Carter had had a taste for alcohol ever since he encountered moonshine in his teens, and his two-year spell in the Army Air Corps towards the end of the Second World War only made it worse. 'You see, Carter, he was the one that was in the battle bad,' said Bill. 'Ralph was in the army, but he wasn't in the fight.'

Music was supposed to be an escape from the hardship of the mountains, but the Stanleys never managed to shake off the shadow of tragedy. Carter got into violent brawls, sometimes with his own band members; Ralph was in a head-on car crash. When the rapid rise of another hillbilly called Elvis Presley rearranged the musical universe in the fifties, the brothers could barely find paying work and the grind only worsened Carter's alcoholism. In another ten years, he had finally and fatally wrecked his liver.

It seemed that Carter never experienced the recognition and reward that came to his brother. Ralph carried on the band after Carter's death, finding fortune, and God. A staunch Democrat, Ralph performed at the presidential inaugurations of Jimmy Carter and Bill Clinton - and even campaigned for Barack Obama. His fixations with death and memory, however, remained. Bill pointed out a modest-looking farm-house down the hill where Ralph's mother once lived; Ralph had kept it exactly as it was when she died, not a saucepan moved from its place since 1973.

Then there was this marble memorial, which had, he once told Bill, cost him five million dollars. Now he had a living legacy too.

'You're saying you never heard Too-ie?' asked Taters. 'Well, we about gonna fix that.'

It wasn't Too-ie, I discovered. It was *Two*-ie, otherwise known as Two, or, more formally, Ralph II. Ralph Stanley's son had been performing alongside him since he was a kid. 'I remember when that little thing first got up there playing the spoons,' said Bill. Now Two had inherited the band. Literally: Ralph had bequeathed him the Clinch Mountain Boys name in his will.

Two's band were programmed to play an afternoon and evening set every day of the festival. These performances were what people left their RVs for, and when the Clinch Mountain Boys played that afternoon, the pavilion was full. The band wore shirts and ties, and Stetsons like the ones I'd seen on Ralph Stanley's head in photographs; Two wore a brown suit and black sunglasses. His voice was a little bland for my tastes, but the band played with a fierce drive, fuelled by an almost manic performance from the banjo player, who whooped and hollered at random.

The crowd ate it up. Sometimes they yelled encouragement mid-song as if they were at a football game. Sometimes they rose to their feet with the solemn dignity of a Carnegie Hall audience that's just heard Yo-Yo Ma. The climax of the set was a song called 'Wave On, Old Glory', which Two had written as a tribute to those who had died while serving in the armed

65

forces, and was releasing on his new album. The Hills of Home Festival was always held on Memorial Day weekend, when the US honours its military dead.

Veterans were invited to stand at the front, facing the audience, while a large American flag was unfurled behind them, and everyone in the place stood to attention, hands on hearts, chins to the sky. When it was over, the servicemen holding the flag folded it into a perfect isosceles triangle and presented it to an emotional Ralph II.

'I don't think I've been more proud of a song,' he said, adding that the flag itself would now be sent to the White House. 'This isn't anything political. Whether you're Republican or Democrat, he's our commander-in-chief, and we're just honouring our veterans.' And as if to prove it he read out the words on the flag case: 'Thank you, President Trump, for Making America Great Again.'

After the set, we headed back to Bill's trailer for a drink. It may have looked small, but it was full of bounty: its fold-out table supported an impressive collection of bottles, from rum and whiskey to a kryptonite-green concoction that turned out to be margarita mix. The pride of the collection was hidden in a cupboard next to the sink – a stack of Mason jars filled with clear liquid.

But the moonshine only came out later at night. For now, Taters set up his deep-fat fryer and cooked us chicken nuggets while he and Bill rescued beers from their cooler and chased them with vodka. They weren't the type who needed alcohol to loosen their tongues, and I enjoyed the gruff confidence with which they delivered their stories: 'Honey, when I tell you something, you can take it to the bank,' Bill declared.

Most were tales about Ralph or Carter. Some were about drinking with Ralph II, and I knew those were Bill's favourites, because I heard them repeated, several times, over the course of the weekend. They also speculated, with friends who dropped by, about the absence of Two's young nephew, Nathan. Nathan had often performed with Ralph and Two in the past and was notably missing from the bill that weekend.

The possibility of internecine rivalry was a major talking point. Nathan had not been shy about his own claim to Ralph's throne. He had released an album entitled *The Legacy Continues*. He'd written songs entitled 'Papaw I Love You' and 'He'll Always Be Papaw to Me'. In the months after his grandfather's death, he'd gone on the road with a show called 'A Tribute to My Papaw'.

Whether there was really any tension or not, the gossipy nature of the campground made it feel less like a festival than a family reunion. Everyone spoke as if they truly were kin to each other, and to the Stanleys. One year on, Ralph's passing was still fresh enough for faces to cloud with grief at his mention. Bands doused their stage banter with nostalgic memories of the brothers. The heavy sentimentality set the tone among the crowd; one audience member even confided to me that he didn't enjoy Two's stuff much, 'but we support him because of his daddy'.

'You try to beat the Stanley Brothers, you're barking up the wrong tree,' said one band leader. That dictum was reflected in the remarkably similar sound of most of the music played that weekend: a strict, old-school approach that paid its own tribute to bluegrass's glory days. The theme of remembrance mingled with a heady military pride. 'Wave On, Old Glory' was played so many times that the veterans began to know their cue.

Several trailers flew the flag of their particular corps; Bill went nowhere without his Marines sweater and his Trump lapel pin. Strangers stopped to ask each other where they'd served, and the encounters were a pageant of brotherhood:

the handshake that turned into a hug, heads held close together in an almost romantic embrace.

The etiquette on these occasions seemed to be to talk about the circumstances in which you left the service, followed by an exchange of opinions on the situation in the Middle East. Trump had made many of the people here happy with his recent bombing of Syria, but even more so with his anti-Muslim rhetoric and his travel ban. The two issues tended to be conflated; one veteran said candidly that he wished he were back in the service so he could go 'over there' and 'kill 'em all'.

I once overheard Bill telling a fellow veteran, 'I don't want praise and glory, I just want appreciation.' I wondered if that was one reason he came here every year. It was hard to fathom what else we were all gathered for. It wasn't the music. I never heard people talk about their favourite songs, only their favourite memories. There were no jamming circles or opportunities to play with others. ('The good Lord made pickers and he made listeners,' said Taters. 'And I'm a listener.') Most of the music was poorly attended. In between Two's sets, people sat in their campsites telling stories of festivals past.

I met Ralph II, eventually. Bill and Taters liked to glide around in their golf cart, waving at folks they saw once a year, like a royal delegation. We were on one of these tours when we caught up with Two on his way to the merch table to sign CDs. He was in visible demand from his many admirers, but he made time for us. There were polite remarks about how hard it had been to do the festival without his father, and how honoured he was by the military flag they were sending to the White House. It must be strange for him, I said, when he knew his father was such a committed Democrat. 'Yes, well, the Democrats have changed a lot since then,' he replied. 'If he could see them now, I'm pretty sure he'd have switched sides.'

I watched him head to the table, where queues of retirement-age acolytes were waiting to shake his hand, and remind him of days gone by. As long as he kept playing, the commemorative cult of Stanley would endure. And why not? The first generation of bluegrassers had reached their natural term limit; Bill Monroe, Earl Scruggs and Lester Flatt were all gone, and now time had claimed the final founding father. Dr Ralph had been canny to raise a son - and grandson, Nathan - who could take over the family business.

Perhaps festivals like this would keep the origins of blue-grass alive. That's not how it felt though. As I drove back through the hollers, it felt like I'd watched as the adherents of a way of life long gone laid candles at its shrine.

A brief and incomplete history of bluegrass, part 3

So, there were these two brothers. It was the 1930s. They grew up on a farm. They played music together. You get the gist.

The brothers were Earl and Horace Scruggs. Horace, the older one, played guitar. Earl played his papa's banjo; his father had died of tuberculosis when he was only four. Earl learned to play with his thumb and his index finger, the way a lot of folk did back then.

He and Horace worked out a smart way to keep their rhythm tight. They'd begin a song standing back to back on the porch, walk around the house in separate directions, and see if they were still in time when they met up again. One day they had a big old row and ten-year-old Earl slammed up the stairs and shut himself in his room with his banjo. He practised for hours until he could hit the strings with his middle finger too. It added an extra note per beat. It helped him play faster. It sounded damn good.

Teenage Horace married and joined the army. Teenage Earl took a job in a textile mill. There weren't many other options for paid work. Except music. Earl managed to get a gig playing for a band out of Knoxville, Tennessee. When that fell through, Bill Monroe – who'd heard about his revolutionary three-finger style – gave him a job with the Blue Grass Boys.

Earl liked playing Bill's music. He got on well with his bandmates, especially Lester Flatt, who played guitar and sang lead. But he didn't like the way Bill worked them. They drove long hours between gigs, crammed next to their instrument cases in the back of a limo. Bill was too cheap to keep the cars running well, so they often broke down by the side of the road. He was too cheap to pay for hotel rooms, so the band had to cover all their expenses out of their salary. It wasn't like their salaries were that great in the first place, either.

After three years on the road, Earl decided to quit the band. Two weeks later, Lester handed in his notice. They said it was a coincidence, but within a month their new band had made its radio debut. Earl's signature tune, 'Foggy Mountain Breakdown', sounded suspiciously like one he used to play for Bill Monroe.

Bill got a new banjo player and a new guitarist. He forbade all mention of Flatt's and Scruggs's names. He refused to play shows where they were booked and tried to keep them off the *Grand Ole Opry*. But he couldn't stop people loving them. Flatt and Scruggs and the Foggy Mountain Boys became famous all over America. Their fans called their music 'bluegrass-style' because it was like the stuff they'd played when they were the Blue Grass Boys.

Bill didn't speak to Flatt and Scruggs for a long while.

CHAPTER 7

Classical music is one of the most vivid, emotional and compelling art forms of this world. Unfortunately, it is also a bugger to learn. It's so complex and exacting that it only works as a form of expression once you've nailed down each exacting semiquaver. Playing *The Nutcracker Suite* isn't about being 'there or thereabouts': at every stage of the page there is only one right note. When you're learning, of course, there are an almost infinite number of wrong ones.

For this reason, the teaching can tend towards the fascistic. When I was growing up, I was lucky enough to have some very kind, encouraging teachers, but I was never left in any doubt as to the discipline expected of a classical musician. At music college, if you turned up late for orchestra you were marked absent because, as the orchestra master liked to remind us, if this was the Berlin Philharmonic you'd have already been fired.

And then there was The Serb. He arrived one day, out of the blue, to replace my much-loved violin teacher, Anna, who had won a fellowship abroad. Anna had encouraged and praised her pupils; The Serb preferred unremitting honesty. His favourite trick was to listen to you play the piece you had been practising all week and then, after an uncomfortable silence, ask: 'Well, do *you* think that was good?'

On The Serb's first week, three pupils walked out of his lessons in tears; by the second, half his pupils had asked to be transferred. He was terrifying, but I stayed with him anyway, through the tears (mine) and the tantrums (his – if he deemed that you hadn't practised enough, he would simply refuse to teach and throw you out of the room). One summer, I broke my wrist ice-skating and showed up at my lesson with my left arm encased in plaster. The Serb was silent a long time, then he turned to my mother. 'She is this desperate not to play?'

But there was something in me that wanted the challenge: of making him smile, perhaps, or forcing a brief compliment out of him. Just the word 'better' was so hard won I grabbed it like a trophy and ran it back home to show my parents. And over time, I grew to understand The Serb. He himself was a sought-after soloist, and his own perfectionism made it hard for him to imagine anything less for his charges. He simply treated every pupil as an adult, and expected them to behave like the professional musicians he assumed they would become.

Perhaps he felt, too, the pressure of his role. The belief that he was supposed to somehow fashion me into an outstanding performer must have been extremely stressful. As it was, my failure to live up to his expectations left me convinced that, while I might be able, technically, to play the violin, I certainly couldn't call myself a musician.

As I set about my task of becoming a bluegrass fiddler, however, I was grateful to The Serb for the disciplined approach to practice he'd instilled in me. Desperate as I was to improve, I spent boring hours closeted away in my room at Andrew and Carrie's. My plan was to memorise tunes until I had a decent repertoire, or until my head spontaneously combusted from the effort. Each morning, when Andrew and

Carrie left for work, I turned on my laptop, found a standard that came up often at the jams, and stuck it on repeat until I could play along at the right speed.

The biggest frustration wasn't learning the tunes; I had a good ear, and could pick up a melody within a few times of hearing it. The problem was that I never sounded anything like the original. I could play all the right notes in the right order. But it was obvious to me - and, I assumed, to anyone else - that something was missing. Nothing I tried sounded like bluegrass. To me, it didn't even *feel* like bluegrass. It was like a school chemistry experiment gone wrong - I'd started with the exact same elements as everyone else in the class, but instead of finishing with the required cobalt crystals and odourless gas, I'd somehow produced a purple liquid and a slight smell of sulphur.

Mindful of Pete Wernick's words - 'The *only* way you'll get better is playing with other people' - I sought out opportunities to pick with others as often as I could. Back home in London, I used to roll my eyes if I had to travel further than a half-hour from my house to meet a friend; but here in the US I had accepted that jamming regularly would mean saddling up the Elantra and getting well acquainted with the rear-mirror-view of a two-ton truck speeding towards my back bumper. Any environmental scruples about a 200-mile round trip for a two-hour session were squeezed into the trunk along with the emergency snacks.

Since I was starting from the bottom, I had no pride: I would go literally anywhere for a picking session. Rotary clubs, farmers' barns, side-of-the-road sandwich stands, didn't matter to me. One Monday morning I headed back to Taylorsville for a jam at the senior citizen day-care centre. It was a good decision: the old folk played slow enough that I could keep up. My appearance there was considered so extraordinary that by the time we were finishing up, the reporter from the local newspaper had arrived; 'English Girl Plays Fiddle' made page 5 of the *Taylorsville Times*.

JM had been right – arriving at a jam with a violin was like showing up with a crate of moonshine. Which often meant that even a fledgling technique like mine was greeted like the second coming of Stéphane Grappelli. You might have thought the situation would give me confidence, but it had the reverse effect and made me acutely self-conscious. I often found myself loathing everything I played, and squirmed with embarrassment when people – whether out of kindness, pity, or genuine appreciation – told me I sounded great. 'But I don't!' I wanted to scream. 'I was out of tune! I was out of time! And everything I play sounds utterly insipid!'

I never felt like that at Murphy's, though. Maybe it was the pizza, maybe it was John's silly songs, but that place felt like family from the get-go. I learned a lot from watching the prodigious talent of Liam and Tray and Eliot, and I quickly grew fond of Zeb and Julie. Julie had long brown hair and glorious teeth, which were regularly paraded in a wide smile. Zeb had a relaxed face, big eyes and a slowness to respond which gave the impression, when you first met him, that he might be stoned. He was just very thoughtful.

Zeb's dad had been a musician too, he told me, in a band called Southern Exposure. 'I think it's the name of a gentlemen's magazine now,' he mused. Like most musicians round here, Zeb and Julie's real income came from teaching and second jobs. He worked part-time at a flower and produce market; she waited tables. They had discovered a recent moneymaker, though, in weddings. With its mountain views and resort hotels, Boone had become a destination for bridal parties. 'A wedding gig's only an hour or two and it pays much better than a bar,' Julie told me. 'You don't have to stay up till 2 a.m. playing till your hands bleed, for fifty dollars.'

I got an insight into their lives during my second week in town. When the Murphy's jam finished at 10 p.m., a select few musicians would take the stage in the sticky bar and play for tips. That Wednesday they were short, and Zeb asked me to join them. I recognised less than one in three songs they played, and even the ones I knew I screwed up, but it was a noisy night and I gratefully realised that no one was listening. Well, no one except one young guy in a farm cap, who seemed to know Zeb, and was cheering on each song with enthusiastic, if ironical, whoops. 'Yeah! Ploughing! Whoo! Retributive justice! Yee *doggie!*'

After two hours of playing to a bunch of drinkers who paid more attention to the ads on the TV than they did to us, Zeb made sure I went home with my twenty-dollar share from the tips jug. My pride at landing my first paid gig was somewhat offset by the thought that Zeb could barely have covered his fuel costs.

Julie suggested I stop by the Appalachian State University library: it had an impressive collection of bluegrass-related materials that was looked after by a friend of hers called Trevor. She and Zeb and Trevor had all studied together at college, and Julie took me to meet him; I recognised the guy who'd been whooping at Murphy's. He showed me around the open bookshelves, then took me through a locked door to the archive, where boxes of papers and artefacts documented the story of Appalachia and its people.

The place was a gold mine. Drawers of CDs housed more than a century of the music of the mountains; every important album I had heard people mention was alphabetically catalogued and ready to be listened to. There were rare live performances, and field recordings, and a raft of DVDs and video cassettes that promised a glimpse of long-gone legends in their prime. I was aware that one of my biggest problems in trying to pick up bluegrass from scratch was that I hadn't heard enough of the masters of the genre. This looked like a good solution.

The real treasure in the collection, though, was Trevor. He had grown up on a hundred-acre farm in a remote part of southwest Virginia, an only child. 'My early social life was church, cattle auctions and cows,' he said, grinning. His voice had a pleasing elasticity that bent the sentences as he spoke; he could make the word 'no' last for four syllables.

Julie told me that when she had first spotted Trevor on campus, she'd turned to a friend and asked, 'Who brought Tom Sawyer?' He still wore much the same uniform as he had then: shirt buttoned to the cuffs (Julie said she'd never seen his arms), and a farm-supply ball cap, beneath which poked some brown sideburns. He had a pencil-shading of facial hair on his otherwise pale young face. A pair of cowboy boots emerged unexpectedly from the bottom of his jeans.

Trevor's first month at university had been an ordeal: trial by town. 'This place was way too fast,' he said, as we looked down from the empty library onto the quiet streets. 'I was having a meltdown. "What is this? When do they turn the lights off?"' His fellow students had been mostly kids from the city and the suburbs, 'And I didn't know what to talk to them about because they were talking about malls and stuff. I'd never been to a mall. Lucky I had music, or else I never would have talked to anybody.'

Trevor had learned banjo and guitar from his hometown barber, Jim, and taught himself to play fiddle. He was twenty-eight now, and taught some of the kids in Boone. So he was full of sympathy for my struggle with the music. I was welcome to use the collection any time, he said, and he'd look out some materials that might help me understand bluegrass better.

It was a healthy change from driving myself crazy with fiddle practice every day. And so the library became my second home. I'd collect a biography of Red Smiley or Jesse McReynolds from the shelves, head to the listening room, assume the university-issue headphones, and dose myself with their songs. (It was around this time that I discovered that Jim and Jesse were brothers, rather than brother and sister.) At lunchtime, Trevor and I would sit in the Boone Saloon, the closest bar to our part of campus, eating sandwiches and soup.

Trevor talked about Southern life the way he approached life in general. He had a mischievous humour, combined with a wisdom and perspective beyond his years. It was as if the two sides of Boone coexisted in him. He got annoyed, for instance, when people said that Southerners didn't get irony – 'We *live* it,' he told me – but he could also appreciate why rural folk didn't find sitcoms like *Friends* or sketch shows like *Saturday Night Live* funny. 'I remember feeling, as a kid, there's no place where people really look or act like that.'

He was especially passionate about history. It was at one of our lunches I learned bluegrass's backstory beyond the mountains – beyond the ocean, in fact, all the way back to the mother country, Great Britain. I was telling Trevor how often, when I met someone new round here, they would instantly want to claim their own British heritage. Everyone round here seemed to be able to tell me about their European ancestors, or name the obscure village graveyard in which they were buried. Even if they couldn't always pronounce it correctly.

Having never had much interest in my own family tree, I was cynical about all this expert genealogy. 'And everyone's always telling me they're three-quarter Scots-Irish,' I said, rolling my eyes. 'What does that even mean? Don't Americans realise that Scotland and Ireland are different countries?'

Trevor looked at me slightly strangely. He was too polite to call me an ignoramus or an idiot. Instead, he put down his beer, and tactfully filled in the details of my own country's history that I had, apparently, never bothered to learn.

I knew nothing, for instance, of the wave of migration from Scotland to Ulster in the seventeenth century, part of King James VI's colonisation of Ireland. Nor had I heard of their onward journey to America, throughout the eighteenth and nineteenth centuries, as a succession of kings cracked down on their dissenting religious beliefs. Or how, searching for their own land to settle, the Scots-Irish had pushed past the now-crowded colonies on the eastern seaboard into the mountains of Appalachia, where life was hard but free.

And that, said Trevor, was where the music of this region had come from. With the settlers was transplanted an entire musical tradition that mingled the storytelling of the Scottish ballad with the jigs and reels of Irish fiddling. The tunes had been passed down, and evolved, through the generations. Ballads began to incorporate stories from their new home – local tales of murder, moonshine and lawless frontier living.

The role of the fiddle, however, didn't change. It remained the lord of the dance. Singing and dancing were the sole forms of recreation in an otherwise tough, penurious existence. The Scots-Irish didn't sound like an especially sociable people – it was said that if you could see the smoke from your neighbour's chimney, you were living too close – but a dance was an opportunity to cast off your cares, however briefly.

And all you needed for one was a fiddle and someone who could play it. Easily portable, a violin could be an entire orchestra – rhythm section, soloist and accompaniment combined. Fiddlers travelled from holler to holler, their instrument slung across their back with string, staging entertainment wherever they were welcome.

By the nineteenth century, the fiddle had made acquaintance with the banjo, inventing America's first popular dance combo; over the course of the next hundred years, the guitar, mandolin and bass joined them to create the string band. The purpose remained the same – to give the hard-working folk something to get jiggy to. Trevor's entire fiddling education had been playing for local dances. 'I just went at it,' he said. 'It's the same the way the first bluegrass fiddlers learned.'

Accompanying dancers required two things above all: you kept the beat, and you never stopped. 'It's like an endurance test,' he explained. 'A dance might go on for ten minutes. You're playing the same melody over and over again, so you've got to make variations on it to keep it interesting while you're still keeping the people moving.' And you needed to be able to foster a boisterous atmosphere. 'If you want to get a crowd of people up on their feet, you've got to be able to tap into the rowdiness.'

I thought about my own fiddling: the nervously careful, note-perfect, weak-ass simulation of the tunes I'd learned. No wonder it didn't sound right. The only dancing I could imagine being done to my playing was kindergarten ballet. I needed to access some of the boot-stomping momentum of the music's roots. I needed to go full *Footloose*.

There were a couple of regular dances in the vicinity of Boone. I chose one that took place in an old dairy barn just outside the town, not least because the land surrounding it looked like set dressing for a period drama. Picturesque farms and pretty red barns, with blackboard signs offering fresh eggs for sale; a creek running by the road, and a crowd of rhododendrons, interspersed with wild lilies.

If I wanted to imagine myself back in the days of the set-tlers, this was my Vaseline-lens moment. The late-afternoon sun caught the far side of the holler, spotlighting a plough left out in the fields as if for show. A blue jay swept past my windscreen. A bunny hopped placidly in front of my wheels.

It only cost seven dollars cash to take part in the dance, but by the look of the room, the organisers were hot-stepping to a fortune. There must have been a couple of hundred enthusi-asts romping across the barn, as a caller, wearing a turquoise tie-dye T-shirt and pyjama bottoms that didn't quite match, conducted the chaos from the stage. The phrases he used were baffling – 'Allemande! Now a clover leaf... roll away!' – and the moves seemed to fall somewhere between square dancing and a Gaelic ceilidh. But the main aim was clear: to swing your partner until you induced internal haemorrhage, or at least some mild ear bleeding.

There were, in fact, regular safety briefings. Participants were warned to keep their elbows in, as bruising may occur; to moderate the size of their steps so that they didn't trample each other; and to be sure, when they dipped their partner, not to 'put their head in a dangerous position'. I had never tried a social activity that came with so many warnings. 'Look out for each other, take care of one another,' said the caller, before the musicians kicked off the next number. Apparently, in the mountains, dancing was an extreme sport.

I stood at the edge of the floor for only a short time before a man with a pork-pie hat, middle-age spread and a heavy Teutonic accent asked me to dance. After ten minutes of twirling, my brain was in danger of coming loose. It was like being on a waltzer at a fairground, if it had no seats, no safety bar, and was operated by an eight-year-old psychopath on a sugar high. 'Za trick is to shnap your het to za left!' barked Pork Pie, as I stumbled, dizzily, into someone else's do-si-do.

I recovered my footing, but a few minutes later I promenaded the wrong way and he was forced to rescue me from being stampeded by the oncoming flank. When the dance was over he bowed quickly and disappeared, with a slightly disgusted expression.

'Some people take it so seriously,' sighed the woman standing next to me. 'Don't worry. Someone else will be along soon...'

She was right. No one stood alone - or stood still - for long, and I was soon whisked back into the fray. Passed from one hand to another, the room spinning in the background, it was an almost hallucinatory experience. Faces loomed towards you through the blur and the heat: some big and round, some small and angular; pinched and serious, or fixed with a rictus grin; bald, or covered in lanky curls; all dripping with sweat. The stamping and whooping was infectious, and the spinning mildly ecstatic. The whirling dervishes of medieval Turkey were supposed to achieve nirvana through their constant rotations; caught up in the dance, a similar euphoria stole over me. I felt as wild and free as I'd ever known.

Between sets, we gasped in damp, hot air, while a pair of electric fans battled pyrrhically to cool us down. Sometimes the caller would try to bring some calm with a waltz, and couples would shuffle around the space, twirling each other intermittently until they got their breath back. The men, who suffered worst, had come prepared, wearing handkerchiefs and bandanas to keep the sweat out of their eyes. One guy had brought a succession of clean T-shirts and changed at the end of each dance, his naked torso winking pinkly from the corner.

Distracted by the complexity of the choreography and deafened by the footfall, you barely noticed the musicians on the stage. Two young men - a fiddler, backed up by a guitarist -

were contriving to sound like a far larger band, their insistent reel driving the dancers on like an electric cattle-prod. Recovering from the last dance, I stood to watch them. The fiddler's body contorted as he played – arching, kicking, curling into a sudden ball then exploding to full height, as if the music were trying to find new routes out, burst from every limb and sinew.

Beat, harmony, and melody came all at once, no string wasted, and his bow never paused, his fingers never tired: he seemed bound to the song from the moment it started to its final note, some quarter of an hour later. The interim was a perpetual movement of flurried scales, breathless variations and impossible segues, the notes tripping from brain to arm to airwaves faster than the speed of conscious thought.

They began a new tune, and the dancers regrouped, oblivious to all but the beat. The musicians didn't care; they gave their all, playing for themselves, for the simple love of the music. I stood transfixed, feeling a curious longing. What I was watching was passion: pure, physical, all-consuming passion. I tried to think if I had ever felt like that while playing my violin, but no memories surfaced. For as long as I could remember, music was hard graft. Could I ever learn to play like this?

A brief and incomplete history of bluegrass, part 4

Before there was bluegrass, explained Trevor, there was old-time. Except, obviously, it wasn't called old-time. Folk here just called it, well, music.

It was the sound of the mountains – the ballads from the old country, the frontier songs of the new one, the fiddle tunes played at square dances. And it was celebrated at events called fiddlers' conventions, where musicians gathered to compete against each other for cash money.

Then Bill Monroe came along with his brash new sound. His band took the instruments and stylings of the old music and turned them up to eleven. They experimented. They improvised. They dazzled. They spawned a generation of imitators.

So now, at the fiddlers' conventions, you had a problem. Because your traditional banjo players, they were playing in the old styles, plucking and strumming the strings the way everyone had before Earl decided to reinvent the instrument. How could these guys compete with the quick-draw bandits of bluegrass?

And your traditional fiddle players: what were they supposed to do? Local celebrities were finding themselves blown out of the water by jazzy Johnny-Come-Latelys who could play all the way up to third position.

The contest organisers decided there was only one fair solution: different categories. So now there were two acknowledged strains of mountain music: bluegrass; and old-time. The old-timers thought the bluegrassers were arrogant show-offs, and the bluegrassers thought the old-timers were persnickety fussbudgets.

They hadn't liked each other for a long while.

CHAPTER 8

On my first trip to North Carolina, I'd met some old-time musicians who had tried to convert me away from bluegrass. The scene was more welcoming, they said; it was less macho and no one expected you to improvise flashy solos. One fiddler, hearing me play, had even suggested I'd be better suited to it. 'Bluegrass is one of the hardest styles in the world to master,' he'd said. 'Perhaps you shouldn't run before you can walk.'

That, I suspect, was where I first got the sense that old-time was for players who couldn't hack bluegrass. In an old-time jam, everyone played the tune together, rather than in sequence, so there was no one-upmanship. It wasn't performance art, it was a participatory experience, and the audience was secondary, even unnecessary. Plus, you were expected to play the tune as it was written, rather than make up your own version. You could add small variations, but old-time was all about being true to the source material. Or in other words, playing the same notes over and over again.

Certainly, the thought of never having to improvise sounded pretty good to me, and there were other benefits too. In bluegrass sessions, the banjo tended to steal the show, but here the fiddle was king, and everyone else was playing backup. The noisy five-string resonator banjos that bluegrassers played were *verboten*, being too late an invention for the music; the banjos played in old-time were open-backed, and played in a quieter, less frenetic style known as 'clawhammer'. Even the singer was an afterthought in an old-time jam – most of the tunes didn't have words.

Old-time was, essentially, a vehicle to fiddle as much as you liked, with no one judging you while you did. I thought hard about what that fiddler had said to me. Maybe I was being too ambitious. I was a decent technical violinist, no more; my playing had no particular creative genius. My character was more suited to the middle of the road, the ordinary, the safe – and bluegrass was none of those things.

And so, while I was staying outside Charlotte on my first trip, with my kind surrogate grandparents, Fred and Doris, I had taken a lesson with an old-time teacher called Adam, who wore a waistcoat, a flat cap, and a piebald beard that encircled his mouth and chin like a sleeping possum. He certainly looked like someone trying to inhabit the 1800s. But he hadn't always been an old-timer. In his twenties he was the electric guitarist in a San Francisco experimental-electronic-industrial rock band, recording albums with titles like *Slow Motion Apocalypse*. Even more surprisingly, he had used to play bluegrass.

'I got tired of the testosterone and the I'm-better-than-you-are,' he shrugged. 'So I dropped out. To hell with all this "Who's the hottest player?" I just like old, corny songs, and pretty melodies, stuff that has feeling, y'know?' He was convinced it was the machismo of soloing that put women off bluegrass, and old-time, he told me, had a much more even gender split. It reminded me of statistics on women in the workplace, and how they are less likely than men to apply for roles or job promotions that they aren't 100 per cent qualified for. That kind of natural self-effacement would certainly be a drawback in bluegrass.

Old-time was traditionally passed down with little emphasis on sophisticated technique. There wasn't a lot of call for it in the music's heyday - mountain fiddlers developed their technical skills only as far as they needed to be able to saw a tune for a dance. They were labourers - most lacked the spare time, or the inclination, to sit around honing their vibrato or polishing their double stops.

Adam hunched over, his fiddle precariously balanced on his collarbone, and played tunes for me to copy, slowly and patiently, phrase by painstaking phrase. My classical technique was, perversely, a drawback: my bowing action was too smooth. Adam would prefer that I throw my elbow about in a fashion that my old violin teacher The Serb used to disparage as 'chicken wing'. Adam was also concerned with my intonation.

'That B you just played - it's supposed to be a blue note.'

'What's a blue note?'

'Somewhere halfway in between two notes. So it's not a B, but it's not a B-flat either.'

'You want me to play out of tune? On purpose?'

I heard the sound of wood splintering as The Serb snapped my bow across his knee and ordered me out of his sight.

The other problem was that I wasn't rhythmic enough. Adam said he wanted me to start thinking of my fiddle as a drum. I felt like those innocents who arrived at drama school, dead excited about becoming the next Al Pacino, only to be told that everything they know is wrong, and they'll spend the next year pretending to be a farmyard animal.

On my way out of the door, Adam handed me a generous stack of CDs: 'This is the real thing, some of the earliest music recordings ever made, all the way back to the 1920s. You've heard of Tommy Jarrell?' I shook my head. Adam looked a little horrified. Tommy Jarrell, he said, had been born in 1901. He'd lived his entire life in the fantastically named town of Toast in Surry County, North Carolina.

Jarrell's fiddling prowess became legendary and while he was rarely seen in public, his mountain hideaway became a place of pilgrimage, drawing fiddlers from far and wide to try to learn his secrets and emulate his style. 'He's long dead now,' said Adam. 'But you listen to those recordings, you can still learn from him.'

Eager to begin my education, I slotted one of the CDs into the car stereo as I drove away. The loud hiss of the record needle and the woody click of the turntable was soon joined by a scratchy solo fiddle. It pulsed away, its insistent, off-key jerks and shuffles repeating their patterns endlessly.

It didn't take long to regret my decision. If there's a more dangerous music to be trapped in a car with, I haven't heard it: after a track and a half I was at the edge of my sanity. It struck me that when The Machines make their bid for world domination, they will play pre-war old-time music across the airwaves, swivelling their CCTV camera eyes in glee as the humans claw at their ears and accelerate blindly into the central reservation.

I hadn't attempted to listen to old-time again since. So I was apprehensive, now, as I pitched my tent at the Veterans Memorial Park in Mount Airy. I had come along with Zeb and Julie to experience my first fiddlers' convention, and Mount Airy - an hour and a half outside Boone, just before North Carolina became Virginia - was a mere two miles from Tommy Jarrell's hometown, at the epicentre of the old-time tradition. The ground was already a few thousand people full, and it was clear, with each new vehicle that rolled in, disgorging fiddle, banjo and guitar cases, that this was going to be a noisy evening.

On top of the hill where we made camp – the only wooded part of the site, and thus the only place offering any shelter from the uncompromising sun – we had a view across the entire park. Below us, a phalanx of RVs framed a large open space; beyond them, separated by a fence, was a small village of tents. Julie interpreted the landscape for me. 'Those tents down by the creek are the real traditional old-timers,' she said. 'The RVs are all bluegrassers. Up on the hill, anything goes.' And what about the big open space? 'Oh, that's where the stage is,' she said. 'But hardly anyone actually goes there.'

The contest had begun already; from an aged PA, you could hear the distant strain of a solo fiddle drift up the hill. Every couple of minutes, the music stopped and low human tones garbled the name of the next entrant. Julie had come here for the old-time jamming, and when she and Zeb joined a cluster of pickers nearby, they invited me to pull up a chair and join in. There was almost no crossover between the bluegrass fiddle tunes I knew and the ones they were playing. Still, inflated by the false notion that this was fundamentally music for people who weren't good enough to play bluegrass, I was sure I'd be able to pick up the tunes as I went, or at least get somewhere close.

I was wrong. I couldn't even pick out the starting notes: the melodies, simple as they purportedly were, were submerged beneath the tide of rhythm. Even more impenetrable was the off-kilter bowing style – a mystery of co-ordination, like trying to rub your head and pat your stomach while balancing a tray of hot coffee on your lap and reciting *The Waste Land*. I watched Julie closely, but when I tried to replicate the see-saw effect she was creating with her right arm, I nearly knocked out my neighbour's teeth.

The tunes went on for what felt like aeons; the longer they lasted, the more people seemed to be transported by them, until their facial expressions suggested they'd left their earthly bodies entirely. Watching them become so serene just made me angry. It felt like someone was playing a trick on me. How could music this dully repetitive be blissing them out?

I held out for an hour or more, keen to be with my friends but feeling more distant from them the longer we played. It was hard to see everyone else having such a great time when I couldn't feel the same way. Uninitiated in this secret society, and feeling like a musical gooseberry, I wandered down the hill towards the RVs. The path took me past the stage - a truck trailer with one side cut out of it - and a set of empty stalls for livestock, used when this place ran auctions and county fairs. There was also an elliptical racetrack, too sandy for athletics, too small for greyhounds. I later discovered it was a new addition to the park, purpose-built for lawnmower racing.

The only people hanging out near the stage were the ones lining up to compete. Disheartened and a little lonely, I gravitated towards the food and drink trucks. There were only two: one sold frozen lemonade, the other something called funnel cakes. The latter turned out to be a sort of pancake that had had a terrible accident with a spaghetti maker. Mine was the size of a dinner plate and the thickness of a family bible; it came covered in sugar, chocolate sauce, whipped cream and shame. By the third bite, I was convinced I felt my health insurance increase.

There wasn't much activity around the RVs - it was a hot afternoon, and lots of people were inside, making the most of their air conditioning. But one awning, stretched between two adjacent motorhomes, had four guys playing beneath it. According to the banner out front, their band was called Never Too Late; I took this, correctly as it turned out, to be a commentary on their age.

On a different day I might have walked by – ageing white men were, as I was discovering, the most common currency in bluegrass. But I really wanted some company, so I stood and listened until they finished their song, hoping they'd invite me in.

'Get that fiddle out,' boomed the mandolin player, from under his floppy sunhat. 'It's doing no good in its case.'

It was a relief to feel I hadn't come all this way for nothing, and my time in the library was clearly paying off: I was recognising not just the songs they played, but the style too. From the quirky chord progressions I intimated that they favoured the bluegrass of the sixties and seventies, when bands like the Country Gentleman and the Seldom Scene moved the genre on by incorporating material (folk songs, Bob Dylan covers) from outside its original canon.

'Do you know this one?' said the guitarist, and launched into 'House of the Rising Sun'.

I threw myself into my playing with a purpose and confidence that felt rather new for me. They, in turn, swiftly adopted me into their wisecracking, box-wine-sipping club. When they weren't playing or drinking, they poked fun at the old-time musicians we were surrounded by.

'I hope you brought your earplugs, Emma...'

'See that lot over there? They've been playing the same tune since last year.'

'They've been playing the same tune since 1901!'

Throwing shade at old-timers was, apparently, one of the customs and great pleasures of a fiddlers' convention – an event, I was just discovering, where people travelled large distances to ignore each other and play music with their friends from home.

The afternoon turned into evening, and I was invited to join the band for their chilli dinner. People began to emerge from their RVs – some to pick, but many more to promenade around the park, listening to the jams. They'd pause as they reached us, and sometimes just the presence of one or two would attract more, and soon we'd have a small audience standing nearby, their arms crossed, their heads nodding along.

Julie had been spot on about the distinction between the tents – home to the old-timers – and the RVs. These commodious, over-equipped apartments-on-wheels were, almost exclusively, the preserve of the bluegrass brigade. I asked the floppy-hatted mandolinist why. 'Because bluegrassers have jobs,' he huffed. 'Old-timers are all hippies with no money.'

This, it turned out, wasn't just another joke, but what Trevor might have called an observable social phenomenon based in historic accuracy. During the folk revival of the late 1950s, artists like Pete and Mike Seeger, with their passion for the music of the people, had sought out and championed old-time. It was a music which had rarely made it out of the mountains, and had long since slipped into obscurity. Through their songbooks, performances, recordings and festivals, they introduced this sound of the South to a new generation of Californian beatniks and coffee-house-frequenting New Yorkers.

A great number of folkies promptly took up their fiddles and open-backed banjos; many descended on Surry County to learn whatever they could from ageing gurus like Tommy Jarrell before the tradition was lost for ever. Jarrell and his friends were thrilled to have someone to take on their inheritance. And so, an unlikely and rather heart-warming bond developed between these mountain men of simple means and old-fashioned values and the long-haired, liberal-minded, college-educated, frankly scruffy young 'uns who ate their food and slept on their floors.

In the end, an entire, obscure musical culture had been saved from extinction by a bunch of hippies. Now the hippies were getting old, and it was they who were passing the music down. They still chose to camp in tents, though - their bones might be beginning to creak, but they were too environmentally conscious (and sometimes too broke) to invest in one of the gas-guzzling road-homes that the bluegrassers dragged out each weekend.

I walked back through the old-timers' tents that night, when it had got too late even for Never Too Late. The sprawling polyester village was largely unlit, and it looked as if its inhabitants had all gone to bed. But there were still people up, playing: it wasn't the melodies I could make out, but the beat, pulsing through the night air.

Threading my way through the guy ropes, I caught a moaning of strings, and saw a clump of silhouettes playing blindly in the dark. I snuck towards them and counted the outlines of nine or ten bodies. Several had dramatic protrusions from their necks that could only be fiddles, and a couple of banjo heads gave off an iridescent gleam.

I was used to orchestras, where the violin section plays as one, their bows pulled seamlessly in the same direction as if by an invisible puppet master, creating a single descant that resonates with the depth of an ocean. To my ears, this ensemble was chaotic. Each fiddler played their own approximation of the notes, while their different styles overlapped and a muddied melody rose unevenly from the pile.

The rhythm alone was a constant, collecting its passenger

tune along the way with the raddled care of a late-night bus driver on his final shift. There was no time to pause or consider: the tune moved on relentlessly until someone said 'Out!' - and, as if they'd just rung the conductor's bell, the music pulled up at its final stop, and everyone hopped off.

There was no comment or congratulation when they finished, just a long silence and an eerily earnest atmosphere. People seemed to be waiting for divine inspiration for the next number; several had their eyes closed, as if it was still not quite dark enough for them. The air of expectancy made it more like a religious gathering than a social event.

The contest went on all the next day. There were numerous categories that covered all the instruments from bluegrass mandolin to old-time banjo, and occasionally someone on the hill would head down to what Zeb called 'the flatlands' for their competition slot. But the supposed main event went unheeded by most people who, like me, spent much of the day alternately napping and jamming and drinking with their buddies.

The hill had a different demographic to the rest of the campsite and was occupied, almost exclusively, by the younger crowd. It had been dubbed 'Hippie Hill' when the Mount Airy convention began in the seventies, and still kept both the name and the low-lying aroma of pot. But really, it was hipster hill, a conglomeration of unmarried twenty- and thirty-somethings, wearing vintage threads and drinking craft beer from their coolers. Several had bankrupted themselves for the month by purchasing their weekend provisions at Whole Foods.

The music up here was different too. It was still predominantly old-time; these younger pickers traded in arcane fiddle tunes with names like 'Glass-Eyed Possum' and 'Dog

Tray Waltz' and 'Rattlesnake Daddy', the more obscure, the better. But they were also fluent in turn-of-the-century rags, and 1920s swing – it was a miracle no one ever broke into a Charleston. One of Julie's friends turned up in a bright yellow school bus – it was, apparently, his permanent address – and hosted a jam jazz in it every night. He had managed to instal an upright piano and a drum set and still leave room for a horn section where the back seats should have been.

It was there that I met Peter. He was an outlier – neither the same generation, nor as eclectic in his tastes, as the kids on the hill. But he had studied deeply in the field of old-time and become a mentor to some of them. I told him that I was struggling to understand the attraction of old-time, and he told me his story – how, after a mental breakdown in his twenties, he had found the music a form of therapy that was as physical as it was psychological.

'This music is kinaesthetic,' said Peter. 'You get a feeling from playing it that's almost like human touch. And that's what I needed in my life, a sense of connection.' I admired his honesty but I still didn't understand. It was all about the syncopation, Peter said – being thrown repeatedly off the beat. He told me to picture a cat sitting on a newspaper, then imagine shuffling the newspaper back and forth. 'It's the loss, and reacquisition, of balance that feels nice. It creates the sensation of being lightly drunk.'

He stopped, as if something had just occurred to him. 'Actually, every old-time fiddler I've studied was a raging alcoholic.'

Wait, I said – you're saying you get a buzz from playing?

'Well, for me it's the feeling of a dog with its head out the car window going, "This is awesome!" For some people it's more Zen.'

Trevor had once told me that he knew fiddlers who went

into a trance-like state when they played. (He himself never had, he said, although he'd occasionally experienced involuntary drooling.) Perhaps this made some sense of why the hippie movement was so interested in an arcane subgenre of centuries-old folk music. It was helping them achieve a kind of transcendental state. They had co-opted an entire genre and repurposed it with the goal of getting high.

I thought back to how I'd felt as I whirled around at the dance, how the physical sensation had taken over and set me free from the tyranny of conscious thought. That wasn't something I regularly experienced; I tended to feel as buttoned up as a frock coat at a cotillion. I envied people like Zeb and Julie who could enjoy that freedom as they played. The idea that music might transport me to a different state of being was one I longed for.

Peter said it was an attribute of old-time that bluegrassers often overlooked, because when they listened to it 'they don't hear any technical wizardry'. 'They don't get what's really there, which is like a piece of raku pottery. It's not highly decorated but it's beautiful in its rough form.'

He talked movingly of the selfless spirit of old-time, as you sacrificed your individual personality to help each other find the common rhythm and be meaningfully present in the moment. 'Bluegrass is like bling,' he said, 'but old-time is like hookah, filling up the room with an invitation to take a hit.'

Peter made it sound like a utopia, and here I had the perfect opportunity to experience it. I could pull up a chair, take out my fiddle, and humbly submit myself to the collective groove until I found nirvana.

I didn't, though. I waited till I'd finished my beer, and then I turned round and went straight back to the RV park. I just didn't have the patience to take on *another* form of music I

97

couldn't play. Besides, I was kind of enjoying the tribalism: it helped me know that I belonged.

I spent the rest of the weekend down with the bluegrass fraternity, drinking wine with the Never Too Late guys, and, in the next trailer along, drinking soda with a teetotal all-Baptist band. I indulged in the common sense of superiority, and laughed at the jokes about the cat-flogging noises from the next field. I may not have been able to call myself a true bluegrass fiddler yet, but I could define myself by what I wasn't. And at least I wasn't an old-timer.

At midnight on the final night, I walked back to my tent. The flatlands were quiet, but a polyphonic hum still resonated from Hippie Hill. The woods were strung with tarps and blankets, magical bivouacs decorated with lanterns and Christmas lights, music emerging from almost every one. Sitting among one tangle of tree roots, a quartet of waifs sang heart-rendingly to no one but themselves from their fairy grotto.

A little further along, under a khaki canopy, I saw Julie picking with a handful of others. It was old-time, but with a modern inflection I'd never heard before, less earthy, more edgy. The melody continually reinvented itself in a constantly shifting soundscape, profound and ethereal, weightless yet sharp as a blade. It responded to no outward instruction but moved entirely by its own spirit, now building in an urgent crescendo, now dwindling to almost nothing. There were no words, and no pre-programmed emotion. This was music that expressed nothing but itself.

I stood a long while, captivated, watching where it went next, hoping it wouldn't end. I had thought it would be hard to fall asleep, up on the hill, where the jams went on till dawn, and their overlapping genres transmitted through your tent like a radio picking up a dozen broadcasts at once.

But the effect was surprisingly comforting, a hypnotic blend of jazz, blues, gospel and string bands, and I drifted away, carried into the same primordial soup that had given birth to bluegrass, seventy years ago.

A top-five of audience requests

There are certain numbers that bluegrass audiences like to hear over and over. And over.

They are, in ascending order of popularity:

5. 'Rocky Top' - The Osborne Brothers first recorded this ditty in 1967. It was adopted as one of Tennessee's state songs in 1982. And no bluegrass musician has successfully managed to escape it since.

4. 'Man of Constant Sorrow' - No one has done more for bluegrass's popularity in the twenty-first century than George Clooney, and he only lip-synced to this song. 'Can you play that one from *O Brother, Where Art Thou?*' asks every person who has ever seen that film.

3. 'Dueling Banjos' - 'Can you play that one from *Deliverance?*' asks everyone else.

2. 'Ashokan Farewell' - Ken Burns made this haunting tune the theme for his epic documentary series on the Civil War. Now people think it's a bona fide piece of Confederate history. It was written by a New Yorker in the 1990s.

1. 'Orange Blossom Special' - This famous fiddle tune requires its player to spend large swathes of their time and energy making train sounds - whistles noises, engine noises and brake noises - before launching into a high-tempo finale of string-crossing double stops and semiquavers. It is the showy encore demanded at almost every gig and no one, it seems, gets tired of hearing it. Except musicians.

Health and safety note: Never, under any circumstance, call for any of these songs at a jam.

CHAPTER 9

No one cursed in North Carolina. At least, not in front of me. Trevor sometimes let loose a 'dang!' to express surprise. If that alone couldn't convey the depth of his emotion, he turned it into a diphthong – 'da-yang!' But I rarely heard a stronger epithet from anyone. At dinner once, Trevor's girlfriend, Savannah, finished a story with the words '. . . and then she told him he could go to H-E-double-hockey-sticks!' I'd never heard the phrase before, and the hockey sticks I pictured were pointing the wrong way, so it took me a moment to figure out.

We British people pride ourselves on our ability to be polite in all circumstances, but the South felt like another level altogether. I discovered that a man heading for the passenger side of his car wasn't planning to hastily remove last night's McDonald's wrappers, but to open the door for me, as if I were a crisp-suited politician in a TV drama. I also learned that being called 'ma'am' was a sign of respect, not a passive-aggressive indication that I was getting on someone's nerves.

And these courtesies weren't just cosmetic. British folk might hold a door for someone in public but we aren't required to smile as we do so. We consider it well within our social rights to refuse eye contact and maintain a tight, even pained expression, highlighting the sacrifice we are making to perform our civic duty. Here, however, people seemed to deem it their greatest pleasure to make your journey to the post-office counter just a half-second swifter.

I hadn't had to pay this much attention to my manners since my parents were trying to get me into nice schools; and I was, inevitably and inadvertently, making some faux pas along the way. I wasn't given to swearing, but even the occasional 'damn' or 'Good God!' that slipped through my lips could evince a wince, especially if there were children present. (There were other words that shocked mixed company; I learned the hard way not to tell people that I was a socialist.)

Another problem was my lack of punctuality. In London you are expected to show up a half-hour after you agreed to meet, and then blame public transport. If I was five minutes late in the South, I'd get a phone call expressing genuine concerns for my safety.

But mostly, I just found it hard to fathom people's intentions. On my first morning in the South, I had stepped into a country store to buy some eggs and bacon for my breakfast, and the man in line next to me had asked me what part of New York I lived in. I looked at him in shock, bewildered by the question, horrified by what it might mean. Did he think he knew me? Or was this some kind of insult about my clothes? He had probably misheard my accent, and was about to launch into a tirade about damn Yankees and their snowflake-loving, Union-minded ways. The thought occurred that I might be in physical danger.

It turned out he had noticed the registration plates on my rental car outside and this was simply his way of beginning a conversation. And that was just the start of my random, brief encounters. It didn't matter where I was - in a store, on the street, on a treadmill at the gym - people I didn't know constantly said hello, and asked questions, and told me about themselves. This is unacceptable behaviour in London, where we are happy to pack ourselves nose-to-armpit in a subterranean tin can to get to work, but possess a ninja-like power to speed through a crowd without ever accidentally catching someone's eye.

Still, I wasn't the only person in Boone who found myself challenged by the locals' friendliness. Andrew, my landlord-cum-housemate, once told me that he could always recognise tourists because they grabbed their children's hands when he said hello. Outsiders like me had to learn from scratch that these bold opening gambits from people we didn't know were not the prelude to some kind of scam or request for money. It took me a while to recognise them for what they were: face-value attempts to connect with a fellow human, and show some kindness in the process.

Trust was extended far more quickly here than in the cold, northern land I'd come from. Friendship was offered almost instantly. People I had barely met invited me out for breakfast or lunch and, when the check came, refused to let me pay. 'Oh, you can look after us when we come to England,' they'd say.

I assumed that the Cane Mill Road boys - Eliot, Liam and Tray, who I still saw regularly at jams - made polite conversation with me because their parents had told them to, or because they were working on a geography project about Europe. Why else would teenage lads waste time on a boring adult? As time progressed, I realised they were genuinely keen to get to know me, and were used to making friends of all ages. Inter-generational relationships were standard here, and communal life was completely different to what I knew back home.

You couldn't walk down the main street of such a small

town without bumping into someone you knew, and people dropped in on each other unannounced, made spontaneous plans. When I asked if someone was free to hang out, I was amazed how often the answer was yes: in London, it can take four weeks to plan an evening, even with your closest friends. Here, they'd stop by at the sound of a beer-can opening. And if I ever did find myself alone and in want of company, I only had to go out to a bar or a coffee shop – there was never any embarrassment in striking up conversation with the strangers I found there.

Social anxiety was just not a recognised condition in the mountains. And whatever herd immunity existed was now at work in me. A sort of thaw set in. I stopped flinching when people spoke to me in the street; I learned to relax and exchange smiles instead of blushing with embarrassment and immediately looking at a distant tree. When people asked me what I was doing in America, I got better at telling them; my inclination to apologise for everything, including myself, began to subside.

So when Trevor invited me along to watch his band practise, the prospect of sitting awkwardly on the sidelines as a bunch of men I'd not met before rehearsed was not as off-putting as it would once have been. He was heading to meet them after work one day, just over the state line in southwest Virginia; his old banjo teacher, Jim, would be there. 'Jim's good people. And it's a pretty place. Lots of Christmas-tree farms.'

The drive north took a little over an hour along single-lane highways, past hills and fields, rock quarries and grazing buffalo. There were more barns than houses along the route; some falling down, some smartly new. Some bore large diamonds in colourful patterns that represented the region's quilting tradition: a symbol of Appalachia. Some carried other signals: a Confederate flag; a Trump 2016 banner.

And then, to our right, we saw an abrupt peak. It was called Mount Jefferson, said Trevor, although historic maps named it Negro Mountain, and a few of the older folk still called it that. It had got the name, supposedly, for its place as an escape route on the Underground Railroad, the trail that enslaved African Americans took as they fled the plantations further south. We passed towns that got smaller and smaller like Russian dolls until we started turning onto roads without signage that threatened to lead nowhere.

'If you carry on that way you get to the place I grew up,' said Trevor, pointing up one of the nameless byways. 'It's called Rural Retreat.'

'Sounds like a holiday resort,' I said.

'And it is certainly not.'

He described instead a farming village in a steep-sided valley: three gas stations, a country kitchen that served breakfast for lunch, and a defunct railroad whose tracks, bisecting the main street, were the only landmark. Trevor's parents kept cattle nearby, and lived in a nineteenth-century farmhouse whose ceiling beams were too low and floorboards too uneven. 'It's worst for my father, since he's six foot four. Once he hit his toe and his head at the same time. He just lay on the floor, yowling.'

We turned into a driveway, in front of a brick building that could have been a small chapel, or a village hall. It was actually a large workshop, its benches scattered with hand tools and unusual machines, a mouthwatering smell of woodshavings hanging in the air. Three men, their hair a varying shade of grizzle, were conversing in a friendly rumble. Most of the members of Trevor's band were in their seventies; he had got the gig on account of a former player passing away.

I stood near the door, feeling like a kid waiting outside the teachers' lounge, until Trevor stepped forward to introduce me. They nodded, and went back to their conversation. One of them, Wayne, was saying he needed a haircut.

'Well, siddown,' said Jim, the music teacher-cum-barber. 'We'll do it here.'

Wayne's hair, which curled thickly from under the sides of his baseball cap, was not as generously apportioned on the top of his head, and as Jim primped it with the clippers and the comb, it began to assume a rather Shakespearean look. 'You want one, Herb?' Jim asked. He snapped the dirty shop rag that had been tucked round Wayne's neck, creating a tornado of sawdust, and the other man took the stool. Herb sat patiently as Jim trimmed his eyebrows and his ears.

'I can do girls too,' said Jim, looking at me.

I stalled. The British me wanted to pass it off as a joke, giggle with embarrassment, and shyly decline. But Southern me wanted to prove I was game, and join the boys' club.

'Why not?' I said. 'It's been getting too long anyway.' Trevor stared at me and shook his head.

When Jim began, my hair stretched down to my shoulder blades; when he finished, the floor was covered in a brunette rug. It was probably a good thing that there weren't any mirrors in the workshop, I thought, although Trevor's face still bore a look of concern.

Wayne and Herb were both luthiers as well as musicians, and this was where they built their instruments. Wayne's guitars, Trevor whispered to me, were so legendary they changed hands for tens of thousands of dollars. His waiting list was said to be many years long. Some claimed it didn't exist at all and was just a fiction to put people off.

Wayne seemed to be the most reluctant master-craftsman on the planet and no one knew exactly what you had to do

107

to persuade him to build you a guitar. Some said the secret was to drop by with home baking or basketball tickets; others said you needed an antique gun or some other rare item to trade. Eric Clapton had only managed to acquire a guitar from Wayne when he agreed to raise money for a charity Wayne supported.

Our collective hair shorn, we took our instruments into the next room so the band could practise. They were booked to play on the weekend at a street festival in the nearby town of West Jefferson, and they needed enough material for a half-hour slot. I had never seen Trevor play before. I couldn't help but notice that his playing habits would have been drilled out of him in a single day at my music school.

He didn't hold his instrument the way an orthodox violin-ist would, at a 90-degree angle to his neck. In classical violin, correct posture is all-important; you sit up straight, feet planted squarely like chair legs, and your left elbow keeps your violin high and straight. Trevor sat with his left leg crossed casually over his right, his chest leaning forward and his fiddle slung so low that his wrist rested on his left thigh. When he played back-up, the fiddle didn't even stay on his shoulder, but slid down to rest on his breastbone.

The sound that came out of it, though, was mesmeric. His style was a blend of two cultures - a rhythmic, slightly rusty sound combined with a bluesy inflection, as if he were playing old-time with a bluegrass accent. They started with a very old fiddle tune called 'Bill Cheatham'; Trevor's bow rocked across all four strings like a shuttle on a loom. His right foot pumped up and down throughout, keeping the beat. It brought back a memory from when I was five, and my toes had involuntarily tapped as I played. My teacher had stood on them.

'That was a little bit rough,' said Trevor, when they'd finished.

'Too fast, wasn't it?' said Herb. And they kicked straight into another.

The band wasn't as slick or regimented as some I'd heard. They seemed instead to be trapping a wild energy that threatened, at any moment, to break free and send the separate instruments spinning off on their own axes. Yet the connection always held, and it was that tension, and closeness to danger, that gave the music its allure.

As if in approval, a black cat with a white chest and white socks on her hind legs wandered in, and rubbed up against Herb's legs as he sang. Out of the window, partially obscured by a lace curtain, I could see a steep slope of firs planted in rows, a vast arboreal army poised to sweep the valley.

A late golden light gleamed through the lace, turning the room into a Vermeer painting, bringing out the deep chestnut tones of Herb's face. It caught the moisture in the harmonica player's eye, and gave an added depth and dignity to his grey-white hair. The furniture in the room, too, seemed to belong to a twilight time. A beat-up brown sofa on which rested a large cowboy hat. A corner cabinet that held haphazard piles of books, five shotguns and a shelf of ammo. A couple of rocking chairs. A grandfather clock whose hands didn't move.

The music saturated every item with nostalgia. There was one particular tune I loved, which made no disguise of its old country origins. It was called 'Hangman's Reel', and it filled me with a flood of images. I felt as if I could hear all the way back to the upstairs room of an eighteenth-century inn, the kind where a young woman of middling means and reputation might meet her future husband at a dance. I pictured a couple, him in uniform, her curtseying as he offered his hand and walked her to the floor.

But as Trevor and Herb and the band kept playing, the pictures gave way to pure feeling. Some of it was written into the music itself. The reel contained a sequence that stayed suspended for a long while on the five chord: a chord that begs for resolution, aching to return to its root. When the tune finally resolved - and the bass played the walk-up to bring the listener back home - it sent a tingle of pleasure down my neural pathways.

A crack had opened in my emotions, and everything else in the room rushed to follow it in. The presence of the black cat, sitting still and shrewd, a witch's familiar. The ease with which the players handed off their solos to each other. The sight of a green shirt, pulled tight over a belly puffed out beneath a chestbone, fabric straining around the buttons. I felt tears springing towards my eyes and hoped they didn't show.

Somehow, even though I wasn't playing, I was experiencing the music not as a critical outsider, but in the ears and the fingers of the players themselves. I wished I could climb inside a fiddle, or place myself at the point where string and bow met - to be able, somehow, to inhabit the notes I was hearing. The music wasn't perfect, but its imperfection was exquisite. So much so that the joy it was causing me was offset with something that felt like heartburn.

It wasn't the first time that music had made me feel pain like this, but it was a rare occurrence and I didn't understand what it meant. Where did the hurt come from? Was it mine, or the music's? It was confusing, and too embarrassing to share; I'd never spoken to anyone about it before.

But the drive home from Wayne's was a late one, and the darkness of the roads, and my newly cropped hair, made me bolder than usual.

'Trevor, do you . . . look, this is going to sound weird. Do you ever find listening to music so beautiful that it hurts?'

I expected a pause, or a worried, sidelong look. I got neither.

'Oh yeah,' he said. 'That's happened to me plenty of times.'

I pushed on, through my own awkwardness.

'I felt something, listening to you guys tonight. I felt a connection to the music that I never feel when *I'm* playing.'

Trevor paused to consider this. So far from any town lights, the sky was a thick catalogue of stars. Even though the moon was nothing but a thin crescent, you could still see its circular outline in shadow.

'I don't get it *every* time I play,' he said. 'But if we get a real good tune going, something with a lot of drive and rhythm, it's there.'

It was as I'd expected. The existence of an entire level of musical experience I'd never had. The proof I needed that I had never really been a musician at all.

'But it doesn't bode well. Whenever I get that feeling, usually I mess up right after.'

A couple of days later, I got a message from the Never Too Late guys I'd met at Mount Airy. They had been booked to play the very same festival as Trevor's band, and wondered if I'd join them on fiddle. The fact that someone actually wanted me in their band brought me an excessive amount of joy: as if I'd been given access to an exclusive club I knew wasn't rich enough to join.

Being in a band had always seemed to me one of the coolest things you could do as a human being, which, I presumed, was precisely why I had never been in one. Sure, when I'd fantasised about it, I'd been striding coolly along pavements with a cigarette hanging from my lips, like Sandy at the end of *Grease*. I'd pictured punky evenings of aggressive noise-making in dingy bars, where guys would buy me drinks and tell me how much they dug our set. My imaginary bandmates weren't all past retirement age and wearing matching XXL T-shirts.

But these were the guys who wanted me. And appearing on a festival stage, I thought, might just confer the honorary status of bluegrasser that I was desperate to earn: playing festivals was what *real* pickers did. Vast numbers of these community events competed for attention every weekend from April to October; towns and counties all over Appalachia and beyond put on their own outdoor entertainments, and they all needed musicians. You could play at three a week and never run out of places to eat corndogs.

I wanted to make a good impression, so I got hold of the set list and went to work learning the songs. There were no plans to meet before the day of the gig – the band had played this same set often, and as the sidewoman, I was expected to turn up like a pro and get it right first time. In other words, I was going to have to wing it.

That Saturday, I drove back north to West Jefferson. It was deep in Christmas-tree territory and, to promote the region's prevailing trade, the town chiefs had given the festival a Yuletide theme, although they hadn't particularly followed through. Under the midsummer sun, occasional outcrops of reindeers and elves looked like they had crash-landed their sleigh on a practice sortie.

It was an eclectic and an eccentric affair. There was a rifle raffle, in which people could win actual guns, and a noisy re-enactment of a local Civil War skirmish, and a man with a metal hook for a left hand selling CDs. When I came across a booth called the John Birch Society, I took them to be a heritage preservation group, and fell into a misguided conversation about history. It turned out they were ultra-conservative conspiracy theorists who believed that the United Nations was the antichrist.

The streets were closed to traffic and, caught up in a back-log of cars looking for parking, I missed Trevor's set; but I soon discovered that pretty much every bluegrasser I knew had been booked to play. Tim was there, with JM and Isaac. Zeb was providing mandolin back-up to a county judge, who turned out to be one of Boone's family collection of Eggers, Eggers, Eggers & Eggers. A beloved local Elvis impersonator fought manfully against the wind, which kept catching his cape and wrapping it forcefully around his face as he sang.

The stage straddled the town's main crossroads; there was a small gazebo behind it where you could set down your instrument case and tune quietly, but you couldn't run through a song without disturbing the main act. A warm-up here meant walking a little way down the pavement, standing under a tree and blasting through the first eight bars with the guitarist.

I had practised plenty in the previous week, but as I joined the rest of the band – a few minutes before walking out in front of the crowd – I suddenly felt only the most precarious grip on the songs. I have never been good at playing my violin under pressure. Hidden in the folds of an orchestra's violin section, I could enjoy playing a symphony knowing that, as long as I kept my eye on the conductor and didn't come in a beat early, my wrong notes would never be distinguished from the throng. But performing as a soloist was another matter.

I'll be honest: I was the kind of person who usually *enjoyed* showing off. As an eldest child I had loved being the centre of attention, and as a rule-following teenager, acting in the school play or crushing it in the debating team was the only high I knew. I thrilled to the adrenaline of performing, inhaling the applause like nitrous oxide. But - violin was different. The further I advanced, the more aware of my mistakes I became, and the more tense I was before I even began. I was once so tight with nerves at an exam that when I picked up my bow to begin I accidentally threw it at the examiner.

The music school I attended had required us to take part in regular recitals and open auditions. Every performance you gave was assessed by your teachers - and with an informal grading system of glances, false praise and snide comments by your peer group. The teacher's notes might have been harsh, but they were nothing compared to the faux-comforting words from your secretly stoked rival, or the snigger from the trombonist you'd had a crush on for months.

For me, these occasions were like the medieval concept of trial by ordeal. In the perfect acoustics of the concert hall, every scratched bow was amplified, and every mis-hit note directly penetrated the ear of the unsympathetic jury. Playing an unaccompanied Bach partita to an audience of fifty of my peers and their parents was the closest I'll come to walking over hot irons.

When we took to the stage in West Jefferson, I headed, instinctively, for the back. But the microphones were set out in a straight row, like stakes you tie human sacrifices to, and my hopes of anonymity were shattered by the MC. 'Folks, I have an exciting announcement,' he told the large crowd, who were, thanks to the family nature of the event, disappointingly sober. 'It's rare enough we see a fiddle player here, and this one's come all the way from the land that gave us the Beatles, so we know we're in for something special. Let's give her a big hand!'

'Can she play "Orange Blossom Special"?' asked a voice from the second row.

I shook my head.

'What about "The Mockingbird"?'

The MC looked at me. I grimaced.

'Er, she don't know that one neither,' he announced apologetically.

'Well,' asked a quavering voice near the front, 'what *can* she play?'

At this point I would have happily volunteered myself for the Civil War re-enactment to end the humiliation, and the dread of more to come.

Sensing that the crowd was growing restless, our guitarist swiftly kicked into the first number. The tune passed around the instruments, and I steeled myself for the moment it would reach me. It was like a game of pass the parcel, only with the foreknowledge that on my go, I would unwrap a terrifying spider that would scuttle up my arm and cause me to lose control of my bladder. I scratched at my strings without enthusiasm.

The guitarist gave me an encouraging smile: my cue to take a solo. I made it halfway through before my mind went blank and my fingers, fresh out of messages from my brain, sputtered to a stop. I looked desperately into the faces of my bandmates, who all looked expectantly back at me. There was a silence that lasted several seconds, before the mandolinist cut in and rescued me.

I waited for the boos and the jeers I was sure would come. I had expected to fail, and, right on cue, I had. My fears that the restless element would stampede the stage and wreak terrible vengeance on the incompetent fiddle player were unfounded – we moved on to the next song without so much as a heckle – but I had lost my nerve. The next time the guitarist offered a solo, I meekly shook my head and continued my oh-so-background playing.

'How did it go?' asked Zeb, when I stepped off stage. He had been tuning up for his own set, and hadn't seen my public failure. My nerves were so raw I couldn't have explained it if I tried. Shame, self-loathing, misery and shock were still duking it out in my conscious mind and there was no room left for language.

'It was fine,' I said.

Zeb must have caught something in my face.

'It gets easier,' he said. 'You just have to learn to let go.'

I had heard this mantra before, from bluegrassers trying to explain to me the mystical art of playing and improvising at speed. The problem was, I didn't have the skill set to do that. If I let go, I fell, and there was nothing there to catch me, no cushiony bed of experience, no refreshing pool of musical ideas. There was just hard, stony ground.

If I was going to get better, there was only one option – push myself harder. I knew I wanted to sound more like a Southerner. But the next call I made was to Boston.

A brief and incomplete history of bluegrass, part 5

Two brothers. 1930s. Farm.

They were called Pierce and Harper Van Hoy. Their dad, HP, was a teacher, and in 1924 he had staged a fiddle contest in the school's gymnasium, on Easter weekend, to raise money for books. It had been such a success that he did it again the next year. And the next. And the next and the next and the next and the next.

By the time the boys were teenagers, HP's fiddlers' convention was the biggest thing that happened in the tiny rural community of Union Grove. There were three separate stages: one in the hall, one in the gym, and one in a big circus tent outside. Pierce was only fourteen when HP told him he had to run one of the stages. Pierce was scared, but he was more scared of his dad, so he did what he was told.

Harper played fiddle and immersed himself in mountain music. Pierce wasn't a musician at all, but he was a good promoter. By the sixties, when HP had handed down the business to his sons, it was attracting visitors in their thousands - including folkies from the north and hippies from the west and bikers from all over. It was getting too rowdy for the school. It was getting too rowdy for Harper.

Harper wanted to downsize the event and take it back to

its roots – smaller, traditional, family-friendly. Pierce wanted a bigger venue and bigger crowds. They couldn't agree.

So, in 1970, Pierce hosted the convention on his land. And Harper ran another one down the road, the very same weekend. They kept up their rival events for a decade.

Harper and Pierce didn't speak for a long while.

CHAPTER 10

There was a delay on the line, and the voice coming out of my computer screen buzzed a little. But still. There was no mistaking what it was saying.

'That's not going to cut it,' the voice told me, in hard-edged, northeastern tones. 'The length of your notes is wrong. The rhythm of your notes is wrong. Nobody ever plays that way in bluegrass. This isn't the second violin part in a Haydn fucking string quartet.'

The Boston number I'd called was that of Matt Glaser. If the best place to learn bluegrass was at your father's knee – and that ship had long since sailed for me – then the second best was the Berklee College of Music in Massachusetts, one of the most prestigious conservatories in the United States. It was responsible for many prodigious talents in the acoustic music scene (Berklee alumni had won hundreds of Grammy Awards between them) and Matt was the director of its renowned American roots programme – and, as it happened, a fiddle teacher.

Private lessons with Matt weren't cheap. And I would certainly be his most remedial student. But I needed someone who could speak to me in a language I understood; and a college professor might be just the right person to explain what was going wrong in my attempt to mimic this music.

A few emails persuaded Matt that I needed his help, and he agreed to a series of hour-long Skype sessions. I knew he had a reputation as the best. I just didn't know he had another reputation as well.

The first three times I brought up his name with people that knew him, I got the same reaction. 'He's a lunatic,' said the first person. 'Utter madman,' said the second. 'Completely nuts,' offered the third. Some even shared stories of bizarre Matt Glaser behaviour, like the time he had whimsically stopped his car in the middle of a main road, causing him to be chased for miles by an angry SUV driver throwing trash.

The man who appeared on my computer screen did not look particularly insane. He had an elliptical head and rimless glasses, and apologised that his emails to me before our lesson had been terse - he was struggling with tendonitis, and needed to keep typing to a minimum. He did, however, talk fast, his speech packed as densely as an A train at rush hour. It was a change of pace from the unhurried speech patterns I'd become attuned to, and I could hear how frenetic it might sound to Southern ears.

Matt had asked me to play a tune for him, then stopped me after only eight seconds to deliver his lacerating judgement. 'Have you heard this phrase: "That ain't no part of nothing"? It's what Bill Monroe said when he didn't like what another musician was playing. In other words, what you're doing has no connection to the musical style he invented. You've tipped your hat as an imposter already.'

I winced, but it was merely for show. I knew I should look crestfallen, or embarrassed, but I didn't feel either of those things. I was *elated*. I'd found what I wanted: someone prepared to call me out on my failures and pinpoint my problems.

'The other big mistake,' said Matt, 'is that you're just too timid. If you're going to play the wrong thing, at least be wrong and be *strong*. Hit it *hard*. No bluegrass fiddler sounds tepid and vague. As someone once said: why compound ignorance with inaudibility?'

The issue, as Matt saw it, was that there was no tradition of teaching bluegrass per se. 'It's difficult to figure out what to practise because the guys who invented this stuff didn't have a practice regimen,' he said. 'They were on the road performing and jamming all the time and they learned by playing with people.'

That was probably why I was finding it so frustrating, he explained. I'd grown up steeped in the orthodoxy of Western European music, where I trod the common pathway of all young violinists, from the studies of Kreutzer to the partitas of Johann Sebastian Bach, improving all the way until I was ready to take on the iconic concertos of Bruch, Mendelssohn or Tchaikovsky.

'So you're going through this vast repertoire of exercises and you have this sense that you're in somebody's hands. But within this American fiddling heritage, there have only been teachers in a formal sense for a decade. When guys like me realised we could make a buck.' He laughed, expelling air in percussive blasts. It made him sound like an actor, reading the words straight off the page: 'Ha! Ha! Ha!'

Matt's background was originally in jazz – he'd played with some 'heavy cats', he told me – and as he spoke about the music, his language oscillated between high academia and a late night in Brooklyn. One moment Matt would be talking about heuristics, tri-tones and modalities and the next he was yelling at me, 'Now feel the groove and *play* that shit!' His teaching method also involved me having to scat a lot more than I expected (Ella Fitzgerald may have been able to make 'ba-da-doo-da-dum-ba-doo' sound like poetry, but I could not). Even from eight hundred miles away, Matt's energy seemed underpinned with a hint of mania. I knew I'd learn a lot, if I could just keep up with his pinballing thoughts.

Matt asked what I wanted to get out of my lessons. I thought about it. And then I realised: I just wanted to be able to enjoy a jam. I told him how, even though I was a competent violinist, I could never relax and have a good time with the music, because I knew I was constantly faking it. 'Welcome to the club, my friend,' he said. 'This is not even a native language for most Americans. Up here in the northern cities, there are a lot of cats like me playing a music that has nothing to do with them.'

To anyone looking at a map of the States, the northeastern seaboard might appear of little importance in the history of bluegrass music. A proudly Southern phenomenon, bluegrass was born out of a specific blend of circumstances – Appalachian tradition, industrial migration, country radio – and remained heavily associated with the South's way of life. And yet the Yankee North could claim a huge debt of honour. It rescued bluegrass from an early grave.

In the fifties, as rock 'n' roll swept the nation, country music responded, electrifying instruments and searching out a smoother, more mainstream sound. Acoustic string music – including that of Bill Monroe, the Stanley Brothers and a generation of bands who had adopted their style – fell rapidly out of fashion. The airwaves were dominated by Jim Reeves, Patsy Cline and the so-called 'Nashville Sound'. Radio stations refused to play old-fashioned 'hillbilly' music, and those whose living depended on it were scrambling for survival.

Then came the folk boom, and the same wave of fascination that had drawn the earliest hippies down to fiddlers' conventions to learn old-time pulled bluegrass into its wake.

The 'hillbilly' music finally made its way north. In 1959, Earl Scruggs played at the inaugural Newport Folk Festival in Rhode Island. The same year, an *Esquire* article introduced bluegrass – which it called 'folk music on overdrive' – to its urban readers. The genre found a new audience just as it was threatening to pass into obscurity, and so the bluegrass artists lived to sing another day.

No trendspotter could have predicted the peculiar cultural exchange that followed. The middle-class city kids encountering bluegrass at college campus gigs shared little common life experience with the blue-collar performers who had worked in mines and factories, or grown up on dirt farms. Not just their upbringings but their political and religious beliefs – not to mention their manner of speech and sense of style – were poles apart. Yet at festival campgrounds, the good old boys of Kentucky, the Carolinas and Tennessee were soon discovering that their new fanbase didn't just enjoy listening to their songs. They could play them too.

This influx of outsiders had consequences that have been fought over ever since. The music's urban aficionados began pushing its boundaries as far as they knew how. And in the northeast, where the jazz scenes of Boston and New York dominated, they pushed them furthest. In essence: those damn Yankees started meddling with the music.

The irony is that Bill Monroe, the man who'd single-handedly invented bluegrass, was one of the first to foster their new ideas. Monroe came across an Amherst student called Bill Keith who played banjo in jazz bands in Massachusetts. Keith's technique – which enabled him to incorporate melodic runs on the instrument – was as significant a leap as the one Earl Scruggs had made when he mastered the three-finger roll. It allowed the banjo, already the most characteristic of bluegrass instruments, to sound more contemporary.

Monroe hired Keith for his band and talked him up as the best banjo player alive – a sharp side-dig at his former bandmate Earl Scruggs, who he still wasn't speaking to. But even a control freak like Monroe couldn't contain when and where people are going to experiment.

Jazz has a natural affinity with bluegrass. They're two of the most improvisatory genres in Western music. They share important features, like their use of pentatonic scales and syncopation. In the seventies and eighties, New York produced an entire scene of musical revolutionaries, many from Jewish families, including banjoists Tony Trischka and Béla Fleck, mandolin player Andy Statman – and my own Matt Glaser. They, among others, saw the overlaps between the genres as something to be embraced and celebrated.

The new direction had a name: 'progressive bluegrass'. It prioritised instruments over the singer. It took tunes as far from their simple three-chord melodies as possible, stretching and testing them like an elastic band. Sometimes, it bent the music so out of shape that it would never go back. It was exciting, it was impressive, and it was, apparently, the future. Some of those players were now canonical figures in bluegrass. Thanks to their influence, the northeast remained a magnet, incubator, and export hub for those who still wanted to take the music somewhere new.

My first experience of 'progressive bluegrass' came on a trip to New York in the early 2010s. A friend had told me about a free afternoon concert that was happening on Staten Island; the band was called Punch Brothers. 'If you like bluegrass, you'll love these guys,' she had said, and since I'd never been on the Staten Island ferry, and I was going to be spending my Sunday alone, I made myself a packed lunch and joined the tourists ogling the Statue of Liberty.

By the time I arrived at the park where the gig was taking

place, I had lost most of my enthusiasm for the adventure. There were no taxis at the ferry terminal, and the walk had taken forty minutes down a surprisingly ugly esplanade. I was sweaty and hungry, I'd missed the support act, and a tomato had exploded in my bag. And then a group of guys in their thirties had walked out on stage wearing archly vintage clothing – three-piece suits, cloth caps – and I'd rolled my eyes so hard I nearly cricked my neck. I'd come all this way to listen to a bunch of *hipsters*? I could have walked two streets from my home in London for that.

The mandolinist began to play before anyone else was ready, a little atonal riff he seemed to be offering up to no one but himself. Was he still tuning, perhaps? The banjo plucked a few unlikely notes behind him. A guitar slid in with an answering run, like a batter stealing first base; the bass player laid down some long bow. I couldn't tell if this was the start of a song or the end of a sound check.

But then the individual noises began to grow and coalesce like a creeping threat. Alien bacteria, perhaps, absorbing their environment and evolving rapidly into something cogent, conscious, dangerous. The sound grew louder, more sinister; a fiddle added urgent spikes of fear; I felt my lungs begin to bubble with anxiety. The music reached a crescendo of terror... and stopped dead. A half-breath later, the guitar kicked up a funky beat, and the mandolin player began to sing about his friend who tended bar.

The next hour was like falling down a rabbit hole and landing in a club compered by Stanley Kubrick or David Lynch. I had no idea exactly what was going on, but I recognised the genius at work. The band's authoritative handling of their instruments matched anything I'd heard in the classical world, but their masterful playing was only the half of it. It was what they were doing to music itself that was extraordinary:

125

bending it, contorting it, dismantling its molecules and creating new elements from scratch like chemistry savants.

Certainly, this was music I could never think or hope to play myself; it's probable that only a handful of people on the planet would have the skills to replicate what they were doing. They were a post-modern firework display, showering their listeners with ideas, allusions and deconstructed melodies that charged the atmosphere with electricity and emotion. When they finished, the air I'd been breathing was stuck in my windpipe like a bruise. After an ovation I didn't think was long or vociferous enough, their mandolin player returned on stage alone and encored with a prelude that Bach had written for violin.

Perhaps the band's influences had resonated with something in my background. Maybe my mind just found comfort and recognition in the brain-boggling intricacy of their work. For whatever reason, Punch Brothers left their mark on me in as unasked-for and permanent a way as those werewolves imprint on each other in *Twilight*. I felt an instant loyalty to that group that never faded. It seemed obvious to me, as apparent as blue is blue, that they were the best musicians I had ever had the fortune to hear.

And for that reason I'd been surprised and not a little deflated when I discovered that my North Carolina friends were less enamoured with them than me.

'Too many notes!' was the verdict of most people I encountered. 'You couldn't *pay* me to listen to that stuff,' said JM. Trevor, who I was sure would share my enthusiasm, told me he wouldn't cross the road to hear them sing. Their voices were too thin, he said, and even when he could understand the words he had no idea what they were talking about.

'But that's the brilliance of it!' I spluttered. 'Some of their lyrics are like a crossword puzzle – it's taken me *years* to work out what they mean.'

He shrugged. 'I can see they're having a good time, but I'm sure not.'

Punch Brothers weren't the only sticking point. When it came to progressive bluegrass, many Southerners just weren't buying it. Herb had told me in his workshop that bluegrass music today had degenerated 'to the point where it's not really music and I don't think it's very good at all'. 'There's no melody you can hang your hat on,' Jim agreed. 'Music has to move or it dies, but some people take it too far.' I asked when they thought bluegrass had started going downhill. 'After Bill Monroe,' Herb snorted.

A lot of the pickers I met told me that if they couldn't play along with the music, they lost interest in it. It was only then that I realised that the aspects that impressed me about this newer style of bluegrass – music that was vibrant and modern-edged, but also complex and note-heavy – were the very attributes that made it unattractive to my more traditional-minded friends. Bluegrass was, to them, a type of folk music, belonging to the people – and smart-aleck instrumentalists like Punch Brothers, who had trained at high-falutin' music colleges like Berklee or Juilliard, took it out of their hands and placed it in the rarefied environment of a concert hall. If that wasn't bad enough, the very people stealing it were northerners who had no heritage rights at all. Why should a bunch of privileged college grads in Boston be the heirs to their music?

This was emotional territory: not just a question of whether these modern forms had merit, but whether they counted as bluegrass at all. After all, bluegrass had rules. Sure, no one had ever quite defined them, or written them down, or asked the listening public to endorse them in a referendum.

But still. There was a general agreement that bluegrass should sound like bluegrass, not like jazz, or classical, or rock, or a mishmash of all three.

People found it far easier to define what wasn't bluegrass than what was. There's an accordion in the band? That ain't bluegrass! The banjo player's strumming? That ain't bluegrass! The fact that Bill Monroe had employed an accordion player in an early incarnation of his Blue Grass Boys, or that the music itself was a portmanteau invention – a wildly creative experiment that fused gospel, jazz, old-time and blues – was beside the point. Its radical beginnings did not give free rein to any and every genre-bender who wanted to advance the music twenty-first-century-style. And that was an absolute truth.

A quick summary of bluegrass song topics

1. The old homeplace: Usually a farm or a cabin, comes with a smattering of animals and at least one much-loved woman, either a mother or a sweetheart. Few bluegrass songwriters seem especially bothered about their dads.

2. Trains: Bluegrass is obsessed with trains, and you can be pretty confident that any number with the word 'special' in the title isn't talking about a lunchtime deal. 'Train 45', 'Brakeman's Blues', 'Mr Engineer', 'Fireball Mail' ... these musicians dedicated a lot of time to singing about a method of transport they never actually used.

3. Cheatin': Doesn't matter whether it's him or her, if it's a bluegrass love song, one of them's probably being unfaithful.

4. Drinkin': Because something's gotta to be to blame for all that cheatin', and because you can't have enough songs about moonshine. Otherwise known as Mountain Dew.

5. Killin': And some of it's pretty gruesome. Pretty Polly begs for her life in front of an open grave. Laurie Foster's

left naked by the side of the road. The Knoxville Girl gets dragged by her hair and drowned. Maybe it's all the cheatin' and drinkin', but there's a heck of a lot of homicide in bluegrass.

6. Chain gangs: The inevitable conclusion of all the afore-mentioned ill behaviour. If you hear someone singing about their nine-pound hammer, you can be fairly certain they're doing time.

CHAPTER 11

As I steered my way through the South, the church offered me guidance, in the most literal sense.

America's obsession with the same half-dozen fast-food chains made turn-offs, crossroads and sometimes entire towns hard to distinguish from each other. Road numbers and compass directions frequently confused me. But churches proved useful landmarks. Not the buildings themselves, which were pretty interchangeable. But the messages mounted on their lightboards.

'Give Satan an inch and he'll be your ruler.'

'Our church is prayer conditioned.'

'The best vitamin for a Christian is B1.'

Once I'd driven past one of those puns, there was no way I was forgetting it. And since every church in the South had their own inspirational motto, I was soon employing them as navigational tools.

A couple of particularly doom-laden messages helped me remember where to turn on my way home. Hang a left at 'You're only a heartbeat away from heaven or hell'; stay right at 'Think before you burn'. Several weeks passed before I realised the latter wasn't erected by the Baptists but by the fire department.

I was a churchgoer myself, and the week I arrived in Boone

I started looking around for a congregation to join. At home, I went to a fairly middle-of-the-road Anglican joint, but I'd experienced lots of different forms of worship over the years, from happy-clappy Pentecostal meetings to austere Protestant affairs. Since I was in the South, I thought I should at least start off by trying a Baptist service.

I knew that Baptists held a more conservative stance than me on most issues, but the ones I'd met, like Isaac and JM, were kind and humble and good-hearted people and I had enjoyed chatting about faith with them. I picked a church not far from where I was living, and went along one Sunday morning. It had been built to the same template as most churches round here – sloping roof and pointy-hatted clock-tower – and I was greeted at the entrance porch by a fairly ancient man who shook my hand as I arrived.

Inside, three or four dozen folk were scattered about the wooden pews, in fashions and haircuts harking back to an older age. I was glad I'd worn a skirt. A printed mission statement hung in large, antiquated type on the far wall; it included strict injunctions against intoxication. The ancient who had shaken my hand made his way to the dais and invited the choir up to lead worship. Half the congregation were in the choir, and I soon understood why – the rest of us were not invited to join in with the hymns.

The pastor sat on the corner of the stage, responding to the music with the occasional 'Yeah!' and 'Amen!' Then it was his turn to command the room. He began with a passage from Genesis, which he punctuated with his own signature phrases and wordless expostulations. 'And God said ... my-my-my ... Let us make man in our image,' he read. 'And let them have dominion over the fish of the sea ... bless-your-heart ... and over the fowl of the air.'

The sermon itself was delivered on the move. He stomped

and jiggled about, working himself into a lather of emotion, sometimes shouting and pointing towards the pews. 'I'm a child of God, my-my-my, there aren't many people in this country can say that. Ha! But you are – ah! – a child of God...' Eventually, requiring an additional outlet, he jumped down from the dais with surprising suppleness and began prowling about the aisles.

I never really caught the gist of his argument. He talked about 'the *res-er-vore* of God's love' but it was hard to summon the image of a beneficent Creator when a man with an angry face was yelling so aggressively that cotton flecks had appeared at the corners of his mouth. 'I don't care how much they preach evolution – ah! – the word of God says – ha! – he made *man*... He didn't make us from *snails*, my-my-my, he didn't make us from *monkeys*...'

The people in the pews meekly took it all, with the occasional head-nod or a whispered 'A-*men*'. I wondered why anyone subjected themselves weekly to this parade of rage. It wasn't just exhausting and upsetting, it seemed utterly futile: a completely literal case of preaching to the converted.

It was a bruising hour, and one I never wanted to repeat. I wished I'd had the courage to ask someone what they got from the experience. Instead I staggered out into the sunlight, punch-drunk, shook hands with the pastor again, and put on my best Southern smile.

Faith was an issue it was impossible to avoid, or ignore, in the place I now lived, even if many church leaders seemed convinced that the population was backsliding and the world was going to hell in a Honda. A lot of my agnostic and atheist friends had grown up in churchgoing families. It certainly felt less taboo to talk about Jesus than, say, Hillary Clinton.

And Christian themes were an integral ingredient in bluegrass music. Hymns and gospel songs were probably the second-largest category in the repertoire, next to fiddle and banjo tunes. At the more traditional festivals, you were never more than ten minutes away from someone telling you how much you needed a Saviour, usually in four-part harmony.

JM and Isaac were great singers. They always threw a set of gospel songs into the middle of a gig, the way Bill Monroe and Ralph Stanley had. Often they would leave their instruments aside, and close in on the microphone all together to sing a cappella. Sometimes the usual vocal trio - lead, tenor and baritone - was joined by a bass, whose low tones lent the songs an added gravity. And the voices moved together with pitch-perfect intonation and meticulous timing, like a human squeezebox.

I was always keen to get in on the close-harmony action. I loved singing, and I really didn't have the right voice to lead a bluegrass song. After my turn to lead at a jam, people would praise my enthusiasm, or the size of my lungs, or my lack of inhibitions. Words like 'gusto' and 'gumption' were used, all code for 'loud'. Sadly, bluegrass singing isn't about volume, it's about timbre. The sound of the holler is a hard, ringing cry, three-parts hoot-owl, one-part sob. Traditional bluegrassers often dismissed their counterparts up north in Boston and New York for this very reason: they might be hot stuff on their instruments, but their voices were soft and puny. Bluegrass wasn't called the 'high and lonesome sound' for nothing.

My singing sounded about as lonesome as the New Jersey Turnpike on a weekend of roadworks. In addition, my accent betrayed me, no matter how hard I tried to bend my vowels. (Someone who heard me sing once told me I needed to get a hillbilly boyfriend, fast.) But my combined years of service in church choirs and the second violins had made me a quick study when it came to close harmonies. And being a girl, I already had a high voice, so it was easy for me to sing the tenor line above the lead singer.

My background in church choirs, I discovered, wasn't so dissimilar from many of the bluegrass pioneers. Bill and Ralph's singing style was rooted in the old forms of mountain worship. People in Appalachia talked proudly of their tradition of shape-note singing, a system which taught illiterate worshippers to read and render beautiful choral harmony. Then there were the simpler vocal practices of the Primitive Baptist churches, where congregations sang in unison, a cappella, because musical instruments were banned (they weren't in the New Testament, were potentially idolatrous, and might lead to dancing).

By the time bluegrass came along, the revival meetings of the nineteenth century had already spawned an entire genre of vocal quartet singing known as Southern Gospel. The songs weren't hymns, per se, but a sort of Christian pep rally. A lot were variations on the theme of 'stop your sinning and do right', but there were also Bible stories, personal testimonies, church discipline instructionals – what to do with drunkards, for instance – and how-to guides for the coming apocalypse. They made up a vast psalmody King David couldn't have bettered. It was these that bluegrass had adopted.

This aspect of the music intrigued me. I could see that singing hymns on Sunday must have been an affirming communal element of life in the mountains, where families were so isolated. But I was still puzzled that sacred songs were embedded in the racier popular music of their day. Why had the early bluegrassers interrupted their regular tales of drunken moonshiners and roving gentlemen callers to include these sudden fits of piety?

Musicians had had a reputation for bad behaviour since pioneer days, and it wasn't entirely unearned. Dances were considered a corrupting influence (to be fair, they did some-times descend into violence), and the men who facilitated them were assumed to be heavy-drinking, daughter-stealing scoundrels. While Bill Monroe wasn't a drinker, he wasn't a devout adherent to the Ten Commandments either. Numbers six and nine, about adultery and not coveting your neigh-bour's wife, were particular blind spots.

He certainly wasn't the only one getting up to no good on the road. From what I'd been reading in the library, from gunplay to domestic abuse, fist-fighting to fornication, those bluegrassers had plenty to repent. And yet their soul music regularly gave me goosebumps. Whenever I put down a biography of another prodigal son to argue this with Trevor, he maintained that all that sinning was precisely *why* they sang gospel music. 'It's two sides of the same coin!' he said. 'They'd done all these things, and they knew it was gonna catch up with them.'

Not many hurried to turn over a new leaf, I pointed out. Trevor grinned. 'All the more reason to make amends quickly.' Bluegrass festivals had even developed the ritual of a Sunday-morning gospel set, allowing hungover campers and musicians to atone for the previous night's shenanigans. Whatever motivated it - guilt, hypocrisy, or just a sort of spiritual insurance - it illustrated perfectly the yin and yang of Southern life.

Bluegrass gospel had become popular enough to earn its own spin-off industry, or at least, its own spot on the CD table and search term on iTunes. There were dozens of spe-cialist acts touring on a well-established church circuit, from humble meeting-places to thousand-seater auditoriums. One of the early models for this sort of pious entertainment was the Lewis Family, who I first came across in a second-hand record sale. Their album cover had called to me because the trio of women photographed in front of a fountain didn't just have matching outfits, but matching hair. It was, in each case, more than twice the volume of their head.

'The Lewis Family Lives in a Happy World' chirped the title, in a groovy sixties bubble-font. The men in suits held a bass, guitar and banjo respectively and did not look the kind who had ever given themselves over to a summer of love. The liner notes told me that the Lewis Family had strummed to fame in the fifties with a weekly TV slot in Augusta, Georgia; a flick through the rest of the 'L's revealed that their career had spanned nearly half a century. Also, that matching outfits were a big part of their brand.

The example they had set showed no sign of petering out in the South. I encountered numerous wholesome family bands, whose blistering picking skills were accompanied by missionary zeal. And they weren't the only ones incorporating altar calls into their performances. Ricky Skaggs, the bluegrass-turned-country star, made my non-churchgoing friends roll their eyes with his frequent pronouncements on faith; Donald Trump's election was, he had told his fans, prophetic.

I felt queasy about it all. Perhaps it was the earnestness of the many home-produced CDs I was handed by well-wishers (typical cover art: a too-low-res image of a church at sunset, or a digitally rendered silhouette of Calvary). Perhaps it was the songs' apocalyptic theology ('He will set your fields on fire'). Or their old-fashioned mores, like the one that wondered what to do about the women in the church with paint on their face. (The answer, if you're interested, was 'Take some water and wash it off'.)

Probably, though, I was just feeling uncomfortable at how politicised Christianity now was in the South. Fellow believers injected my Facebook feed with daily doses of encouragement and outrage: today, an uplifting Bible verse next to a picture of Mike Pence; tomorrow, a screed about foetuses being people too. The implicit message: *true* Christians were pro-life and - like Pence - anti-gay marriage.

I knew these people. Good folk with genuine convictions, whose kindness and generosity I had benefited from. I rarely saw them proselytise or browbeat - except, obviously, on social media - and I only heard things I didn't like when I brought up an issue myself, like asking why women shouldn't be priests, or why Jesus wouldn't believe in welfare and environmental regulation.

Still, some of the conversations I had with other Christians made me so angry I replayed them in my head when I was alone, desperate to prove the other person wrong, if only to myself. And some conversations scared me: I was afraid that if I started pulling at too many threads, my own faith might just unravel in front of me. What if they were the ones in the right, and I was a bona fide heretic?

Just outside Boone was housed the headquarters of an evangelical organisation called Samaritan's Purse; I often came across people who worked there, and was friends with a couple. One had risked her life serving wounded combatants - including ISIS fighters - in a field hospital in Iraq. The organisation did seemingly wonderful charity work in parts of the world that desperately needed it. It was also run by Billy Graham's son Franklin, who had called for Christians to vote Trump, and who regularly argued that Muslims and gay people threatened America's way of life.

My faith is a foundational part of who I am. The problem was that I didn't *want* to have anything in common with someone preaching the things that Franklin Graham did, or anyone convinced that Donald Trump was endorsed by an intelligent God. For so many of my Southern friends,

138

bluegrass and belief went hand in hand, but those close ties were making me question my own identity. Faith was supposed to be a way to connect with something bigger, outside myself. Here, it was making me feel hemmed in.

There was, naturally, a bluegrass gospel song that offered its own wisdom on the situation, called 'You Go to Your Church, and I'll Go to Mine'.

*The Lord will be at your church today, but he'll be at my
    church also
You go to your church and I'll go to mine, but let's walk along
    together*

But I carried these contradictions with me like a nagging injury. And now when I drove past one of those church signs, I felt a little lost.

CHAPTER 12

There was one place near Boone where I encountered a more liberal outlook. Asheville, two hours west into the mountains, was known as North Carolina's music city - which was particularly confusing, since it was very easy to mishear as Nashville, Tennessee's rather more famous Music City. To bluegrassers, however, it was just as significant. It was in Asheville that Bill Monroe had first assembled his Blue Grass Boys.

Most of the folk I knew in Boone made a trip over there at least a couple of times a month. There was a weekly bluegrass jam which, Tray and Eliot had told me, hosted some of the highest-grade picking in the whole of North Carolina. So I drove over to check it out. Having been told Asheville was the ancestral home of bluegrass, I'd expected some actual ancestors, and pictured a small town built of timber and grandfathers, where the shops sold fishing tackle and the teeth were few. I was not expecting a youthful, cosmopolitan city, where the musicians were trendy-haired singer-songwriters and the windows were full of contemporary art and gluten-free muffins.

This was a city that wore its cool on its sleeve - or rather, emblazoned it on an ironic T-shirt and accessorised it with a FUCK TRUMP button. Every other store was a bookshop or a coffee shop, or both. Students lounged on distressed leather sofas discussing HBO programming and the latest piece of street art. Walls were a fluttering mass of flyers, advertising a curious blend of rural, spiritual and musical activities. 'Aaron Welding: for all your welding needs!' sat next to the promise of yogic enlightenment for nineteen dollars a week. Beneath, a simple hand-scrawled message read, plaintively, 'Want to form a band! Help me!'

To say that the streets were full of aspiring musicians was no empty cliché: the city was so thick with buskers that you couldn't park your car without a soulful soundtrack. On the afternoon I arrived, I immediately ran into a couple of college kids picking their hearts out on guitar and banjo. The guitarist wore a trilby and sang with a tortured expression; the song was so fast it was impossible to make out the lyrics aside from the odd, heartfelt, swear word.

They introduced themselves as Chad and Pete and I asked whose songs they were singing. 'Mine,' said Pete. 'We're busking up the money to be able to record them.' He said it with such enthusiasm that I instantly worried for him. When I mentioned I'd a fiddle in my car, they insisted I bring it out and pick along; for the half hour we played together, they didn't make a single buck. Feeling guilty, I slipped them a twenty-dollar bill, and wondered as I left if I was the first person to *lose* money busking.

By night, the same streets literally hummed with the live music spilling from the city's hip bars and clubs. Walking the streets gave the effect of a radio tuning in and out - a waft of a country song, a mumble of interference from the pavement, followed by a sudden salty blast of rock. The jam Tray and Eliot had recommended took place at the Isis Music Hall, a 1930s movie theatre that had recently been restored and reopened. The fact that it had kept its original marquee and name was, everyone agreed, a bold move.

The hall itself was a large space - darkly lit, I suspect, to keep its diners and drinkers from noticing just how unfinished the decor was. A cocktail bar ran down one side of the room, and a handful of pickers commanded attention from a lofty stage. The bartender, seeing my fiddle case, pointed me towards a back door - 'That's where the musicians go' - and I passed through it to a green room, cluttered with sofas and cases and guys.

The men were all young-ish - in their twenties and thirties - with beards in different states of scruffiness, and an overall lean and hungry look. There were no women. Most of them looked round to register my arrival, then went back to their conversations. A couple in a corner were running through a song; when a curtain behind them opened, revealing the door to the stage, they exchanged a few words with the players making their way off, and went up to take their place. It seemed that the jam was a sort of free-rolling performance, to which any were welcome to contribute. Any, that is, who could keep up.

I could hear, through the wall, the beat of the bass. It sounded impossibly fast. I couldn't tell what song they were playing, but I didn't know any that went at that tempo. Feeling self-conscious, I busied myself with my instrument, which meant that, far too soon, I looked ready to play. The only clean-shaven chin in the room noticed this. He was about to go on, he said. Was I ready? Since my only other options were to sit friendlessly in a room pulsing with male buddydom, or beat a humiliating retreat, I said yes.

We joined a guitarist and a banjo player who were already out on stage. 'Got one you wanna play?' asked the guitarist. I named a Bill Monroe number, 'Road to Columbus', which

I'd begun to work on in my lessons with Matt. At least if I stepped up and kicked it off myself, we'd have to play at my speed. And I was actually pretty pleased with my effort, until the tune passed on to everyone else.

I'd never really understood the term 'shredding' until I saw it there. The musicians around me shredded that tune like a piece of A4 in a copier jam. Like a woollen scarf caught in an escalator. Like a fraudulent tax return when the Feds come knocking. Once we were done with 'Road to Columbus' and the rest of the group were choosing the tunes, and the pace, I knew I was out of my league. I'd never played anything I *knew* at their speed, let alone improvised on ones I didn't.

The urgent push of the bass and the furious chunk of the mandolin made my heart race so hard I thought I might go into cardiac arrest. But a sort of survival instinct kicked in; I ground my teeth and bore down on the fiddle. I might not play anything pretty, but I was damned if I was going to crumble in front of these guys. I stuck it out for four or five numbers – enough to look like I wasn't quitting – then staggered backstage.

Instead of sanctuary, I found the male clique back there engaged in a jam even more intense than the one out front. The green room thrummed with ingenuity, but it was also electrified by the spirit of competition. This was a throw-down, a face-off, a creative rodeo. As the breaks were passed around, they grew ever-more outrageous and avant-garde. You could hear each player straining for the original, the unexpected, or at the very least a little shock value.

I sat and listened until they were done, wondering if it was possible to passively consume testosterone. Later, I heard a few of them discuss their plans for the week, and it told me everything I already suspected. The guitarist was auditioning banjo players for a new band; the clean-shaven guy, who I'd learned was called Caleb, was recording his 'psych-synth' EP. Everyone here was a gigging musician, home between tours, hustling for work. The Isis was where they came to play for tips, and blow off steam, and see who else was around: an unofficial, underground network for those who dreamed of making it big.

I liked Asheville and I made it back there often - not so much for the Isis jam, which remained as intimidating as its name, but for the gigs that happened all over town. Sure, it often felt like the *Portlandia* of the South. I saw people too young to get a mortgage smoking Sherlock Holmes pipes, and I once ran into a street poet who sat behind a typewriter composing verse to order (when I said goodbye he'd responded: 'The future's a big place, I'll see you there'). But it was also a place where every type of music was welcome, and where genres fused in a celebratory melee. Where bluegrass felt as much a part of the future as the past.

CHAPTER 13

Progressive bluegrass had one big advantage, for me, over the traditional kind. It was indisputably, quantifiably out of my reach. There was no possible way that I could perform the pyrotechnics of the Punch Brothers, or keep up with the crazy chord changes that Caleb liked to throw into a song. This was the kind of music I could listen to in wonder, without ever expecting myself to replicate it.

Traditional bluegrass, on the other hand, was based on simple principles which, after three months of total immersion, I ought to understand pretty well. And yet I couldn't hear myself getting any better.

I did the homework Matt set me, and took a masochistic pride in the hours I spent each day on tedious rhythmic exercises. I eagerly awaited the magical moment when I'd sit down with Zeb and Julie and Trevor and suddenly unveil my new powers. I even pictured their impressed faces, and heard their words of congratulation: 'Dang, Emma, you just about tore that thing up!' But the reality, whenever we played together, was that I felt and sounded as stilted as I always had done.

At jams I strained for some kind of authenticity. Each time my turn to solo came around, I hoped something new and unexpected would emerge, and that I'd find myself fluent in the musical language everyone else was speaking. All I ever managed were the same couple of trite phrases I'd used a hundred times, like an exchange student in Paris stuck at 'Ça va bien, merci!'

While I was playing, the frustration would build up in my chest and find an outlet in my reddened cheeks. The rest of the time, it filed itself in the base of my brain like a half-forgotten obligation. The more desperately I wished for a breakthrough, the more elusive one became. By my third lesson with Matt, I'd noticed a distressing phenomenon. All the conscious thought I was giving to the things he'd been teaching me had caused me to lose hold of even those elements I *had* mastered. I telephoned him in a funk: I actually sounded worse.

'Of course you sound worse!' he barked at me. 'A couple of months is no time at all. Over the course of the year, *maybe* you'll notice *incremental* changes. I sound worse today than I did years ago...'

Matt segued into a story about when he'd played with Stéphane Grappelli and by the time he circled back, he was comparing bluegrass to yoga. 'A lot of things that are fundamental to this music are very elusive and tackling them is like doing your downward dog or whatever that shit is. Some days it's completely fucked up and others it's really great. So I'm sorry to disabuse you, but you have to get rid of that whole idea of achievement. You don't master this music, you master it each day.'

This was not what I wanted to hear from my guru. I didn't need a spiritual journey of enlightenment, I just needed my bowing arm to start doing what everyone else's did. Nothing Matt had said made me feel the tiniest bit better. In fact, the knowledge that I couldn't expect any dramatic improvement sank down into my intestines, where it sat like a large rock. If

146

I wasn't going to get any better at this stuff by the end of the summer, then why was I bothering in the first place? Why would I even *care* about bluegrass?

I always had a sulky, offhand relationship with music. You might even call it dysfunctional. The honest truth is, eight-hour orchestra rehearsals aside, I had never spent much time listening to music at all.

I wasn't someone who listened to the radio, or bought CDs. This had, in the past, made for difficult moments at college or wedding discos, when some iconic hit would suddenly fill the floor, and I would have to mouth awkwardly along without letting on that it was the first time I had heard it. But it wasn't an all-consuming passion for Mozart and Mahler that distracted me from the pop charts, or kept me from becoming an indie kid, or a metalhead, or an official member of the Janet Jackson fan club. I didn't listen to classical either, unless I had to.

My issue wasn't genre snobbery, or failing to find my tribe. I just didn't really *need* music – not the way a lot of people I knew seemed to. My school and college friends weren't able to get through a day without a fix of their favourite tunes. But I always resisted a soundtrack to my life. Music wasn't some kind of emotional proxy or sacred space for me; I never retreated to my bedroom and blasted the walls, or begged for an iPod for my birthday. If I wanted an escape from the world, or just some distraction on a long train journey, I would read a book.

If music is vital to a human's well-being, it was simply another of those healthy options that I chose to ignore, along with salad and running. I always thought people rather over-stated the claims for music – the belief that it could touch us more deeply than any other art form, or that it was an emotional language we all understood without having to learn. Listening to music never moved me in the same way as a great piece of theatre, and I was far more likely to cry at a movie than at a concert.

That's not to say I *couldn't* be moved. I got a surge of pleasure from singing along to a song I knew well, although I put that down to familiarity rather than anything more profound. Certain types and pieces of music did fit my mood better at some times than at others. But when I listened to it, music was a tool calibrated to my purpose, not a joyride to an astral plane.

Take my iPhone, for instance. When I arrived in the South it contained, besides the bluegrass I was learning, a smattering of different music that represented particular functions in my life. There was some indie rock for moments when I felt keyed up or angry - the White Stripes, Franz Ferdinand - and songs from musicals to cheer me up if I was sad. The light dusting of punk was there for when I needed a confidence boost, or to stay awake on a late-night drive.

A lot of the songs on my phone never even got played. Many were too familiar (bored now!), or not familiar enough (bored already!). Several were classed as off-limits because of their associations with periods in my life I would rather not revisit. There were, for instance, falling-in-love songs I hadn't found an excuse for in a long while, and a couple of leftover break-up songs that had proven valuable as purgatives in the past. The latter remained on my playlist in case of future relationships/relationship disasters. Until then, the Pretenders' version of 'Angel of the Morning' rested behind imaginary glass, to be smashed only in case of emergency.

I didn't count music as an emotional pursuit so much as a cerebral one. From the moment I'd first heard bluegrass, it had spoken to me on a technical level; it was a puzzle to be solved, a ladder to be scaled. The songs and tunes, like the classical compositions in my life long ago, were an intriguing prospect with a set of rules I could learn and conquer. Their mathematical flourishes were their appeal, not their melancholic nostalgia for little girls in Tennessee and mothers six feet under. I'd barely related to pop songs about my own generation; I wasn't going to be too invested in 'Little Maggie' and 'Darling Corey' and 'Nellie Kane'.

And this was how I continued to pursue my painful and peculiarly dispassionate bluegrass education. Until, one day, Tray introduced me to someone who saw through me in minutes. His name was Dan and he ran the degree course that Tray was taking at the nearby East Tennessee State University, a job he combined with playing guitar and fiddle in a touring band. Dan listened to my complaints about how hard I was finding bluegrass to learn, cocked his head to one side, and asked: 'Have you ever heard of imposter syndrome?'

I sighed. 'I don't need anyone to tell me I'm an imposter,' I said. 'I'm fully aware of that fact.'

'That's not what I meant,' said Dan. 'I'm interested in why you *feel* like one.'

'Because I sound like a classical violinist trying to sound like a bluegrass one.'

Dan nodded. 'So tell me: why does Carter Stanley's music stand the test of time? Why can Bill Monroe's voice cut right into your heart?'

I shrugged like a moody teenager.

'This music came from people who were living poor and worked hard for everything they have,' he said, looking at me hard. 'Bill Monroe used to run a team of mules. Kenny Baker was a coal miner. Playing in a band just might earn them a little more, but they didn't have anything to fall back on. They had their instrument and their clothes. Their music *was* their life, and it was how they spoke to others.'

149

He paused, and looked at me to see if I understood. I didn't. He carried on.

'If you come from money - I imagine, I don't know what that's like - you don't have to worry. And you don't have to play a crappy instrument, because you can have a good one straight away. And you can pay to take lessons from someone. Or you can study at Berklee for sixty-five thousand dollars a year.'

I blushed, as they say here, seven shades of purple. I hadn't mentioned that my teacher was from Berklee.

'That's not the way this music was formed,' he said. 'It's not like we have to go through hard times or become drunks to know what it was like . . . but you *do* have to somehow connect with that experience. Sometimes musicians over-intellectualise the process and get so caught up in what notes they're playing that they miss out on the human interaction.'

Dan coughed, and excused himself. 'What I'm saying is' - and here he turned to me with a kind expression - 'you have to play music that has guts, not just notes.'

I felt humbled. And exposed. Dan was right: I didn't *feel* the music when I played it. It was an academic exercise, a self-serving goal. As for Bill Monroe and the bluegrass originators, they had always felt pretty remote to me. I'd kept an ironic detachment at Ralph Stanley's family farm, and I'd enjoyed Monroe far more as a caricature of orneriness than a man of flesh and blood. Their almost schmaltzy love of home, and country living, was something I couldn't connect with, and it had made me suspicious. I had assumed, without realising it, that I wouldn't particularly like these characters if I got to know them.

Maybe it would do me good to walk a little in their shoes.

A small but representative sample of banjo jokes

What's the definition of perfect pitch?
When you throw a banjo into a skip and hit an accordion.

What's the difference between a banjo player and a large pizza?
The pizza can feed a family of four.

What do you say to a banjo player in a suit?
Will the defendant please rise.

What's the difference between a harmonica and a banjo?
When you play harmonica, you only suck half the time.

What do you call a successful banjo player?
A guy whose wife has two jobs.

What do you call a beautiful woman on a banjo player's arm?
A tattoo.

What's the best way to tune a banjo?
Wire cutters.

How do you get a banjo player off your porch?
Pay for your pizza.

CHAPTER 14

Kentucky didn't look that far from Boone on the map. To reach it, you just had to cross the narrowest taper of eastern Tennessee. But the mountains were in the way, and the hundred or so miles of road took three hours before depositing me in eastern Kentucky's coal-rich, dirt-poor hills. I had always thought that this was the area Bill Monroe was from, since he sang so much about the hollers and the mountains, but I was wrong. Bill had spent his childhood in the western part of the state, near a tiny place called Rosine. To get there required another five hours' driving.

I planned a round trip, taking in first the Monroe homeplace, and then the annual festival on the campground Bill had owned, and bequeathed to his son, in Indiana. The Appalachian Mountains, I was discovering, were an incomplete geography of this music. The word 'bluegrass' itself referred to a prevailing forage crop in the pastures in the central region of Kentucky, a species more accurately called *poa pratensis*. Monroe's parents had been farmers, and he had named his band after his literal home turf.

As I started out down the Kentucky highways, I squeaked with fan-girl gratification each time I saw a sign to a local business – a Bluegrass RV Park! The Bluegrass Health Clinic! – but half an hour later, by the time I'd reached Bluegrass Business

152

Supplies and Bluegrass Portable Restrooms, the novelty had worn off. I did, however, lengthen my route so that I could make a journey down the Bluegrass Parkway. Tall-growing grass carpeted the meadows to each side in a thick shagpile. It covered the gentle rise and fall of the land like the hair on a sleeping dog. But it was not blue. It was, quite emphatically, green. On a colour chart, it sat somewhere between Emerald Isle and Kermit's Ass.

This discovery didn't entirely ruin the romance of the road trip. Other Kentucky icons were less disappointing, like the white-picketed paddocks that frequently lined the road, denoting the state's most famous industry – horse breeding. Occasionally I'd spot a couple of these slick-looking animals, their handsome features beaming with health and privilege, like equine subscribers to Goop. The Parkway also took me through the epicentre of Kentucky's other great export: bourbon. Every few miles brought a turn-off to a distillery, and I'd be lying if I said I ignored them all. In fact, I got completely waylaid, stopped over at a hotel, and didn't make it to Rosine until the next day.

By the time I reached Ohio County, Bill's birthplace, the landscape had changed. The beautifully groomed paddocks and thoroughbreds had given way to wild woods and rough agriculture. The chi-chi towns that welcomed tourists on the bourbon trail – selling them high-dollar, small-batch liquor and local artwork – had disappeared, replaced by pawn shops and papered-over windowfronts.

I pulled up in a place called Hartford, thinking to get gas, but there was not a single other being in sight. As I began to walk down Main Street, wondering where everyone was, a warning siren cranked through a PA, the kind installed in the fifties to warn residents of impending Armageddon. It was impossible to know if this was a drill or an imminent

153

alien attack, especially as the rest of town was clearly in the bunkers already.

Maybe my own presence had triggered the alarm, and somewhere in a secret command centre the mayor of Hartford was running my image through facial recognition software for credible threats. Either way, I was freaked out enough to abandon my walk, jump in my car and drive away as fast as the speed limit allowed.

The Monroe homeplace, just outside Rosine, was preserved as a site of historic interest and open to the public. I arrived to find a group of visitors being welcomed with lemonade and iced tea, while a guitarist and mandolin player performed for them on the porch. It was a church tour party, and a local dignitary had arranged to show them both the house and the other nearby sites connected with the Monroes. Their host, an amiable man in his fifties, invited me to join them; his name was David, although I noticed that everyone called him 'Judge'. He seemed delighted to have another person to talk to about Bill and his family.

The house was a modest, timber single-storey, with four bedrooms and a kitchen. It seemed, from the fireplaces and the woodstove and the quilted bedspreads, to have been a comfortable dwelling, although it would have felt pretty small with seven children in it. The judge told us that James and Malissa, Bill's parents, were decently off compared to many, and James had employed a number of locals on his 360-acre farm.

But Bill had had his own sorrows, said the judge; as the youngest child, he was often ignored and left to himself. He had poor vision – his left eye was turned inwards, a condition folk round here called 'hug-eyed' – which made him even more isolated. 'On the other hand, it might could have improved his hearing.'

We wandered past walls where framed black-and-white photos showed Charlie, Bill and their older brother, Birch, instruments in hand. In typical youngest-child fashion, Bill only learned to play mandolin because his brothers already had a guitar and a fiddle which they wouldn't share. 'And even then, they made him take four of the strings off it, because they didn't want him playin' too loud,' said the judge.

On one of the beds were displayed the records Bill had made with Charlie in their early act as the Monroe Brothers. In pictures of the two of them, Charlie often stood, smiling and relaxed, while Bill, shorter than his brother, leaned or sat, with a serious, self-conscious expression (Charlie always looked the more affable, and eager to entertain you). On another wall was a printed sheet containing the names of every player who had been a sideman for Bill and earned the title 'Blue Grass Boy'. There were 161 of them. He clearly operated a revolving-door policy.

My fiddle case was strapped to my back as we emerged on to the porch – I never left it in the car, not because I was afraid of it being stolen, but because an average summer's day in the South would have melted the glue and caused the entire wooden edifice to collapse. The guitar and mandolin duo waved me over. 'Wanna pick one?' they asked. I was all but ready when the judge explained to them that I was from London, England. The guitarist snorted. 'I won't ask what you think about your mayor,' he said.

I bridled. I knew what he was referring to. Earlier that week, there had been a devastating terror attack near London Bridge; President Trump's response had been to disparage London's mayor, Sadiq Khan – a man I'd gladly voted for – on Twitter.

I told the guitarist I thought our mayor was a good man.

'Really? He's the one letting the terrorists in,' he replied.

My left hand gripped the neck of my violin far more tightly than it was supposed to.

'Your president is mistaken,' I said.

'I didn't think it had anything to do with our president.'

We stood within touching distance, glaring at each other. Our audience had gone quiet. The wooden balustrade of the porch began to remind me of the ones that bystanders leap behind in Westerns, the moment the gunfight breaks out. I didn't have a six-shooter to reach for, but my trigger finger was hooked apprehensively around the end of my bow.

And then someone from the tour group coughed. 'Perhaps y'all could play "Jerusalem Ridge"?'

I put my fiddle under my chin and kicked off the tune. It was a good choice, a haunting and dramatic fiddle piece named, by Bill Monroe, after a nearby escarpment. Some of my fury made its way into the notes, and I played with an edge I'd never found before. When we reached the end, there was applause.

'See?' the guitarist announced to the assembly. 'Ain't never seen each other before in our lives, won't never see each other again. We might disagree completely about politics. But we can still make music together. And that's the true beauty of bluegrass.'

Still, I was relieved to move on to our next stop - a replica of the log cabin Bill had lived in as a teenager. His mother had died when he was only ten, and his father followed six years later. With his older brothers away in Detroit working for a motor company, the orphaned Bill moved in with his Uncle Pen, a fiddler who funded their extremely basic lifestyle by trading small goods and playing for square dances.

Cramped and sparsely decorated, the cabin lived up to the frontier-style existence that bluegrass songs so often evoked: two rooms - a bedroom and a kitchen - once lit by oil lamps, and a collection of Bill's personal effects that included a hand-saw and a bullwhip.

'Bill loved his Uncle Pen,' said the judge. 'It was his time here that turned him into a true musician, so they say.' Pen took Bill along to gigs as his back-up guitarist, and through him the younger man met other musicians, like Arnold Schultz. Arnold was an African-American labourer who played the blues in a style that intrigued and inspired Bill. And when Bill finally rejoined his brothers, who were now working in oil refineries in northern Indiana, he had already encountered many of the influences that would inform his later creations.

We headed on to the cemetery, in a convoy of cars so long we looked like a funeral procession ourselves. You couldn't miss Bill's grave; it was the only one marked by a ten-foot-high obelisk. As we gathered around it, the judge reappeared. With a guitar.

'I just want to say a few words about Bill's mama,' he said, pointing to a headstone brightened by a colourful arrangement of artificial flowers. 'Malissa Monroe was a wonderful woman and she's the one that first taught the boys to sing and play the gee-tar. So this one's for Mrs Monroe . . .'

Well, I left my old home back in the mountains
For mother and father had both passed away . . .

The quality of the judge's singing was dubious, and he was missing a couple of important chord changes. Also, this was exactly the kind of mawkishness I found hardest to stomach in bluegrass. But now, as I stood there, I thought of a sixteen-year-old who hadn't seen his mother since he was ten, and had just lost his father too.

. . . The birds will be singing while mother is sleeping
They will sing o'er her as the grave sinks away

Bill had joined his parents here in 1996; he had lived to the age of eighty-four. Not long after he was buried, the judge told us, they had found his grave covered in quarters. It had been a habit of Bill's to keep a couple of rolls on his person, and hand the coins to children at his gigs. It had always sounded like canny PR to me, rather than generosity, but now, in the place where so many had come to pay him back, I wasn't so sure.

We stopped by one more grave. 'Pendleton Vandiver' it declared, '1869-1932'. Underneath were the words of a famous Monroe number, one he had written nearly two decades after his uncle's death. It was a song I loved, even though I found the fiddle part fiendishly tricky; it memorialised Uncle Pen and the tunes he had played, all night long, to keep the dancers busy.

Late in the evening about sundown,
High on the hill above the town,
Uncle Pen played the fiddle Lord how it would ring,
You could hear it talk, you could hear it sing

As I walked away, I was surprised to discover that my heart felt full, and my eyes just a little moist.

The judge, I discovered later that day, was no legal expert handing down weighty decisions from the bench. His title was Judge Executive, a particularly Kentuckian term for the chief administrator of the local government. Ohio County, which the judge had been elected to oversee, was, he told me, a struggling region; 20 per cent of the population lived in poverty.

Rosine, one of its typical communities, had once been home to a pickling factory, a baseball bat mill and several schools. Now, thanks to rural depopulation, the town was home to forty-one people and its only amenity was the Blue Moon Grocery Store whose half-empty shelves stocked snacks, drinks and toiletries. Some even had the supposedly reassuring words 'NON SALVAGE' written on them in marker pen.

Still, they did have plenty of music. Every Friday after work, people came together at the barn for the weekly 'Jamboree', where a string of bands played half-hour sets to any who wished to listen. That night, the church tour group and I were doubly blessed. Because at the close of the Jamboree – featuring an exceptionally cute band of pre-teen siblings who had to have the microphone specially lowered for them – the annual town festival was taking place in the park.

By 'park', the organisers meant 'basketball court', and by 'festival', they meant 'single local act playing in the bandstand'. And by 'bandstand', they meant a rickety pavilion built presumably to give parents shelter from the sun as they watched their kids shoot hoops. But more music was more music, and we settled our blankets and camp chairs on the asphalt as the sun began to set.

After three months, I had some appreciation of how high my novelty value was in the areas I was travelling through. It didn't throw me, any more, when I found my presence officially announced at a jam or a gig or a church service; the words 'we have a special visitor with us today' had become as much a part of my daily routine as waving at other drivers as they passed, and eating pig. The band had been playing for just over an hour when I saw one of the church tourists get up from their seat, walk to the bandstand and confer with the lead singer in between songs. There was a half-amplified mumble from the stage – 'Well, has she got her fiddle?' – and within seconds I was being ushered up to join the band.

The lead singer wore a Stetson. I don't know how many gallons it was, but you could certainly have hidden a teapot under it.

'Have you ever met a bunch of dumb rednecks before?' he asked.

'Sure she has!' shouted someone from the audience. 'She's just been at the barn!'

The band asked what I'd like to play; I trotted out my 'Road to Columbus' and, as an encore, 'Bill Cheatham'. Then I moved to the back of the stage, as the etiquette of these situations demanded, and began the routine of putting my instrument away.

'Where are y'all going?' asked the singer, whose name I now knew to be Josh. 'You're sounding great! You gotta stay up here!'

And so, I stayed; and when he asked me to sing one with him, I sang three. Josh had a decidedly handsome face, and his Stetson and stage banter combined to give him a rascally charm. The band was set up the old-fashioned way, around a single mic, so that when a player took a solo, they had to squeeze past the other instruments to grab prime position. It also meant that, when we sang harmony with each other, we were leaning in until our faces were a quick lunge away from kissing. I couldn't help but wish I'd chewed some gum before I'd got up there.

Whether it was all the enforced proximity, or the brownness of Josh's eyes, I can't tell you, but something unexpected happened on that stage. I felt connection; not just synchronicity, or togetherness, but a blissful sensation which

160

might have been like an ecstasy high, if I'd ever had one to compare it to. A palpable bond had formed between us, and it was too dynamic to admit anything like fear, or nerves, or self-consciousness. I had no thoughts of what I was playing, or how well. I was in the moment, and I wasn't there alone.

It had always struck me how the good musicians I knew, like Zeb and Trevor and Tray, could inhabit each other's spheres so completely as they played. They were just as into the next person's music as their own, supporting, encouraging, shaking their heads in awe. They exchanged smiles and silent jokes and eyebrow raises. And every now and then, a look might pass between them that suggested relationship far beyond their daily friendship.

I'd seen those moments often, at gigs, between the musicians I admired. Their bodies leaned unconsciously towards each other, and their faces lit up with delight, caught in the unselfconscious and deep pleasure of the world they were inhabiting. The intimacy they shared with each other in those instants looked deeper than any I'd experienced in my entire life. I envied it from the bottom of my heart.

When I caught Josh's eye, I knew that we had the same look on our faces. And I understood, for the first time, what it was. You could take the greatest satisfaction I'd ever felt from playing, and you could triple, quadruple, square and compound it, and it still wouldn't reach what I was experiencing in that moment. This didn't feel like achieving or conquering anything. It felt like being in love.

At 11 p.m., the playground was in total darkness; I hadn't noticed that the audience had left, and we were playing to ourselves alone. No one wanted to stop, but the band had a gig in Tennessee the next day – they needed to load up their bus and hit the road. Josh asked if I'd like to join them. But I was headed north to Indiana, for the annual Bill Monroe

Memorial Bluegrass Festival. And besides, I didn't want to ruin the magic. This had been the greatest night of my musical life - I didn't want to be eating breakfast with the band the next morning and discover that they were Flat Earthers, or that Josh's Stetson hid a large bald patch.

Before they left, I asked Josh why the Kentucky bluegrass wasn't blue. 'But it is,' he said. 'I'll tell you when it happens. When the sun goes down at the right time of the day, and there's a big field with the light coming across it, you'll see a glimpse of blue. It's like spotting a rainbow.'

Maybe I'd still get my chance. I did notice a full moon on my way back to the motel. 'Blue moon of Kentucky, keep on shining,' I sang, pleased with the serendipity, as I drove through the songwriter's hometown. I wondered if Bill was busy bossing people about in heaven, or if he might have looked down and noticed me.

CHAPTER 15

A handpainted sign on the Rosine Barn had claimed it was the 'Home of Bluegrass'; Ohio County had gone as far as trademarking the phrase on its marketing material. But I wondered whether Kentucky could really lay claim to the music. When you listened to bluegrass, you realised it wasn't the sound of home at all, but the sound of longing-for-home. Songs that depicted the family farm, or the cabin on the hill, or the angelically patient sweetheart, all recalled them from a distance. The singer was separated from them by miles or years or both.

Take 'Blue Ridge Cabin Home', where the writer's thoughts 'wander back to that ramshackle shack in those blue ridge hills far away' – hills, he readily admits in the chorus, he hasn't seen in a long while. One of Mac Wiseman's most famous recordings wonders 'how the old folks are at home' precisely because its protagonist has buggered off and left them behind; The Dillards' 'Old Home Place' is the tale of someone who 'ran away' to work in a sawmill in Charlottesville, and returns ten years later to find himself with no girlfriend, money or family farm, somehow surprised that they weren't shrink-wrapped and awaiting his return.

To me, many bluegrass lyrics sounded like a form of emotional hostage-taking; and the secret behind that lay not in Rosine, but on my drive north. It was a journey Monroe must have known well. Bill Monroe had followed the same bearing when he left Uncle Pen to work in the oil refineries of Whiting, just outside Chicago, in 1929. He was a young man joining the many thousands who migrated from the rural South to the industrial cities of the North, often their only option in Depression-era America. When Bill and Birch and Charlie entertained the workforce at the local dances, they played for people like themselves. People who had left behind all they ever knew - open country, closeness to nature, a simple way of life - for a new world of belching chimneys and crowded modernity. No wonder they sang mournfully of home.

No wonder, either, that once Bill was finally making money as a musician, he bought his own farm outside Nashville. Not long after, he purchased land in Indiana. He and his Blue Grass Boys appeared on the bill at the weekly Brown County Jamboree in Bean Blossom, Indiana, in 1951, and Bill enjoyed it so much that he bought the barn, along with its fifty-five acres of park and woodland. Today it was known as the Bill Monroe Memorial Music Park, and it hosted the longest-running bluegrass festival of them all.

Driving through the gates, I expected to see my odometer spinning backwards in the style of Doc Brown's DeLorean. Nothing here had been updated since the 1950s. Not the signage, which had yellow-and-red circus lettering, and told people that the show would go on 'snow, rain or shine'. Not the booths, which sold pretzels and coffee and not much else. And not the bathrooms either. There was, as I soon discovered, no hot water plumbed to the showers. It was either a classic piece of Monroe stinginess or a pious attempt to keep festival-goers from impure thoughts.

Most people, however, had their own showers: the RV

brigade was here in droves. They parked up in a bloom of cul-de-sacs named after their heroes – Kenny Baker Avenue, Roy Acuff Drive – and next to their giant metal ships were docked smaller tenders, the ubiquitous golf buggies with which they shuttled themselves to and from the stage. This was an epic, eight-day festival, and many arrived the week before to secure their favourite spot and stake their place in the audience. Under international bluegrass law, once your camp chair is in position and fully unfolded, no one has the right to move it, even if you leave it empty for 95 per cent of the week.

The handful of punters who planned to sleep under canvas, or whichever flame-retardant polymer substituted for it, were invited to pitch their tents on the side of a steep hill. Trevor had lent me his, as he said he never used it, and I could see he was telling the truth when I prepared to secure it to the ground and discovered he had no pegs. Luckily, the pair of teenage boys in the neighbouring tent were under the ongoing supervision of their mother, who checked in on them several times a day and had brought spares of everything they might need. She helped me secure Trevor's tent to the ground, but she couldn't do anything about the gradient. I woke every night having slid to the bottom corner in a painful arrangement of limbs.

The organisers certainly didn't want anyone complaining that they hadn't heard enough bluegrass. The stage was occupied twelve hours a day; they must have sequestered every banjo within a 500-mile radius. Each evening set included two or three acts who would have been name-brand headliners on any other bill; and in seventy-two hours I almost halved my wishlist of bands I wanted to see live.

My favourite discovery was Michael Cleveland, a thirty-six-year-old fiddler from southern Indiana whose playing seemed to defy the laws of physics. His bow moved so fast it ought to have broken the sound barrier. His inventiveness appeared infinite. And yet while he handled licks and riffs at speeds that his predecessors might never have dared imagine, his music carried within it the sound of bluegrass as it was played in its earliest incarnations. His band was called Flamekeeper, and his mission was clear: to absorb, master and elevate the entire canon of bluegrass fiddle.

Keen to see what Cleveland was doing up close, I risked exploding my eardrums by stealing a seat directly in front of the speakers. He had an unusual bowhold, and when he backed up the rest of the band, he did it with a violence that only added to the drama. Playing the rhythmic offbeats was commonly known as chopping, and I'd never thought the word so apposite: Cleveland hit down on his strings as if he was trying to snap his bow in half. At the end of the set, his bass player led him to the centre of the stage to take his bow and I realised that Cleveland was blind.

As I headed back to my tent on the first night, I was disappointed not to find any jams going on. I'd been tucked up in my sleeping bag a full three hours when I heard the unmistakable thump of a stand-up bass. While I wanted to ignore it and go back to sleep, I also hated the idea that I was missing out. So I forced myself blearily into my clothes, checked my watch - 2 a.m. - and levered my body, which was as stiff as my fiddle case, out of the zippered flap. I walked around that unlit campground for nearly thirty minutes trying to trace the source of the phantom bassline. I never did.

What I found instead, the following day, was Michael Cleveland's own bass player, the young man who had acted as his guide on- and off-stage. He was called Ty, and he was staying in one of the holiday cabins just up the hill from my tent, with his uncle, Roy. I ran into the pair of them as a rainstorm was sweeping across the site, and they ushered me under their awning and offered me a beer.

It was only lunchtime but I suspected, from Roy's joviality, that he had already had a couple himself. Both men had the same dark brown hair and teddy-bear physiques. They were Bean Blossom regulars and since it was too wet to submit ourselves to the open-air seating, they offered to drive me down to the music park's museum, built by Bill Monroe and his son, James, in 1986 to house the Bluegrass Hall of Fame they had inaugurated.

It was a curious building, combining stone cladding and a chalet-style roof with some cheap-looking Roman pillars. Inside, walls and cabinets were crammed with photographs and memorabilia. The costumes of a number of country stars were displayed on mannequins which leaned so acutely it seemed that the headless ghost of Hank Williams was lurching at me asking for a swig; Dolly Parton's double-Ds had never felt so threatening. The whole effect was a charmingly homespun shrine not just to musicians, but to the festivals that had been their second home.

'Wouldn't none of us be here without Carlton Haney,' said Roy, shaking his head. 'The music wouldn't have survived.'

'Who's Carlton Haney?' I asked.

'Only the guy who invented the bluegrass festival!' said Ty. 'He's the one who started it all, back in '65 . . .'

They told me how Haney had come up with the idea when he'd seen Bill Monroe jamming backstage with his former bandmates Don Reno and Jimmy Martin. Haney was Bill's booker. He also managed Reno and Smiley, the popular bluegrass duo that Reno had formed with Red Smiley after his stint as a Blue Grass Boy.

Bill Monroe's Blue Grass Boys had a large pool of previous alumni, many of whom were now stars in their own right.

In the past, bluegrass bands had rarely appeared on the same bill, and some of them - thanks largely to Bill - refused to share a stage. But Haney, a canny businessman, realised that if he could convince them to perform together, the way they jammed backstage, people would pay good money to see it.

He spun the festival as a tribute to the father of bluegrass, and charged six dollars for a weekend of camping and music at a horse farm near Roanoke, Virginia. It was a timely experiment. The same year, Bob Dylan went electric, and the folk revival that had saved bluegrass itself subsided, overtaken by an invasion of Beatles and Stones.

Haney's multi-day format was copied all over the South and Midwest, and eventually all over the world. It inspired a uniquely social form of music: the campgrounds were democratic spaces where the performers picked all night with the punters. When Ty, Roy and I returned to their chalet and took up our instruments, we were carrying on a tradition that was still bluegrass's spine, sustaining both its community and its economy.

These days, Ty and Roy pretty much lived on the festival circuit. They'd started going to them together when Ty was a teenager. One of his relatives had needed bone marrow, and Ty had been the donor, and as a reward for his bravery Roy had taken his shy, quiet nephew to an event in Tennessee. Ty had always been a good picker, but the late-night jamming had transformed him as both a musician and a young man.

'Used to be he wouldn't say boo to a ghost,' Roy told me.

'I got much more outgoing,' Ty agreed. 'I was so desperate to keep playing I'd carry my bass around on my shoulders at three in the morning, looking for a jam.'

Ty's big break had come when Michael Cleveland heard him picking and asked him to join his band on the road. The last few years of touring, and seeing the different ways people jammed all over the country, had taught him a lot about musicality. 'These days it's easy to learn all the technical stuff you can ever need on YouTube,' he said. 'But you've got to have emotion. There's people who can burn it up on their instruments, but then you'll see a guy who only knows two chords and can make you cry.'

I asked if he had any tips for dealing with my nerves. 'Yes,' he said. 'Get angry. Music's a mind game - with yourself, with the audience, with the band. I get myself angry before I go on just to give me the edge this music needs.' Ty had such a warm smile and a gentle vibe I couldn't even picture him mad.

'Blimey,' I said. 'What does it take to make you angry?'

'Ah, sometimes just wearing a suit in the heat and humidity is enough.'

I enjoyed hanging out with Ty and Roy; they didn't take anything too seriously, except picking, and even then they didn't mind when I couldn't keep up. In the evenings, we sat in the audience - what Roy called a 'cottonfield', because when you looked out from the stage all you saw were white heads - and watched the other bands.

And while the audience might have been ageing, I had now seen so many contemporary bands playing traditional blue-grass - and each with such large followings - that I refused to believe the music itself was under threat of extinction. All of them were writing new songs, and adding to bluegrass's ever-expanding repertoire, although they also played a good proportion of oldies. Of course, performers at the Bill Monroe Memorial Festival were under an unspoken obligation to oblige their audience with a strong quota of Bill Monroe tunes.

Bluegrass festivals were a pretty weird proposition, all things considered. I tried to imagine a rock festival where everyone was expected to make at least half their set Lynyrd Skynyrd covers. Where every act played from the same repertoire, on the same instruments, in an attempt to capture exactly the same sound. But that's what people came for. And when the bands weren't singing old songs, or new songs crafted to sound like old songs, they were singing songs about how no one sang the old songs any more.

We got too far away from Carter and Ralph
And the love of a sweet mountain girl
We're way down below that high lonesome sound
And a far cry from Lester and Earl . . .

I thought of Trevor: I knew that the bluegrass-on-bluegrass phenomenon caused him great irritation, because he regularly complained to me about it. 'Whenever you turn on the radio there's all these songs bragging on how great the music used to be,' he would grumble, 'and how it isn't like it was in the old days. And *all* those bands are playing it like it was in the old days!'

As a country kid, Trevor found this particularly annoying because early bluegrass tackled topical rural concerns. 'There was a lot in there about fear of urbanisation, about "how do we hold on to who we are?" But no one sings about real issues today.

'All those things that caused people in the South to vote for Trump - the opioid crisis, the collapse of the rural economy, how tough it is to run a farm because of the dairy levies - bluegrass might could be a place to express them. But instead they keep churning out songs about how no one will ever live up to Bill Monroe.'

Maybe that was why, after a few days, the quaintness of the Bean Blossom set-up began to curdle for me. The last act

I saw was a duo called Dailey and Vincent, famed for their close harmony singing, and whose set featured soupy songs about doing unto others as you'd have them do to you. I could tell they were a big deal because their bus, which was parked behind the stage, was wrapped in a giant photograph of their faces, next to a large logo for their principal sponsor. They closed it out with a number called 'America, We Love You', along with their thanks to God and the good people of Springer Farms for their 100 per cent antibiotic-free chicken.

The festival still had several days to run, but I was craving a hot shower and something other than pretzels for dinner. And Tray and Eliot had been in touch to tell me that Cane Mill Road had just made their first CD, and were having a party to celebrate. So when the rain returned in earnest, I took it as my cue to say goodbye to Ty and Roy, and get back on the road.

Strange how your phone can know something before you do. It had pre-calculated the route to Boone without me even asking it. My robot navigator spoke her stilted prophecy. 'You are. Six hours. From home.'

CHAPTER 16

Life in the mountains was a lot wilder than the one I'd left behind in London. Not in the partying sense; a big night out in Boone was when Trevor and Savannah and I headed to the bowling lanes *before* going to Murphy's.

But the sheer amounts of roadkill I saw – be it possum, groundhog, skunk or, on one tear-jerking occasion, baby bear – confirmed how much animalia I was sharing these hills with. I became acquainted with birds of varying ringtones – blue jays, robins, the haunting whippoorwill. I learned that the weird ululations that came from the woods by day were turkeys, and the howls at night were coyotes.

Sometimes, it felt like I wasn't in a nature documentary so much as a Disney princess movie. Walking through even short grass would release dozens of butterflies in plumes about my ankles. Bunnies bounced and chipmunks skittered and deer chewed nonchalantly through people's front gardens, until someone reached for their air gun. In the evenings, fireflies – or as they called them down here, lightning bugs – blinked out their phosphorescent messages at dusk. I always thought they were magical creatures. Then one flew into my face as I was falling asleep, and I murdered it in panic. Its body lay on the pillow beside me emitting a reproachful, fading green glow for a good quarter hour, because I was too scared to touch it.

There was, however, far creepier stuff out there. We never heard or saw the mountain lions – they were silent hunters – but there were scare stories about them stalking little kids along their school bus route. Vulgar vultures looked up at you with their mouths full as they tore the entrails from roadside carcasses. And then there were the vast, dirty webs I saw everywhere, wrapped round tree limbs like stumpy bandages on field amputees. I had no idea what monstrous eight-legged fiends were capable of spinning them, but the prey they were digesting seemed more squirrel than fly.

One of the most extraordinary sights to be had in the Appalachians didn't belong there at all. I didn't notice it at first; you don't when you're driving. The colours outside your window stay the same and so does the outline. It dawns on you slowly, with perfect horror-film pacing. The trees have disappeared. The street lamps have disappeared. Everything has disappeared. In its place is a smooth, bubble-edged simulacrum of a landscape, a nightmare realm. The world you can see has been covered – yarnbombed – with a monstrous green monoculture. I was surprised that Andrew didn't have a DVD in his collection of scary B-movies entitled, simply, *Kudzu*.

The alien vine, a piece of 1950s optimism gone horribly wrong, had swallowed large tracts of North Carolina. It had been imported from Asia, thought to be a useful plant until its triffid hunger began to redecorate the South. I passed great slopes and lagoons of it wherever I went. Kudzu was capable of causing some truly bizarre and trippy sights. Telegraph poles became ladies in ball gowns; cypresses turned into brontosauri.

The games it played with reality would have been funnier if it hadn't been smothering everything it touched. But this unearthly vision was like a doomed peek at a post-human future. The kudzu was unstoppable. It wasn't malign, but it couldn't help itself: the more compatible it found a place, the more it cloaked and choked and strangled everything it met. Wherever I encountered it, it made me feel anxious. *Et in Arcadia ego.*

Appalachian weather had its own micro-patterns – a mix of heady sunshine and late thunderstorms that sent the sky apocalyptically purple and veined it with forked lightning. Carrie loved the rain, and we'd sit on the porch to watch its monsoon blanket fall. On hot days I'd go with Zeb and Julie to a nearby lake to bathe and swim. Trevor never joined us; it was rumoured that so much sun exposure would crumble him like a vampire.

Boone life felt easy, made sense. I liked who I was here. It reminded me of the early flush of a love affair, when you discover you want to be a better person. Suddenly, acts of kindness and generosity didn't seem so difficult any more. And my new friends, who didn't know better, treated me as if this sympathetic, thoughtful, big-hearted version of myself was the only one. Andrew told me how wise and comforting and compassionate the surrounding mountains had always appeared to him, and I wondered if this was their influence.

The epicentre of musical life – and all our lives – was the Jones House, a historic building near the post office, in the very centre of the main street. In the nineteenth century, it had been the home and surgery of the local doctor, and it had been preserved by the town in its original, timber-slatted state; its front parlour was still furnished with antiques and an upright piano.

Small as it was, the Jones House had become the town's de facto cultural hub, running music lessons and concerts and exhibitions and symposiums. Trevor, Julie and Zeb all taught their pupils out of the upstairs former bedrooms. Every Friday night in summer the lawn filled with folk coming to hear the free gigs that bands played from the porch. The house was always full of kids and teenagers and adults and seniors, all hanging out together. And it was where Cane Mill Road had thrown their album party.

Releasing a CD wasn't unusual in the bluegrass world, which operated its own cottage recording industry, but the boys had somehow commanded enough pre-sales to take them to No. 9 in the official bluegrass charts. We'd gathered beneath the dining-room chandelier to watch them perform and eat layer cake with their official band photo on it. Andrew and I had stood at the back of the room, consuming segments of their frosted faces, while the real versions wore expressions of supreme concentration, determined to give their guests a good show.

Liam closed his eyes for his mandolin solos, lids fluttering as he played a fast tremolo on the strings. Next to Tray and Eliot stood a young man with a pudding-bowl haircut. 'That's Casey,' Andrew whispered, 'their new guitar player.' Casey had taken on some of the lead-singing duties from Liam; he had a voice so old it seemed it must be coming from someone else in the room. And I wondered how a kid who couldn't grow facial hair could be responsible for a sound so deep and soulful.

I couldn't avoid noticing how many bluegrass prodigies there were. Each town in the mountains seemed to have raised its own dedicated genius, whose extraordinary abilities were either God-given or a sure sign of demonic possession. At one local festival I'd been walking round the grounds when I was drawn to the extreme energy coming from one of the outer stages. I couldn't see the band, but I could hear their flashy instrumentals and snappy vocals driving a crowd into a frenzy and I followed the sound until it deposited me in front of a smart-suited group of schoolkids. Two of the four hadn't hit puberty.

The guitar player, I discovered, was a twelve-year-old called Presley Barker – a protégé of Wayne, the luthier with the Shakespearean bonce. Presley had won most of the prestigious guitar contests in North Carolina and Virginia, destroying his adult rivals, Wayne included. And the fiddle player? He was thirteen, and he'd been playing the Grand Ole Opry for the past three years.

Even among the pupils at the Jones House there were some outrageous talents. A pair of fifteen-year-olds called Willow and Kathleen whose string band played at major festivals; an eleven-year-old fiddler called Asa, who gobbled up the youth prizes at every fiddle contest he entered. There were probably a hundred or more like them in the three neighbouring counties, Trevor reckoned. 'Monsters', he called them, although he was referring to their picking ability, and not their personalities.

Trevor thought it probably came down to the way the music was passed on. 'Playing guitar round here, it's like breathing,' he said. Youngsters were welcomed into the circle as soon as they could string a few notes together. No one told them to go away or keep quiet. 'There's a lot of positive reinforcement round here, and these kids are like, "OK, I *can* do it!"'

I tried to recall anything from my own childhood that felt like what Presley, and Asa, and the Cane Mill Road boys were growing up with. For me, music may have been, in the strictest sense, a social activity, but it wasn't a sociable one. Classical music didn't encourage informal, spontaneous gatherings. The smallest of groups, like quartets, trios and duets, still needed infrastructure: stands, sheet music, lots of practice. We didn't hang out and play just for fun; we didn't veer off-script and see what we could create when the adults weren't looking. We didn't try to teach each other tricks, or do our best to make someone else sound better.

Where I went to school, music was as competitive as sports. There were national music exams that you took to demonstrate how far you had progressed. There were school prizes and merit badges and honourable mentions at morning assembly: all sorts of external markers of achievement to acquire, or fail to acquire. To me, these were outward indicators of the one *really* important question: how good were you compared to everyone else?

I wasn't the only young musician to spend my teenage years acutely aware of my place in the pecking order. As Matt Glaser pointed out, classical music had a strict pedagogy; it was obvious, from the repertoire that you were playing, where you stood with your peers. And that was an extremely motivating factor for a naively suggestible and approval-hungry kid like me.

Orchestras, though, were the real arbiter of self-worth. Don't let the delicate refinement of Handel's Water Music or the lush romanticism of Tchaikovsky's *Romeo and Juliet* fool you. To ambitious young musicians, especially those who may be dealing with major existential issues brought on by hormones, playing in an orchestra is less about art than it is about survival. The orchestral stage is a brutal gladiatorial arena, often overseen by a narcissistic tyrant of a conductor, who feels nothing as he crushes you with a fatal thumbs-down.

My well-funded school managed to maintain three separate orchestras, a series of increasingly elite ensembles that you had to audition to join. Think of it as working your way into the first team for football or hockey. Unlike a sports team, however, you hadn't made it once your name was on the sheet.

Every orchestra is its own enclosed society and as hierarchical as a naval ship. If you're the French horn playing first chair, you are higher status than whoever's in the second chair; the same applies throughout the brass and woodwind sections. Among the strings, the better players are the ones sitting closest to the conductor - the further back you are from the rostrum, that all-important seat of power, the less you matter. If that weren't feudal enough, the outside chair, closest to the audience, takes precedence over the inside one. The player on the inside must turn the pages for her partner, pencil in the conductor's instructions, and offer up her own instrument mid-performance if, heaven forfend, a string should break.

The violinists feel it most keenly of all. There isn't just one section of violins, there are two, a rustling plantation of ids and egos. The newbie arrival sits in the back row of the seconds. From there, a timber landscape stretches out ahead of her, one she will traverse with glacial movement. Like a gamer setting out in a newly minted universe, she must begin as the lowliest of creatures, earning credits and building up her status until, one day, she can fight for the ultimate prestige - leader of the orchestra.

Whether the impact of all this on my psyche was unusually deep, I don't know. If I think back to those days - of grey, stippled plastic chairs with aluminium legs, a box of rosin tucked between them within easy reach - I can still feel the straightness of my back, and the light pressure of my violin's end piece as it rested on my thigh. I hear the tightly kept silence of fifty youths, well drilled as any cadet corps, while the conductor complains to the oboes about their tuning. I feel the electric bristle as he barks a bar number and the entire room quickly reaches for their instruments, ready for the downbeat – no seconds wasted. Order and quiet, and a slowly numbing ass.

Rehearsals were long periods of boredom, while other sections' issues were dealt with, interspersed with intense periods of concentration, when the focus switched to your own. The conductors I played under may have been teachers in their other lives, but in the practice hall they were god, and rarely a merciful one. Many loved to show off their omniscience and pinpoint hearing by identifying exactly which of the dozens of violin desks was getting it wrong – then forcing the unfortunate pair to replay their weak attempt in front of everyone. The sound of the baton tapped rapidly against the conductor's stand, calling a halt to a run-through, signalled that he'd found a new victim. Humiliation was only ever a stick-wave away.

No wonder, under these circumstances, that our finer human traits did not shine through. I made the occasional friend in orchestra – usually a desk-mate with whom I had shared an especially traumatic term, who had become an ally in the trenches. But fear and ambition made me suspicious and judgemental of those even a few feet away. I was barely seven when I first saw a conductor make their underage charge cry. And I was part of the cold, unmoving mass that didn't even offer her a tissue.

I don't look back on my musical self with a great deal of pride. Of my own abilities, I was simultaneously vain and unsure, in craven need of validation. Of others', I was either painfully aware or briskly dismissive. I had little generosity or encouragement for players of a similar standard to me. That proximity was dangerous, and I sensed, like two racing cars approaching a corner neck and neck, that there was only room for one of us to make the inside line. As for those players who were demonstrably better, I ached with envy and longed to hear of their mistakes.

I had enough self-awareness to know that I should try to disguise these impulses. Still, they leaked out in a fondness for gossip and bitching, which, it turned out, was not mine alone. There were plenty of ruthlessly insecure musicians alongside me in the hothouse, a place of superficial smiles and backstabbing comments and double-edged friendships, brittle as bone. 'Do you mind playing a little more quietly?' one of them once asked me, with a pitying smile, as we rehearsed a quartet together. 'It's just so hard to stay in *tune*...'

Reaching the front of the first violins was the work of my high-school career. I was so keen for my music teachers' good opinion that I was an easy mark: when they needed someone to help out in the junior ensembles or fill in for flakier individuals, I'd give up even the rare evenings I was supposed to have free. But that didn't earn me their respect, or their endorsement, or any of the things I was striving for. When I was finally invited to lead the orchestra, I was told the position had to be shared - with the girl of the pitying smile.

In my last year at school, the headmistress gave out music colours for the first time. I didn't receive them. My stalwart service, as instrumental fodder for whichever branch of the music department that needed me, obviously didn't make me *that* valuable. Other students were handed the star solos and the applause and the conductor's congratulations at our end-of-term concerts. My lessons with The Serb and my Saturdays at music college seemed pointless, now. The message was clear. Whatever I had to offer, I still wasn't good enough.

CHAPTER 17

Since I'd been in the South, most of the places I'd eaten out in were breakfast, burger, or BBQ joints. In fact almost everywhere I ate, and my friends gigged, served some sort of meat in buns. Often it was accompanied by a slew of baked beans and creamed corn and mac'n'cheese. Sometimes it was served with a piece of cornbread the size and density of a bath sponge. For variety, Tom and JM had once taken me to a service station plaza with an all-you-can-eat buffet called a Golden Corral. It remains the only place I've had my steak with a side of cheesecake.

So when I heard from Wayne that he and Presley would be playing at a fancy out-of-town restaurant, I asked if I could join them. I had not yet encountered the wealthy end of Southern living, although I had seen inklings of it. Golf-course manicures and exotic flowerbeds spilled down from the porticos of the houses in the resort towns outside Boone. Private roads and electronic gates hinted at secret communities in the hills – El Dorados for those who occupied them just a few weeks a year.

At an isolated, five-star inn on the grassy banks of a mountain tributary, I finally stumbled on their hidden tribe. They drank from large glass goblets and sat out on the lawn in the white chairs people use for wedding parties. Waitresses

181

in little black dresses wove between them, conveying tiny asparagus spears on silver trays. Peachy tones of Sauvignon filled the air, and the gentle flap of linen.

On the porch overlooking the lawn, the two guitarists had the air of court musicians. Presley wore jeans, with a crisp shirt and a wholesome smile. His face was handsome and freckled under a stiff quiff. There was an aura of goodness about him so powerful you could have dropped him into an eighties kids movie and known, instantly, that the gang were going to be OK in the end. Wayne, meanwhile, wore his plaid shirt and his work boots and his Red Sox cap, and might in other circumstances have been shooed off the premises.

When Wayne took a break, Presley watched the older man with unrestrained affection. When it was his turn to solo, Presley's gaze moved to his hands - sometimes the one shifting surely around the neck, sometimes the one that was picking the strings so fast you knew you were just imagining the movement, like watching a baseball travel between the pitcher's hand and the slugger's bat. The tone and volume coming from his guitar made the goblets quiver in sympathy. The country casuals murmured to each other how awesome the kid was.

The faces of those closest to him - the early birds who had snagged the rocking chairs on the porch - worked hard to balance their natural expression of indulged content with a look of tutored appreciation. I found a spot of floor near his feet; it was like sitting with my ear pressed against a speaker. The vibrations from the guitar travelled through me to the wooden decking and ran to earth. I noticed the beginnings of fuzz on Presley's upper lip. When he came to a lick he liked, he couldn't help himself, and his blinding smile broke out. The porch swooned.

In between sets, as the audience revived itself with

expensive wine, I talked with Wayne and Presley and his mum, Julie. Julie had always liked to dance, which was Presley's introduction to music. 'Ever since he was able to *talk* he wanted to play something,' she told me. 'He wanted trumpets, he wanted drums, a banjo, a flute ...' He started picking a guitar when he was seven; by the time Wayne met him, two years later, he had already worked out how to play complex fiddle tunes on it. Julie shrugged - it wasn't anything to do with her. He just loved his guitar, and he'd spend two or three hours a day practising it - more, if he didn't have to do schoolwork or chores.

Presley didn't have a phone, or an iPad. He liked to ride his bike, played a bit of basketball. He went to a public school - his dad worked there - and he got straight As, even though he did a lot of his schoolwork while he was out on tour. 'We'd never travelled, or been anywhere at all out of the mountains, before he started playing music,' said Julie. 'So he's taken *us* a lot of places.' Presley was modest about himself, deferent with adults, and conversed happily with everyone. He looked like an easy son to raise.

But then, so did Asa, and Eliot, and Liam, and Tray; so many of the kids I had met seemed plucked from a storyline in the *Andy Griffith Show*. Maybe that wasn't a coincidence, either - Andy Griffith was originally from Mount Airy, where Zeb and Julie and I had gone for the fiddlers' convention, and which his fictional TV town of Mayberry was based on. One of the old guys I jammed with once told me that the youth here were different to city kids. 'The way I put it, we're twenty years behind the rest of the world,' he said. 'There's still a lot of the old values - church on Sunday, keeping up your heritage.'

Perhaps it was because the scene was so inter-generational, I said, and the Southern tradition of respecting your elders still carried weight. Perhaps the study of music instilled discipline. Or maybe it was self-selecting, and the young people this music appealed to were the kind who were already brought up the old-fashioned way? The old guy had nodded. 'Plus, there's more belts to them in this county than there is in the whole of Charlotte,' he said. 'The kids in Charlotte'd probably try to sue 'em over it.'

I couldn't argue that there was no hothousing here in the South. The contests scene was known to be awash with pushy parents, and there were numerous stories of talented child musicians who had burned out under the applied heat of touring and familial expectation. I met one man who had performed all over the US as a teenager and now, in his mid-twenties, could barely bring himself to pick, even with his best friends.

Still, it seemed as if the humble setting of this music kept its young folk relatively honest, and limited how much of an arrogant asshole they could become. After all, even being the best bluegrasser in the entire world wasn't going to guarantee you fame or fortune. The best you could hope for was to entertain. That's what Presley enjoyed doing, he told me. 'I like giving people a good time, y'know?' he said, with his effortless beam. 'It's more fun than competing.'

There was a Friday-night concert that week. The act was a family band led by a fiddler with a big reputation, who I'd been looking forward to seeing for months. Trevor was visiting his girlfriend's family over in Asheville, and Zeb and Julie both had paying gigs to play that night, so I went alone – no way was I missing it.

I found an empty seat in the front row, thrilled to be at such close range. There were six of them on stage, three women in floaty dresses and the men each sporting a different kind of hat: trilby, train driver, flat cap. For a while, I was distracted by the confusing family dynamics. A range of ages made it hard to tell who belonged to whom, or whether everyone on stage was the progeny of the fiddle-playing patriarch.

Then the mandolin player, whose goatee made him look like a teenager wearing a disguise, began singing about life on the road, and its lyrics and wistful melody made me instantly melancholy.

Got aches in my back, aches in my heart
When the music ends, the hurting starts . . .

It wasn't as if it was a blindingly original subject for a song. But the fiddle coloured in between the lines of the simple country melody and its yearning tones caught me at the throat. *Oh lord*, sang the younger man. *Oh lord, I'm running low.* I felt raw and exposed. I was being ambushed by my own emotions.

The family joined in with the chorus; they smiled at each other as they sang. Was this homesickness I was feeling? Loneliness? Why should I feel lonely, anyway? It wasn't as if I hadn't made friends. I was happy. Things were good. No need to feel like this. Stop being silly. Just stop it. My eyes welled. My stomach heaved up sighs. *God*, I thought. *Please let this be my hormones.*

The band moved on to a couple of bluegrass standards. At times, three of them were all playing fiddle - their own little chamber orchestra. Their different styles highlighted the different sounds of their instruments: this one dark and treacly, that one sparkling like champagne. The performers were so in sync they could finish each other's musical thoughts. They hung on chords like a group of acrobats on a single tightrope, countering each other's weight with miraculous precision.

The more brilliant they got, the worse I felt. I could hear someone tapping their feet and it prickled my skin like sunburn. Distracting. Bad manners. I glanced down my row for the culprit then looked back to the stage. The band leader was tapping his foot too. He put down his fiddle and began a guitar duel with one of the young men who might have been his son. The audience giggled appreciatively; the two men were laughing too.

The music was dynamic, playful, clever - all the things I loved. But right now, it was making me miserable and anxious. I sat in my black fog, and every ingenious new lick they invented left a papercut of envy. Why couldn't I just enjoy myself? What was *wrong* with me? Why did this family's joy in each other need to make me feel excluded, left behind? In their good looks and easy flair, I saw myself reflected back - a struggling mediocrity. I watched them swap instruments with abandon and berated myself for not having learned guitar, or mandolin, or anything else. Heck, I still couldn't play fiddle, and I'd had all the advantages a musician could want.

I felt a weight on my chest and a tightening round my heart. An inverted cone reached down my windpipe, a stalactite of some emotion I couldn't make out. My thoughts spiralled until they arrived at the question that, I realised, had always been there, hiding in plain sight. If I couldn't be *good* at music, how would I ever enjoy it? And if I couldn't enjoy it, what did that say about me?

The duel had morphed into a daisy chain of flourishing cadenzas, and now the star fiddler had returned to his violin. Chords and riffs tumbled out of the man like happy accidents; he gleamed with the light of each new discovery. The solo heated up; my heartbeat, hijacked by the tempo, was forced along for the ride. Two rods of pure envy inserted themselves either side of my breastbone. I had to stop myself yelling out in pain. The music was exquisite. The music was torture.

I didn't stay for the encore. When the people around me jumped to their feet, I bolted for my car. I rested my head on the steering wheel, and sobbed until I was almost empty.

A brief and incomplete history of bluegrass, part 6

Sam Bush didn't have a brother. He had sisters. But still. They all loved music. They all grew up working their parents' farm.

Sam started picking mandolin when he was eleven. He lived in Kentucky, so of course his hero was Bill Monroe. Once he was old enough, he started making the 200-mile round trip to Bill's Sunday jamborees in Bean Blossom, Indiana. He spent his vacation at Bill's bluegrass festival.

But Bill's music wasn't the only kind Sam liked. He loved the Beatles, and Jimi Hendrix, and the Allman Brothers. The world was exploding around him. Young men were being drafted to Vietnam. It was hard for a young guy to stick to songs about living in a cabin on the hill. Sam and his friends weren't living in a cabin on a hill. They were living in the throes of a social revolution.

When Sam was eighteen, he went to the fiddlers' convention at Union Grove: not the small, traditional one run by Harper, but the giant, noisy one, run by Pierce. He made friends who played bluegrass but loved rock too. They started a band of their own. They called their style 'Newgrass'. Bill Monroe heard it, and hated it.

Sam's band played festivals all over the country. Bill told

them he wouldn't book them at Bean Blossom unless they cut their long hair.

Bill and Sam didn't speak for a long while.

CHAPTER 18

I never saw Denver. The road west from the airport slung me straight into open country, as if the city was just a myth. Not even a wink of steel in my rear-view mirror. Just acres of brownish turf, and even more of sky, all the way to Boulder. After months in the mountains, the absence of forest offended me. The landscape looked naked-ugly, not so much unfinished as barely started.

It was two weeks since I'd last picked up my violin. Everyone – Trevor, Carrie, the barista who had mistakenly asked me, that morning, how I was doing – agreed I needed a break. Andrew had diagnosed my problem as that of the novice runner who was beating herself up for not being Usain Bolt. 'You've just got to start with a 5k, like everyone else!' he said. I nodded, but something inside me, padlocked and straitjacketed, made a stifled, desperate struggle.

A friend who lived in Colorado had invited me out to stay for a few days; there was even a bluegrass festival that happened just down the road from her, she said, in the little town of Lyons, on the edge of the Rocky Mountains. It felt good to sit in her house that night, breathing the mile-high air and eating crisp vegetables from the farmers' market.

The next day as she went to work I headed into Lyons, which comprised some nice places to eat, a couple of yoga studios, and a trio of marijuana dispensaries. The latter advertised home-grown, eco-friendly cannabis with names like Lamb's Breath and Golden Goat, and offered deals on products called 'wax' and 'shatter', whose purpose I couldn't decipher. I was not educated in the ways of the weed.

A river, the St Vrain, carved a trench to the west of the businesses, and a bridge across it brought me to the festival grounds. Down in the South, I heard people speak of Colorado as if it were paradise regained. The touring musicians I met loved or longed to play there. Friends had driven three days straight from Tennessee and North Carolina in order to reach its legendary bluegrass gatherings. There were two that sold out months before they opened. One took place in Telluride in the far southwest of the state, 500 kilometres across the mountains from Denver, a journey that didn't seem to put anyone off. The other was this one: Rockygrass.

A few steps beyond the gates, it was easy to see what made Rockygrass so popular. This was a rare festival that lived up to its good-looking marketing photos. Past a cluster of vendors selling snacks and vintage clothing, the site spread out to form a giant gully, backed by sandstone cliffs in a shade that wavered between red and brown. At their base, the river drew a perfect horseshoe, and the stage sat in its heel, a timber construction designed to blend with the magnificent backdrop. A yin-yang symbol was mounted just beneath the roof.

Around and behind floated happy campers on giant rubber rings, drifting between the top and bottom banks like musical notes across a stave. The ground itself was a patchwork of tarps and blankets and rugs and tablecloths. They interconnected all the way to the river's edge, so that not a spot of grass could be seen. The crowds were nothing like the 'cottonfields' I had left behind in Kentucky. Girls in flowery dresses and hempy skirts crammed my vision; women with armpit hair and nose rings, and men carrying babies in slings. There wasn't a pair of bib overalls in sight.

I searched for somewhere to stand or sit and found a patch of tree root too lumpy for anyone to claim. A fraction of a set had passed when my eyes began to leak. I scanned my emotions – I wasn't sad, or angry, or in pain. I wasn't even hungry. But my tear ducts were definitely being stimulated by something. I tried squeezing my eyelids shut. The liquid just congregated in pools behind them, before pitching down my cheeks in a hot cascade. I must have rubbed sunscreen in my eyes, I decided, and tried to wash them with some water from a bottle. It didn't work. Within ten minutes, my eyes were so shot I could barely keep them open.

When I realised the situation was not going to improve by sitting, embarrassed, under a giant cottonwood tree, I rose clumsily and stumbled over people's picnics towards the exit. From behind my curtain of lacrimal fluid, I could just make out a painted red cross. I arrived at the first-aid tent like a third-act Oedipus. Thankfully, they had seen the symptoms before. 'A lot of people struggle with allergies round here,' they said, sympathetically. 'We've got a pollen that's pretty unique. Can we show you where you can find a pharmacy?'

Half an hour later, I was back under my tree, dosed with powerful antihistamines. A guitar and Dobro duo were commanding a surprising power for two acoustic instruments. From this far away, I could only see the outline of their faces, and my brain filled in with the closest likenesses it knew; the Dobro player became a forty-something Kurt Russell, and the guitarist Samwell Tarley from *Game of Thrones*. Kurt stood slightly upstage, his resonator-guitar projecting flatly from his hips, hung at his neck like a tray of ice creams. He watched Samwell singing with almost paternal pride.

I leaned back into the trunk and wiggled until I found a

comfortable niche. It was hot, but I had shade and breeze, and as I closed my eyes a waft of pot glided under my nostrils. In my already woozy state, the plangent sound of the Dobro was both epically distant and intimately close, as if I were hearing it through a telescope. Samwell was singing a Grateful Dead number – 'Friend of the Devil' – and after a couple of choruses he fell back to the guitar, following the notes in whatever direction they took him.

A thick stupor crept over me, gluing my head to the bark of the tree. I heard notes drop from the guitar like seeds, growing instant shoots that curled and twined together. I saw riffs and phrases stacked in ever-increasing towers, as Samwell's fingers moved faster and faster on the strings, building a skyline of melody. Just when I thought the guitarist had reached his physical limit, the notes would split into triplets, or burst into tremolo, as if he had nothing to do but turn on a sprinkler, and let them rain. Drowsed with Benadryl, I seemed to be walking through a world he'd built, streets he'd populated with living ideas, until I realised he was no longer on stage, and hadn't been for some time.

My quasi-high lasted for the next two sets, fuddling them together into a cloud of sound until I fell asleep. I dreamed that I was playing fiddle with Isaac, but I'd forgotten to rosin my bow, and no sound came out at all.

Thanks to my general Girl Guide approach to life, that afternoon ranked as one of the trippiest experiences I'd ever had. I loved it. I stuck around for the evening acts; the head-liners were what everyone here referred to, knowingly, as a 'jamgrass' band. It wasn't like any of the jamming I'd seen. A light show turned the stage from a downhome porch into a *Close Encounters* spaceship, projecting psychedelia onto the surrounding box elders. Glow sticks and balloons appeared en masse in the audience. A guy next to me sparked up a huge blunt.

The music itself was an electric blast, a rock fantasia as brought to you by banjo and mandolin. Dry ice cloaked five shadowy figures, whose instruments all seemed to be turned up to eleven. At their centre, picked out in the purple-pink-red lighting, was a fiddler. It was clear to him - and to the rest of us - that he wasn't *actually* playing violin. He was on electric guitar.

I couldn't really hear what the band were singing. The lyrics I did catch seemed to be about feeling free or letting go or being blown about by the wind. I don't remember Flatt and Scruggs ever finishing a number with a chant of 'boom shaka laka boom shaka laka boom'. But the songs just seemed to be a vehicle for the players to take off on long, experimental excursions up the necks of their instruments.

The fiddler channelled Jimmy Page, his solos raging and ecstatic. A mountain breeze stood in for a wind machine, blowing back his chin-length hair as he threw himself about. It was hard to discern any actual melody, but this was music to build an atmosphere, not tell a story. You didn't follow it; you bathed in it.

Peppermint candy stripes of light enveloped the stage, and the players began to disappear into the dry ice until they were no more than nebulous outlines. The sound kept on, budding, swelling, bulging and distorting. The longer it lasted, the more I wished I'd visited one of those dispensaries beforehand. I lay on the towel that I'd brought, like a galactic hitchhiker, letting the symphonic tsunami crash over me. It was too vast to think about. Its amplitude was strangely healing.

Hooked on the vibe, I heard a lot more jamgrass over the next forty-eight hours. The concept was simple: you played long numbers and medleys and you didn't stop the party for anything. Colorado, I discovered, was its epicentre. The bands had kooky names like Leftover Salmon and Trout Steak Revival and Trampled By Turtles and they had the festival crowd rocking out before midday. Until now the only time I'd seen a bluegrass festival brought to its feet was for the national anthem. And it took the audience a while to lift their replacement hips out of their camp chairs.

But this was another demographic altogether. The festivarians, as they called themselves, wore T-shirts that said 'I Stand with Planned Parenthood' and 'Make America Sane Again'. I ran into Pete Wernick, my old Hawaiian-shirted camp instructor, who had lived in Colorado since the seventies. He had moved here from New York at a time when the Grateful Dead were having a big impact on bluegrass - Jerry Garcia was a dedicated player of banjo with his own all-star bluegrass outfit, Old and in the Way. 'And people liked to jam out, you know?' said Pete. 'They liked the freedom. They heard all these new cool sounds and they wanted to play that way too.'

Before I'd come to the States, the word 'Deadhead' was nothing but a gardening practice to me. But still, there was something about the music here I recognised. Something about the sound that reminded me of home.

In my household, the members of my family had each enjoyed music in their own uncool way. My mother had dabbled in trumpet and flute, and listened to radio stations that played popular classics - orchestral numbers you could hum along to, delivered in bite-size movements. My sister was a musical-theatre fan-girl, and many a family road trip was made to the sounds of Andrew Lloyd Webber power chords. In her teens, she had developed a belt to rival Barbra Streisand, making the car too confined a space to be trapped with her and the soundtrack to *Cats*.

Of the four of us, only my father had no specific musical

ability. In fact, he had a strange form of musical dyslexia: he could hum or whistle a tune quite competently until the moment that someone else joined in, at which point he would leap to a completely different note, like a lemming hurling itself off a cliff. His musical taste was even more bizarre than the rest of ours. It was founded on a much-loved collection of seventies prog-rock LPs, which he would insist on playing on Sunday mornings when everyone else was trying to sleep in. Experimental rock and psychedelia always seemed an odd choice for our conventional, mild-mannered father. But he would wander about the house to the strains of Pink Floyd, declaiming 'We don't need no education!', while sending his two daughters to expensive private schools.

Dad was no record collector, but he preferred them to cassettes, and each vinyl was handled with the deft care of a butler: its centre rested on his fingertips, balanced, at the edge, by his thumb. He would sweep the record delicately with an anti-static brush before positioning it on the turntable and lowering the needle with meticulous care. Then, as the drums kicked in, we would watch him bounce his arms up and down a little and twist at the waist – this his concession to dancing – before the age-inappropriate lyrics spilled happily and incongruously out of his mouth.

His tastes reached to some of the heavier stuff from the period – Led Zeppelin, particularly – and it took a special parent to feel no embarrassment or concern when singing in front of his children, 'Hey, mama, said the way you move / Gonna make you sweat, gonna make you groove...' In retrospect, it was adorable how much joy he found in his music. At the time, all my sister and I experienced was a synthetic whine we both hated. Mum also despaired of it, and many a row began with Dad's innocent failure to understand that

Jean-Michel Jarre was not a relaxing accompaniment to family dinner.

Hearing the faint echo of these seventies sounds – played on bluegrass instruments, for sure, but with the same earnestly esoteric approach – gave me a warm familial glow. Transfigured by nostalgia, noises that would once have given me bona fide earache were now bizarrely comforting. A whole era of music revealed itself to me, like an angel previously disguised as a hobo. For the first time, I understood what my dad loved about his records.

It wasn't just the skill or stamina that could sustain a twenty-minute instrumental solo, although that certainly blew me away. Somehow, out here under the vast Colorado sky, I could finally appreciate the magical power of a music that eschewed subtlety to drop-kick you in the gut. A music that wanted to wrap you in a blanket of stars, and was prepared to give you a concussion first if that was what it took. Stop trying to drive the car, it seemed to say. Take your hands off the wheel. Let us shoot you into outer space instead.

I heard the message, and I wanted to respond. I looked around me, at the smiling, multicoloured festi-verse. The blissed-out, bikinied bodies that floated along the river seemed to epitomise the spirit of the place. It was time, I decided, for my own epiphany.

Andrew and Carrie and Zeb and Julie had often raved about tubing, an activity which sounded uncomfortably medical, but which they described like heaven on a stick. So I had borrowed a giant inflatable ring from my friend's ten-year-old son, determined that this was the place to make my maiden voyage. 'Make sure you go with someone,' he had told me. I thanked him for the tip, then ignored it. I was an adult, after all.

I picked a secluded spot upstream for my launch; I wasn't

quite sure how this was going to go down, and I didn't want the indignity of onlookers. The water was cold, although that wasn't the chief discomfort. The shale was like crushed glass under my feet, and the bigger flatter rocks were slippery enough to brain me with a single false move. Dropping into my giant doughnut was a relief.

For approximately ten seconds. That was how long it took for me to realise that the current that had looked like kindergarten fun from a distance was, at least to my untutored helmsmanship, a seething torrent. My tube was picking up speed in compound time. I careered towards the unyielding cliff face, bounced off, and headed back towards the shallow bank, where my butt scraped along its jagged bottom.

Thus I pinballed, between literal rocks and a hard place, for the remainder of my terrifying, mortifying ride. I whizzed past strangers who, seeing my tortured facial expressions, shouted advice from on land. 'Lean back!' they said. 'Steer with your hands!' One guy stuck out an arm in an offer to haul me in. I got nowhere near him. The sandy beach, my planned exit point, sped past without pity.

I had no idea what was further down the river, and I didn't care to find out. I had been in a state of rigidity since I hit the water, entirely preoccupied by the thought of how I was going to stop. Now my mind panicked that I might find myself borne along all the way to Nebraska. I could be careering towards a waterfall, like Annie Edison Taylor in her airtight barrel. The thought jolted me from my paralysis. I made a supreme effort, and flopped myself out of my tube like a live fish ejecting itself from a frying pan. It took me some time to drag myself and my vessel back to the shore against the cold current. A couple of little kids floated past me in a state of serenity.

The barefoot journey back to my towel and my clothes –

through the thorny fringes of some woods, and up the long gravel road through the campgrounds – took longer than I'd been in the water. The campsite was a hipster's hippie Narnia: not an RV in sight, but plenty of Airstreams and campervans and the general atmosphere of a circus. I passed a jam that a shirtless ponytailed man was accompanying by spinning poi balls. Someone had projected lights onto the ground that made the grass sparkle like tinsel. Further along I came across a clump of bodies entwined on a double-sized Twister mat. 'Left hand blue, good fucking luck!' I heard. A guy in a sequinned silver cape wandered by and nodded a greeting.

Dry and dressed and heavily chastened, I ran across Pete again. He was with his bandmate, Tim, and it took a moment before I recognised Tim from the thirty-year-old video clip that I'd watched at Pete's music camp: the mandolin-playing Napoleon Dynamite. He was quieter than Pete, but with eyes that suggested buried reserves of unspoken thought. I told them about my nightmare river cruise, and vowed never to go tubing again without a mentor, preferably a ten-year-old. Tim gazed at me the way a tribal elder might ponder a distant flock of birds. 'You went alone?' he asked. 'Oh no, you gotta go *with* someone.'

Like Pete, Tim had moved to Colorado in the seventies, after an unsatisfactory year of college back home in West Virginia. 'It's bred into us in America, that idea of "Go west",' he said. 'I was into camping and the outdoors, so I went to Jackson Hole to be a ski bum. But I never made enough money to ski.' Through bluegrass's 'underground telephone' – the incorporeal, reciprocal network of musicians struggling to get by – Tim heard there might be band work in Boulder. It turned out to be the perfect college town to learn his craft. 'There were a lot of people who wanted to go out, tap their foot, dance around and have a few beers, and if you fell on your face, you could get straight up again.'

But Pete and Tim were never jamgrassers. 'Bluegrass bands back then, there was two kinds,' Tim explained. 'There were white-belt-white-shoes-matching-shirts-and-pants bands, and then there were the hippies in T-shirts and jeans and long hair, like Sam Bush.' When their own attempts at experimentation didn't go over so well, Pete and Tim created a counter-revolution, wearing suits and ties and writing new songs that sounded like old ones. 'When Hot Rize started in '78, we were the traditional band around here. But we'd play the same music and wear the same clothes east of the Mississippi and we were considered the progressive renegade band because our hair was too big and our ties were suspicious.'

I noticed Pete was wearing yet another Hawaiian shirt. I asked if he had an entire wardrobe of them. 'I do,' he nodded. 'They all belonged to our guitarist, Charles. I like wearing them to remember him.'

'Charles was a great guy,' said Tim. 'He was like a spiritual mentor.'

'He would teach folks guitar . . .'

'. . . But he ended up being their life guru.' Tim recalled the time a talented young guitarist, frustrated that he wasn't getting any better, had asked Charles for a lesson. 'And Charles said to him, "You look like you smoke pot, right?" And the guy said yeah. Charles told him, "Don't touch the guitar. Go smoke a bunch of pot, lie down, and listen to Monroe records for a whole day. Just let the music flush through you."'

'Did it work?' I asked, wondering whether this should be my next move. Tim shrugged. 'I guess. The dude never came back for another lesson . . .'

Pete and Tim had fulfilled their on-stage obligations for the day, but they weren't rushing home. This was the kind of festival where musicians liked to hang out with each other. Friends gatecrashed the ends of each other's sets; creative collaborations were born at backstage hangs. Their good buddy Sam Bush was flying in that evening and they didn't want to miss the chance to jam with him.

I'd seen Sam Bush live before. It was actually hard not to; the sixty-five-year-old seemed to be constantly on the road. He headlined shows all over the country, infusing everyone with his youthful rebel spirit. Sam Bush couldn't seem to get enough of performing, which was impressive, considering how long he'd been doing it. He had been bringing his nuclear energy to bluegrass since before I was born, when his band Newgrass Revival first began tearing up the rulebook.

Forty years later he still looked like someone making a point of protest. He wore jeans and sneakers and was invariably the scruffiest-looking feller on stage; his T-shirts did not exclude the occasional tie-dye. Whatever he had treated his hippie hair with back in the good old days – conditioner, eggs, or nothing at all – had worked. It remained thick and curled and respectably brown, a shoulder-length reward from the peacenik gods for a lifetime of service to counterculture.

These days he was as eminent a name as bluegrass had to offer, but he still liked to maintain the illusion that he was outside of the establishment. Today's T-shirt read 'PEACE' on the front and 'FREEDOM' on the back. He made self-deprecating jokes about his use of electrified instruments, and introduced the audience to his 'nine-times award-winning bluegrass drummer of the year'. Climate change was more likely to turn hell into a continental ice-shelf than the bluegrass authorities were to endorse such a category.

The mandolin is a petite instrument, and, I had always thought, suffered a certain emasculation by comparison with its colleagues. The acoustic guitars of bluegrass were big and macho, and the ability to speed-pick your way around them was extremely sexy indeed. The banjo had a large head which hung right in front of your crotch, and required a slight thrust of your hips to hold in position. The mandolin looked like your mum had shrunk it in the wash. It seemed delicate and not a little fiddly.

Sam Bush, however, attacked a mandolin as if he was in a fight with a grizzly bear. He strode about the stage, wrestling it under his control, his upper body rocking back and forth in giant arcs. Sometimes he jammed the instrument against his thigh so he could strike it harder. Even accounting for the amplification, it was a surprise to me how big a noise he could get from a few fragile pieces of wood that wouldn't fend off a burglar for more than five seconds.

The band leader urged on his players with a medical-grade enthusiasm; by the time his banjo player had worked his way up to the top of his fifth string, Sam looked like he might explode with gratification. More was definitely more. In the early days, the length of bluegrass songs was governed by the amount of time available on early ten-inch discs; three minutes was the maximum, and that brevity had become a part of its songwriting tradition. This set had *drum* solos that lasted twice that long.

Wolf howls started up between songs, a request for the band's big hit, 'Howlin' at the Moon'; Sam pretended to mis-understand and theatrically checked his flies. In the middle of the number he broke a string, and held his mandolin high above his head in a Freddie Mercury pose until a technician ran to replace it. The crowd ate up the stagemanship and orgasmic delivery, despite the fact that most, like me, were far too young to have been around for his heyday.

In front of the stage, a group of devotees were attempting

to dance to the music, and the sight confirmed something I had long suspected. The human body was not engineered to move to a bluegrass beat. Limbs leapt at random, unsure how to articulate the groove or to keep pace with the roistering tempo. Their owners looked like jointed mannequins who had, through the power of some mischief-making sorcerer, just been given life. And now wanted to crunk.

It was the worst dancing I'd seen in my life, and that included a lifetime of middle-class English weddings. You could have filmed the entire scene, overlaid a soundtrack of screeching strings and repurposed it as a zombie movie. But I couldn't fault their enthusiasm. I thought back to my dad, playing air drums on his knees, singing his atonal duets with Robert Plant. There was freedom here, and you didn't need to be high to feel it. I pushed forward and threw myself into the throng. And then I leapt about like a Mexican jumping bean.

CHAPTER 19

'So, when are you going to enter a fiddle contest?'

It was the question that had been stalking me all summer. Ever since I'd arrived in North Carolina, people at jams had been encouraging me to compete - it was considered almost a rite of passage. For most, it was simple economics: festivals and conventions usually gave you your entrance fee back once you'd crossed the stage to perform. After all, you were providing the free entertainment, whether performing your individual showpiece, or joining up with a few friends to enter the band contest. And entering wasn't just financially responsible. For youngsters, it was a useful gauge of their progression; for veterans, a reason to keep pushing themselves.

Whenever I demurred, I was told I shouldn't be worried. It wasn't a big deal, said Andrew's dad, John, who was used to entertaining the Murphy's crowd with his novelty songs. 'It's all your friends in the audience anyway,' he told me. 'They don't care how y'all play.' He was such a sweet man that I couldn't admit to him the real reason I didn't want to compete. Which was, bluntly, that I didn't want to enter something I couldn't win.

I knew from what Trevor had told me that the battle for prizes was hard-fought. 'There's an entire set of people who devote their weekends and their lives to this stuff,' he'd told me, as we sat in the library staffroom eating doughnuts. 'For them, music is all about "Can I win the next convention?" And that spirit's kept that whole world of fiddling alive.'

Trevor had been judging a contest the previous weekend: somehow, he said, his name had gotten on someone's list. 'It's a ridiculous job really, you're judging apples and oranges.'

'Then how do you make your decision?'

He swallowed another bite of doughnut. 'I just look at the audience, and if they're into it, and the music's solid, I'm going with them.'

'Appalachian X-factor.'

'Some of the string bands are out for blood, which is kinda funny when you think how small the prize money is.' Trevor told me he'd once given a band second place to their deadly rivals. 'Dang, these guys were ticked off. And I coulda just handed them all fifty dollars apiece, and I'd only have been out two hundred! But the bragging rights mean so much.'

I respected my friend's judgement on music and many things beside. But he was also the man who had once convinced me, driving home from a jam through pitch-black backwoods roads, that he'd lost his way and we were running out of gas. Who had shown up to a dinner party with a plate of pork scratchings topped in mayonnaise and pickle, calling them 'hillbilly hors d'oeuvres'. I tried to imagine him implanted in an environment that took itself so seriously. I decided that, faced with a fistful of angry locals, it was a miracle he'd got away at all.

The most cutthroat of contests took place in Galax, a small town in southwest Virginia that boasted the longest-running fiddlers' convention in the world, hosted every summer since 1935. It was also, said Trevor, somewhere a lot of country folk went to 'drink beer and cut loose'. Less than thirty miles from Mount Airy, Galax shared much of the same musical tradition, although apparently the locals wouldn't thank you for saying so. 'They're at the top and bottom of the same mountain, but they like to keep up that there's all this distinction between their styles,' Trevor told me, rolling his eyes. 'At a certain point, you're splitting hairs.'

All my musician friends knew which week 'Galax' took place; everyone raved about the late-night jamming, and encouraged me to make it a fixture in my calendar. A few days beforehand, it became apparent that none of them were actually going themselves. Not really their scene, said Zeb and Trevor. Not enough old-time, said Julie. It was left to my African-American friend Tray to tell me what the others hadn't wanted to. 'It's got me feeling weird a few times,' he said. 'It's some good picking, but there's a real rednecky vibe, lots of rebel flags hanging up.'

So I made the hour-and-a-half drive alone, through deep mountain territory, where rusted cars and rotting cabins were interspersed, every now and again, by the bright red shutters and lemon walls of a home from *House Beautiful* magazine. I passed free-roaming goats and donkeys and ducks and chickens, and a sign on the road that urged me to 'Stop feral swine: report hog sightings!' At a gas station I ordered breakfast from a girl who gave me a blank stare, then disappeared and came back with her boss – it turned out she needed him to translate my accent. The eggs and bacon and biscuit and toast and coffee didn't break three dollars.

The town of Galax was secluded enough that it came as a surprise. A sudden run of storefronts selling gifts and pork barbecue; a 1930s theatre hugging a corner, with a music shop nestling under its protection. Within a mile the businesses had left off, and the town was throwing out its final enticements, an open-air swimming pool (open five hours a day) and a 28-acre municipal park, advertising a three-hole Frisbee Golf course.

A couple of grey-haired gentlemen set up at a booth by the park entrance took my wad of dollars and waved me in. Admission was six dollars a day, and a camping spot for the week was eighty. As vacations went, it seemed pretty reasonable. The site was already full to bursting. The guys on the gate told me that a lot of the RVs had waited in line for the past week, parked in a stationary convoy through town until the gates opened. The sheriff's department was, apparently, cool with all this.

Instead of joining the muddy melee at the bottom of the hill, I pitched my tent in a slightly remote, shaded spot that overlooked the site. (Trevor had warned me that Galax knew only two types of weather: drenched in rain, or 'hotter than Satan's house cat'.) Sounds floated up from the basin: a welter of string music, a stab of high-pitched laughter. Across the PA an old-time fiddle was playing the national anthem, to the background roar and shunt of an industrial plant.

A ribbon of road led down the slope from my spot to the motorhomes, whose can-of-spam regularity was interrupted only by a patch of tennis courts. In the bottom left corner of the park was a grandstand. By the time I had made my way down to its bleachers, the bluegrass fiddle category was just beginning.

An hour in, my ears were ready to sue for emancipation. The entrants were terrible. They were - and I can think of no kinder way to say this - as pleasant to listen to as an angle grinder meeting concrete. They played fiddle tunes with three-quarters of the notes missing, although whether through design or amnesia was not apparent. They played waltzes that would have required the dancers to move in super-slo-mo. One of them delivered 'Amazing Grace' in a tempo so lethargic it seemed possible it wouldn't end before the Second Coming. The final verse – 'When we've been here ten thousand years' – had never felt so literal.

I couldn't understand it. Winning Galax was supposed to be the ultimate trophy for a fiddler. But this was a sequence of sonic horror that could match anything John Carpenter ever composed. My teeth felt like they were being approached with a high-speed drill, and the misery didn't look like stopping any time soon. A line of hopefuls holding their weaponised instruments snaked out from the back of the stage.

It seemed obvious: the only way for me to avoid further hearing damage was to join them. Sure, I hadn't worked up a showpiece, and I didn't have anyone to back me up on guitar. But against this standard, I still had a decent shot. I picked up my case and meandered to the large covered area behind the stage, where an old fellow sat behind a desk with a clipboard. I told him I'd like to register to compete, and he asked my name.

'Emma John,' I said, confidently.

'Joan?'

'John.'

'Jones?'

'John. Like the man's name.'

'Oh. *Jaarn.*'

He started running down the printed sheet in front of him.

'Oh no,' I said, 'I'm not on there. I'd just like to register.'

He looked at me with confusion.

'Are you saying you're not pre-registered?'

'I'm not,' I said. 'I'd like to put my name down now.'

'Honey,' he said, 'we don't take walk-ups.' He gestured at the long line, which I estimated, at three minutes a tune, was worth at least three more hours of stage-time. 'These here are all pre-registered. Deadline was a month ago. Come back next year.'

I returned moodily to the bleachers, mentally punching myself in the nose. I'd been an idiot. Now I had no choice but to sit and listen to a series of incompetents, like this one who'd managed to break a string by catching it with the sharp heel of his bow. On his very first note.

In an effort to disengage from the on-stage carnage, I focused on my surroundings. To my right was a parade of food stands offering Bourbon Chicken, Jalapeno Cheddar Hush Puppies, and something unfathomable called Bloomin' Onion Deep Fried Pickle Chips. Hotdogs, a sign said, were provided by 'The Ladies of the Moose'; it sounded like a matriarchal hippie commune, or possibly a boast about the contents of the sausage.

In front of the bleachers a slick square of orange earth – there had been hard rain all week – was decorated with the usual squadron of empty camp chairs. The stage itself was the open porch of a timber-framed lodge. In between each performance a large, overalled man, whose tattooed biceps popped from his cut-off sleeves, reappeared to adjust the microphone. Sometime during the second hour, he was replaced by a young woman. She sat at the back of the stage ignoring the music and reading a thousand-page novel which she had only just begun.

By hour three, a new thought had occurred to me. Either the playing was getting better, or I was developing Stockholm Syndrome. My shoulders were no longer hunched in a defensive cringe. When two sweet-looking kids walked on stage, I steeled myself for some amateur sawing; but the blond-haired fiddler sounded like Paganini. It turned out he was the thirteen-year-old kid who regularly played on the *Opry*; his back-up guitarist was Presley Barker.

It was as if all the really heavy talent had settled at the bottom of the pool; the last half hour was a deluge of fast and furious fiddling. How the judges would choose between them I couldn't guess. My personal favourite was a scraggy-looking guy with white hair from his temples to his shoulders, whose shirt hung off a bony frame, and who gazed at the end of his fingerboard as if he'd left something down there but couldn't remember what. Nothing about his playing seemed pre-destined or rehearsed; he played with a hint of swing, and an effortlessness that almost disguised the complexity of what he was doing.

My body numb from an entire afternoon perched on a concrete block, I bought a Lady-Moose-dog and took a walk around the campsite. It wasn't long before I spotted Ty and Roy under a canopy, picking with a few friends. On banjo was Michael Cleveland, whose fiddling had floored me in Indiana. He was sickeningly excellent on the five-string too – and, I soon discovered, on mandolin and guitar, his brilliance nonchalantly interchangeable between all the instruments.

Ty waved me in and mimed a bowing action, but I shrank at the thought of playing my fiddle in front of his genius friend. Instead I sat and listened, while Ty ran up and down the mandolin and Roy kept a lively beat on bass. When the music wound down, we talked; it turned out this week at Galax was Michael's official vacation from his busy summer touring schedule.

'But you could be on a beach!' I said. 'Or at Disney World! Isn't the point of a holiday to have a rest from your day job?'

He turned his head towards me. 'Man, if there ain't nothing going on, and nowhere I have to be, I'd just as soon jam as anything.'

I liked Michael, with his round face and his artless grin. When I asked him what was going through his head when he played, he said, 'Most of the time, I'm just hanging on and trying to keep up with everyone else.' It tickled me to discover that we had that in common.

During the week that followed, I never failed to see him with an instrument in his hand. The man had a childlike enthusiasm for playing, and a palpable lack of ego about his own skill. He seemed to enjoy other people's breaks even more than his own; head bent towards wherever the music was coming from, he'd beam – sometimes even chuckle – with pleasure.

I never got up the courage to jam with him myself. I was sure he'd have been encouraging rather than judgemental, but I enjoyed talking to him too much to dare complicate it with my own insecurity. He told me how he had grown up in Indiana, just across the river from Louisville, Kentucky. His grandparents had been big bluegrass fans who went to jams every weekend, and started taking him along when he was only six months old.

'Oh man, I had it coming out all sides,' he said. 'I had this eight-track with big speakers and I would lay my head on the speaker, and fall asleep right there listening to it. I was ate up with it. Still am, really.'

He started playing at four; I told him how shamefully envious I felt towards child prodigies. Michael gave a surprising snort. 'When you hear people say, "Oh he was so talented, he just picked up the instrument and started playing," you *know* that's a bunch of crap. Most musicians it's a lot of work. My parents said that it was two years before I could play anything. It was slow going.'

I realised the crass assumption I'd been making – that blindness had given the young Cleveland aural superpowers – and confessed as much. 'Yeah, people often ask me about that.' I detected a phantom of a sigh. 'But how do I know? I've never had sight, so I can't compare.'

What he did know, he said, was that he'd never found music so pressurised that he'd lost his initial love of it. 'Some of the other kids, their parents pushed them so hard. There was one kid I used to know, his parents would say, "If you don't play good you're going to get it tonight." I see a lot of 'em, man. "How can I make my kid practise?" and "What can I do to get my kid interested in the fiddle?" It really frustrates me. Because there's so many times when the kid ends up living the parents' dream. I always knew I was playing because I wanted to, not because I had to.'

Michael had a number of pupils who were trying to convert a classical technique into a bluegrass one, like me. I told him about the struggles I'd been having, and he was a good listener. Words spooled out and piled in a stringy muddle between us, finishing with my guiltiest secret. I wasn't even sure why I *wanted* to play bluegrass, I told him, hoping that the prickle in my eyes and throat wasn't obvious in my voice. Everyone else seemed to have this pure love for music, and me - I just needed to prove something. I didn't even know who to. No wonder I never became a musician.

Michael's eyes were half-closed behind his tinted glasses, but I felt him looking at me all the same. 'Look,' he replied, 'I guess no one's reasons for playing are probably all the same. But one of the reasons we all play bluegrass is that it's *cool* to do this stuff. Heck, I started because I heard a cassette tape of Benny Martin playing "Orange Blossom Special" and I just wanted to be able to do it too.'

He paused, and seemed to consider his next words carefully. 'The fiddle's a very intimidating instrument. They don't call it the hardest instrument to play for nothing. It all connects after a while, and sometimes it *is* a while. It's frustrating while you're waiting. But I'll tell you one thing. You came all this way to play fiddle, it don't matter what you think. You *are* a musician.'

CHAPTER 20

The manufacturing plant that abutted the park made furniture – a last remaining outpost of the region's once-booming textile and timber businesses. This one was clearly trying to compensate for something. It billowed steam twenty-four hours a day, and its production noises continued all night, rolling up the hill and into my tent, which I rarely returned to before 4 a.m.

There was something unsettling about Galax's circadian rhythm. By day, the grounds were almost abandoned. I never managed to figure out where everyone was hidden, although it was conceivable that they were standing in the endless line to compete. The judges started early, and each morning at 11 a.m. the PA would wake me with the un-welcome news of, say, the autoharp competition, followed by the even less desirable sound of 'The Stars and Stripes Forever' rendered in its tinny tones. A minister gave a prayer of thanks for the Moose, which was far less trippy once I discovered that the Moose Lodge was the name of the organisation that hosted the event.

The sky was overcast and ever ready to throw down. The couple of times I bothered to drag myself down the hill during daylight hours turned into lonely trudges through sneaker-destroying sludge, past unnervingly empty campsites.

I quickly learned to spend the afternoon at the swimming pool instead. Only at night did the park come alive.

It was then that the more popular contests were scheduled – guitar, bluegrass band, old-time band – and the locals poured in. From 6 p.m., the grandstand filled with unironic Stetsons. T-shirts with fishing jokes ('Return of the Jockeye') and NRA slogans ('The Second Amendment: The Original Homeland Security') wandered down the asphalt, holding cardboard trays of fries and their children's hands.

From the speakers came a contiguous murmur of music and words – broadcast-ready sentences, delivering the name and hometown of every contestant to syndicated radio stations across the region. The announcer listed their call signs like a mantra – WFDD, WNCW, WBRF – and padded the changeovers with public information. *Tickets for the raffle to win a hammered dulcimer are still available for a dollar apiece from the Ladies of the Moose, just behind the John Deere tractor...*

While the visiting spectators made for the booths and the bleachers, the serious pickers headed in the other direction. Come nightfall, the serried grid of motorhomes turned into a minuscule musical metropolis. The entire field broke out in string bands. Along each row of tents and trucks, every third or fourth plot pulsated to the bluegrass beat. It was as if an underground spring of music had overflowed, and now bubbled up wherever it found an outlet.

Ty and Roy helped me decode the scene. It was a choose-your-own adventure; you walked around until you heard something you liked and asked to join in. If you wanted old-school Flatt and Scruggs, you headed to the big yellow tent where the East Tennessee students hung out, nicknamed 'Camp G-String'. Hard-core fiddle tunes happened at 'the crossroads', where the meeting of two asphalt tracks left plenty of room to square dance. The trailer with the plastic

215

flamingos and the illuminated palm tree hosted a session that welcomed novices: the picking wasn't always top quality, but the barbecue was.

There was a swingy jam, a stoner jam, a jam where everyone played Beatles and Stones covers. Ty's favourite was the one at Camp Cigar, a blistering affair where Michael Cleveland and various of the contest winners could be found mixing it up in the early hours. The spot was unlit and relatively hidden, but each night drew a large, enraptured audience. The players disappeared behind a thicket of shoulders; by 3 a.m., when you thought they must have exhausted their best material, they were only just beginning to explore new galaxies.

My own preference was the tent that titled itself the International Kazoo Championships Headquarters, whose eclectic spirit might, on any given visit, encompass a Casio keyboard or a flute or a packing-crate drum. I once walked past to the strains of a Bill Monroe tune called 'White House Blues', and realised that the singer had rewritten it as zombie horror. *McKinley's in the graveyard, he's taking his rest, Gonna eat your brains . . . Gonna eat your brains!*

At exactly midnight, folk would gather behind the Kazoo HQ for the nightly 'soup kitchen', when a woman called Mary appeared with two deep pots of scalding grey liquid she ladled into plastic cups. She apparently began this nocturnal ritual twenty years ago, the prophetic outcome of a late night staggering about with the munchies. Mary's soup may have tasted like dishwater filled with small pebbles, but it had become such an institution that now a whole roster of volunteers helped her chop the carrots and onions which bobbed and sank in the pallid broth.

More spontaneous jams mushroomed in the middle of thoroughfares or outside the bathroom blocks – then vanished again, the music they produced as evanescent as quantum matter. (Schrödinger's banjo joke: If you trap a banjo player in a soundproof box with a bottle of poison, how do you tell if he is alive or dead? Answer: It doesn't matter, so long as the box stays closed.)

These standing circles were less benevolent than the seated kind. The males comprising them suddenly grew much bigger than their half-folded versions. Their guitars and banjos crowded together nose to tail, an interlocking chain that kept pretenders out. You couldn't hang around the fringe, hoping for an invite. Either they saw you coming and hollered at you – 'Got your fiddle?' – or you were expected to keep walking.

When I did get the nod – vouched for, implicitly, by Ty or Roy – few of the guys would stretch to eye contact. The sole acknowledgement of the female interloper was usually a brusque and slightly resentful 'What you got?' The question meant twice as much as it suggested: *What tune do you want to pick?* and *Can you pick at all?* Still, I preferred that to the alternative. Sometimes I was absorbed entirely without remark: my alien presence tolerated, but entitled to neither vote nor voice.

It was vital for a woman to prove herself fast in these bro-jams. Fear and false modesty were the enemy. I learned that the first time I found myself in one: the guys talking over my head about people I didn't know, choosing songs in a shorthand I couldn't follow and kicking off the tune without warning. Everything was in an up-tempo B major, and B is a hard key for a fiddler. Unnerved, I played so timidly that my skin stung with their unarticulated contempt. When a second fiddler joined the group, this one male, the rest simply ghosted me until I murmured a pitiful excuse to no one and withdrew. The circle closed itself up behind me.

By the middle of the week I'd adopted a new tactic: shock

and awe. Instead of attempting to secure my acceptance through a defensive, attritional humility, I attacked first. Pulling the pin on all my showiest tricks, I lobbed them into the centre in a multiple grenade-burst. It wasn't subtle, but it worked: a single strong break in the first number could earn my place in the group. If I was lucky, I might even catch the eyebrow raise that signalled it had.

Later, Ty taught me that these macho jams had their own name – 'mashing'. You could identify a mash jam, he explained, by the heavy-handedness of the guitarist, thrashing at his strings; by the fact that the tunes rarely moved out of B (which was easy on the male voice); and by an utter lack of taste.

Hanging out with the mashers may have failed to do much for my musicality, but it did teach me a raft of dirty and dubious songs that could still make them guffaw the fourth or fifth time round. 'If I'd Have Killed Her When I Met Her I'd Be Out of Jail By Now'. 'I Can't Get Over You (Til You Get Out From Under Him)'. A banjoist called JB tried, and failed, to introduce me to the ways of 'dip', aka dipping tobacco. 'It'll put hairs on your chest and make your babies born naked,' he said, passing the pouch. 'It'll put strength in your pecker.' He looked at me. 'Or in your case just grow one.'

Older female pickers I came across at festivals had told me their stories of how hard it was to break into the all-male world of bluegrass when they were coming up. One remembered having to literally elbow her way into circles; another said that, whenever she joined a jam, it would mysteriously disperse, only to reconstitute itself somewhere else without her. Sometimes it was the other players' wives and girlfriends who had snubbed them, suspicious of their intentions. I'd certainly had it easy in Boone, surrounded by welcoming friends. My only real enemy had been myself.

218

At Galax, there was no room for self-doubt. If I wanted to be in, I had to be all in. And that was just the experience I needed. For months, everyone had been telling me to let go, to stop over-thinking everything, but they might as well have told me to swim across the Sahara or grow a yucca plant out of my head. Gripping tightly was what I did. Over-thinking was who I was.

But in Colorado, I'd sensed a spark of liberation. Something in me was ready to change. I'd carried that flicker with me to Galax. I was ready to stop worrying. I was ready to stop hanging back. So I drank beer, and I cut loose. I wandered round the site, carrying my fiddle with a confidence I siphoned from the can of Pabst in my other hand.

It can't be true that the more I drank, the better I played, but at times it sure felt like it. And the ability to hold your drink counted pretty highly in a place where the picking went on until people's instruments were wet with morning dew. Technically, the 'public display' of alcohol was illegal, so we cloaked our beer cans and bottles in coozies, and the sheriff's deputies who patrolled the site were obligingly uncurious.

There hadn't been a police presence at any other events I'd been to, but Galax, I discovered, had form. The tennis courts had often been used as a processing pen for drunk and disorderlies; some years the site had even had its own wooden jail cell and on-site judge. The atmosphere, one officer told me, could be febrile. 'But not this year,' she said proudly. 'We've had a few knee-walking drunk so far, but we haven't had to arrest anyone yet.' She sucked in her cheeks thoughtfully: 'It's probably the rain.'

Back in the seventies, there had been a little friction between the long-hairs and the bib overalls. A woman I met called Pamela who had lived in Galax all her life could remember when the hippies had taken up an annual residence in

219

the horse stalls that lined the fiddlers' convention field. 'They used to wash in the creek at the back,' said Pamela. 'It was the first time I'd seen a naked man who wasn't my husband.'

I ran into one of those former stall-dwellers, Rodney, calling the dances at the crossroads. With his smoothed-back white hair and an even smoother smile, something told me that 1970s Rodney had done all right with the ladies. He told me how the fiddlers' convention used to draw crowds of one hundred thousand at a time. But after a disastrous festival called Stompin 76, which blocked the roads for miles around and caused near-riots, the locals had had enough. 'People freaked out,' said Rodney. 'The next year, they'd torn down the stalls, and they were arresting people for anything. They didn't want to be a refuge for these outsiders and northerners.'

The locals' victory was complete: Galax was no longer contested turf. Unlike the nearby Mount Airy convention, there were no hippie enclaves, no tie-dye or batik on display. There were, however, a handful of Confederate flags, draped over tarpaulins, mounted on aerials.

The sight had been such a common one in my travels that I was becoming a little blasé about it. My brain still registered a twinge of concern whenever I saw a Southern Cross - the uneasy sensation that someone nearby was looking for an argument, and wanted you to know. But it was impossible - or at least futile - to feel worked up with righteous liberal anger every time. Maybe that made me part of the problem.

Roy didn't hang a Confederate flag. He had a synthetic banner depicting a cartoon mule, around which was written the words: 'If You Don't Like My Rebel Flag, You Can Kiss My Ass'. He liked to point to it, with a giggle. Plenty of people - all white, all men - had been keen to educate me on why the flag wasn't a celebration of slavery, but a symbol of Southern pride. I had listened to all the apologist arguments.

One night, hearing the same spiel at the campsite, I mentioned Tray. 'Forget the politics,' I said. 'What about the personal? Seeing those flags makes a talented young banjo player feel unwelcome. That's not right.'

'But *everyone's* welcome here,' someone called Donnie assured me. 'Having a Confederate flag doesn't mean people are racist. And yes, bluegrass is very white. But then rap is very black. I don't know how welcome *I'd* feel at a rap concert.'

There were, in fact, a couple of people of colour at the campsite. I had a long chat with a man called Alex, ethnically Latino, who had been adopted into a white family at birth. He was even more evangelical about bluegrass's open-mindedness than Donnie. Alex wanted me to know that he'd never experienced any racism in this musical community. Well, until yesterday, when a passive-aggressive stranger had asked Alex when he'd hopped the border.

Happily, Alex had been able to tell this threatening figure both the floor and the address of the hospital he'd been born in. 'I've *never* had to do that before,' he said, as if that proved his point. 'And he was somebody my own age.'

This, to Alex, was evidence that the media and others with ulterior motives had stirred up a previously non-existent racial divide. I found his logic baffling, but Alex was adamant that I shouldn't believe the 'racism rhetoric'. 'People think that I'd be afraid to walk into a small Virginia town because of my skin colour. But that's not the case. Everyone has treated me incredibly well.'

Certainly Galax seemed a familial place. The bluegrass world was not a large one, and I had reached the stage where so many bearded older men asked me how I was doing as they passed that I often couldn't remember when or even whether we'd met before. I always smiled back, just in case;

it was possible that I accidentally flirted with several people's grandpas.

But I'd spent enough time in the South to learn that there was always something going on beneath the surface. The better I got to know the folk I was playing with, the more likely I would hear things that made me want to walk away. 'At least Trump is trying to do something,' Roy told me once after a few beers. 'I can't stand all these protests. That makes me angry. If they don't like it, they can go home.'

'Roy, you can't say things like that. Who are "they", in your scenario? And where are you suggesting they go home to?'

He huffed. 'Well. All these people said they're gonna leave the country if Trump comes in. *They're* still here. Why don't *they* go?'

The convention ended in anti-climax. Capricious mountain weather chose to drench the finals of the old-time band contest, although the avid cloggers who had come to dance to the music clung tenaciously to their fun. Clogging was an Appalachian tradition I had long struggled to make sense of. It was a method of dancing to old-time music that involved shuffling and stamping your way through a tune, often on a wooden board you'd brought with you for the purpose. 'Flatfooting', as the style was called, wasn't dissimilar to Irish dancing, but I'd always found its jerky mechanism completely unappealing, except perhaps as a high-intensity lower-body workout.

In the Galax downpour, hooded and poncho-d, the cloggers laid down their boards on the soupy ground like soldiers shoring up their trenches. Ty and I passed them, sipping coffee as we prepared for one last all-nighter. I had never seen so many flatfooters in one place. They kicked and skipped on their precarious platforms, sliming them with orange mud, their legs swinging loosely at the knees.

Individually they were strange enough, but in this vast company they made me think of those medieval tales of mass hysteria, where townsfolk, infected with a sudden collective mania, jived till they died. There was no synchronicity of style between one dancer and the next. This one kept up a gentle shuffle-ball-change; that one stabbed at the floor with her heels and kicked at an imaginary assailant. Another flailed her arms and turned in a slow but constant circle, stuck on an invisible spindle. No one co-ordinated with anyone else, or even seemed to notice they were there.

'I don't see why they do it,' I told Ty, dialling up all my bluegrass scepticism and anti-old-time sentiment. 'It looks idiotic, and everyone's just stuck in their own little world.'

'That-all's the point,' he said, refusing to indulge me. 'It's nice how into it they are. It's like that sense you get when you're playing, that you're flying above the music. You know that feeling?' Of course; I'd been chasing it for months. I shut up, chastened.

We stayed to watch the awards ceremony – all the week's winners, from first to tenth place, announced in a tedious epic that lasted over an hour. Presley Barker had, to no one's surprise, won the guitar contest; a makeshift bluegrass band that had co-opted Ty as bass player had placed third. We wandered back to the tents as the rain let up, hunting for a session. Disappointed faces, heading the other way, paused to share intelligence.

'Anything down at the G-String?'

'No one around. What about Camp Cigar?'

'They've packed up already.'

A pair of rubber boots joined the conversation.

'What's going on?'

'Nothing, man. Swingtown's dead.'

'And it's too early for Soup Kitchen.'

223

'This is what always happens. Everyone arrives so excited, and by the weekend they're burned out.'

A little later, I found a jam everyone else had overlooked. The pickers were all in the fifty-plus bracket, and I recognised them as the Baptist group I'd played with at Mount Airy. Their matching blue polo shirts were embroidered with their band name, Gaining Ground. Unlike the young ragers who'd hit it too hard all week, these soda-drinking retirees were still going strong.

Their bass player, Lynne, beckoned me in. There wasn't a full-time fiddler in their band – their mandolin player Wendell took on the role when needed – and I was considered a desirable addition. Wendell, a gentle man with a Colonel Sanders face, chucked me on the shoulder and murmured kind words about how my playing was coming along. At least, I decided that's what he was doing. His accent, a thick curdle of vowels, was almost impenetrable to me; most of the time I just pretended to understand.

We were finishing up a fiddle tune when I noticed a figure standing close by, not quite reached by the light from the RV. 'Get over here, John!' said Lynne. 'I want you to hear this girl. She's really somethin'.'

'I know,' said the voice. 'Why do you think I came over to listen?'

He stepped out of the shadow, and I saw the man I'd admired on stage the first day I'd arrived, the fiddler whose style had seemed so uniquely free. Up close, he had keen, dark eyes and a wiry intensity. His white hair was trapped beneath a straw hat, and his beard was closely trimmed.

I told him how much I'd enjoyed his playing.

'More than the judges, I reckon,' he said, with a sardonic smile. 'You compete?'

I shook my head.

'Should've. I heard you from my trailer over there. You got chops.'

I stammered thanks, a feeling in my chest that was halfway between warm treacle and heartburn.

'Shooz layk lazzzl,' said Wendell. *She used to play classical.* John nodded. 'Y'all going to Happy Valley?'

'Where's Happy Valley?'

'North Carolina. Last fiddle contest of the season.'

I shrugged; his laconic manner made me shy, and reluctant to ask more. But he looked like a man who had seen the world, and he probably recognised the eager body language of someone who wanted the chance to impress. Perhaps he had read it in my eyes – the blinked message, *I want to play like you.*

Either way, as he left, he threw down a casual offer. 'Well, I'm fixing to go. It's still a ways away. If you wanted to compete, I'd be happy to help get you ready.' He turned to walk away. 'Think on it.' And his tall frame faded into the darkness, like the Man with No Name.

Ty and Roy were still sitting by their coolers as I headed back to my tent. Somewhere, a solitary guitarist picked a half-speed 'Hotel California', the last song of the night. We talked politics for a while – Roy's disgust at the tax burden, mine at for-profit healthcare – but our hearts weren't really in it. Eventually we just stopped and listened: to the crickets, on a 5 a.m. timer switch; to the background boom of America's dying manufacturing industry.

The stars were eclipsed by the dawn, and a red sun rose behind the mountains. But if I thought that this romantic wake-up call would be the week's final word, I was wrong.

A one-sided history of the banjo

In the first half of the seventeenth century, an English explorer called Richard Jobson travelled along the Gambia River in West Africa, looking for gold. He didn't find any. But he did come across a native instrument, he wrote later, 'made of a great gourd'. It had a neck and strings like, say, a lute. Jobson didn't find out its name, but by the time it was observed again, in the Caribbean fifty years later, it was pretty well known as the banjar.

The banjar hadn't just appeared in the Caribbean, of course. It had travelled there, on slave ships. The people that England and France had duped, kidnapped, bought and sold to work on their sugar plantations were finding ways to recreate the music of their lost homes. And when the slave trade moved on, to the East Coast of America, so did the banjar.

For more than a hundred years, the banjo - as it became known - was an instrument played almost exclusively by African Americans, sometimes for each other, sometimes to entertain their owners, and their owners' families, and their owners' friends. It gave white families something to dance to when they wanted to take their minds off business, or give their kids a chance to meet a suitable spouse.

And then, in the 1820s, a young farmer's son called Joel Sweeney learned how to play banjo - from the African Americans, he said, where he lived, in Virginia. And he started to play it to people at the courthouse, and then at the circus, and finally all over the world, in his own minstrel show. The banjo saw some upgrades over the years: the gourd became a wooden drumhead, the neck was given frets, a fifth drone string was added. And thanks to the minstrel craze - who *didn't* love a white guy putting boot polish on his face and pretending to be black? - it became a beloved item in parlours across America and England.

It also became less appealing to African Americans, who were not only being ridiculed in the minstrel shows but who were also banned from entering the contests at fiddlers' conventions, and whose recordings were sold as 'race records'. They began to prefer guitars. For more than a hundred years, the banjo was an instrument played almost exclusively by white folk.

And no one talked about that for a long while.

CHAPTER 21

No one had mentioned Charlottesville that week, not even the cops. I only found out what had happened there because my mum texted me from the UK. The headlines about riots in Virginia had panicked her: Britons rarely comprehend how vast individual American states are, and she was concerned that Galax might be dangerously near the action.

I sucked up dregs of information from the radio as I drove back to Boone. A march protesting the removal of a Confederate statue had taken place two days before. No one at the fiddle contest seemed to have registered that, two hundred miles north of us, neo-Nazis had taken to the streets carrying torches and chanting racist slogans. If anyone at Galax had seen the news, it hadn't merited comment; neither the fact that one of the far-right sympathisers had driven into the crowd, killing a woman, nor that the sitting president had claimed 'both sides' were to blame for the violence.

My journey home took me past Wayne's workshop, and I stopped in to say hi. Wayne was used to visitors at all times of day; his workshop was practically a social club. He clapped me on the shoulder and said he was setting up a guitar for a client he expected any moment. Did I want to head to the vault? There were a few folk there already.

Wayne walked me through the house, beyond the room

where Trevor's band had rehearsed, past a small kitchen, to a metal door the colour of a roulette table. A three-point turn-handle in shiny silver stood out from the middle, like the ones from every heist movie I'd ever watched. Wayne turned the handle and ushered me into a large, comfortable room, where three young men sat on stools and leather cubes, trying out instruments. The walls were slung with priceless banjos, guitars, mandolins and more – Wayne's personal collection. 'Help yourself,' he said as the heavy door shut behind him.

I recognised a couple of the guys – they too had come straight from Galax. Their chatter was excited and a little gauche, like kids comparing new toys.

'This is *solidly* one of the best mandolins I've ever played.'

'Holy shit, have you *seen* this banjo . . .'

'I can't believe he's just left us in here with ten million dollars' worth of guitars.'

'I'd want this one, and this one. Then this one. No, wait, *this* one . . .'

Since I've never been able to play anything with frets, I took up a stool in a corner to enjoy the experience by proxy. A dozen antique shotguns and a rack of expensive-looking wine cosied up next to me; a signed baseball bat and ball hovered above the door. Wayne clearly traded in more than instruments.

The young men in the room continued to experiment, noting the different accents of the rosewood, the mahogany, the sprucetops. Their own accents were equally diverse: Illinois, Michigan, New York. One of them, a junior doctor, told me he arranged his shift rotations so he could spend every weekend travelling to bluegrass festivals.

'You're not married, then,' I joked.

'No,' he said. 'I've got a girlfriend, but she doesn't like coming to these things.'

'She's not a bluegrass fan?'

'She's Indian,' he said. 'I mean, she was born in the States, but the few times she's come, she's felt very ostracised. People are looking at her all the time.'

I told him I was sorry to hear that, and relayed my conversation with Alex, and the positive experience he'd had. The young men looked at each other, awkwardly. Then the junior doctor spoke, in a tone of apology. 'Maybe people wouldn't do it to his face, because he's a good picker. But... we heard bad stuff this week. Calling people wetbacks. Using the n-word when the black guys were right there, picking in the same circle. It's depressing, but it's the truth.' The stories from Charlottesville, so objectively distant on the radio, lunged closer.

The subject of Confederate monuments was stoically ignored at bluegrass jams for the next few weeks. It was quite an achievement, in its way, to blot the topic from conversation so completely, when the words 'Charlottesville' and 'statues' were implanted on TV chyrons in every bar and living room. You didn't mention current events like these in mixed company, only with friends you were sure agreed with you.

But we all knew, via the telepathy of social media, where each other stood. My own online feeds had quickly become a vertiginous trampoline of competing reactions. Asheville acquaintances immediately planned acts of mild vandalism on the town's statue to segregationist governor Zebulon Vance. Conservative friends demanded a returned respect for history, authority, military sacrifice and God. Scrolling made me feel sick and anxious. Trevor said this was exactly why he wasn't on Facebook.

Every degree of my own liberal bias was confirmed when I met a couple of teenage boys, walking through a forest not far from Andrew and Carrie's house. They were wading through a creek chasing fish when I first spotted them. Later, as I walked back to my car, they re-emerged on the path, rods leaning on their shoulders like rifles. We fell in step and chatted about school – both were about to leave, so I asked what they were looking forward to.

The younger one told me he was excited to vote; his friend had been old enough to cast his ballot at the previous election.

'Doing my public duty,' the eighteen-year-old smiled, bashfully. 'Making America great again.'

Well, I thought, at least they're politically engaged.

'Does it worry you,' I asked, 'what's just happened in Charlottesville?'

The boys shook their heads: confident, optimistic, unbothered by the horror of the world. 'What can those protesters do?' asked the older one. Words flashed in my mind – *mob, maim, murder* – but he was already continuing. 'The worst they can do is tear down a monument. They're not going to divide the country.' I had that miniature moment of freefall you get when your foot reaches for a step that's not there. Our words – our worlds – had missed each other by miles.

I picked with plenty of people who thought that the issues surrounding the Civil War's legacy were overblown: that if everyone just stopped talking about racial tensions so much, the problem would go away. Some would even tell me that 'slavery was over long ago', delicately forgetting that segregation hadn't been dead fifty years. Thanks to my outsider status, I often received impromptu lessons on American history. Secession was about states' rights, not slavery. Did I know that George Washington had owned slaves? And that Lincoln was a *Republican*?

The Appalachians themselves had never had a large

231

African-American community - the plantations were all to the east, and the mountainous landholdings were too small to need slave labour. Still, I noticed that whenever I visited parts of the South where fortunes had been built through slavery, I was always reminded by tour guides and docents that the workers had been treated worse somewhere else - in the next estate or town or county along.

It was hard, clearly, to know what to do with an un-comfortably recent history of apartheid and oppression and injustice. Some of my friends, usually the older ones, found it best to assign it to the distant past, and grumble in private that affirmative action policies were unfair. I couldn't count the number of people who told me that they didn't care about skin colour, that it was what was on the inside that counted, and that race relations had been fine until the media and Black Lives Matter had started stirring things up.

'This stuff is being designed to create dissent and to create a gulf,' I was told by one band leader who had a huge follow-ing on the bluegrass scene. 'Anyway, if we want to talk about the problem we've had with races being mistreated, I think we really need to start with the American Indian, yet nobody does.'

I thought of Tray, and how naive he said he'd been when he first started playing bluegrass. When people had made him feel uncomfortable at jams - even trolled him on Facebook - he thought it was just people being jerks. 'I'd never dealt with the racism thing before,' he said. Still, it was only a few, and bluegrass was a mostly accepting world. That was one of the reasons he tried not to make a fuss. 'I want to advocate for people, but at the same time I don't want to cause a big problem. People are going to look at you worse if you do something, so mostly I've just had to bite my tongue.'

Tray hadn't even heard a banjo when Boone staged the

first-ever Black Banjo Gatherings more than a decade ago. The Appalachian State University - the same one whose library I was such a regular visitor to - had hosted them to promote awareness of the many African-American contributions to old-time and bluegrass music. The Gatherings had recognised the uncelebrated legacy of black musicians and inspired contemporary musicians, like Rhiannon Giddens, to rediscover the music's black roots. Giddens' band, Carolina Chocolate Drops, went on to win a Grammy award with its reinvention of black string band music.

It was obvious, when you turned the microscope on bluegrass, that it was never purely 'white'. Its rhythmic complexity, syncopated beat and improvisatory style were all hallmarks not of European but of African music, whose influence had reached it by way of jazz and blues. There were echoes of African spirituals in the call-and-response structure of its songs, and even some of their lyrics. Joining the dots - reconnecting the music to a wider history of humanity - felt particularly worthwhile in a world where it seemed so difficult, still, for the white establishment to look its past full in the face.

Although not in every case. The week after Charlottesville, a man called Will - who I'd met at Pete Wernick's camp - had taken me to a jam near his home in Virginia. On the drive there we'd talked about Trump, and Hillary Clinton, and what he called 'the old Southern attitudes'. Will told me about how when he was a child his mother had employed a black cook - 'for virtually nothing, probably thirty-five cents an hour' - who had gone on to work for the family for twenty-five years. The cook had a nephew, gentle, thoughtful, scholarly, who had been one of the first black law students admitted to his college. 'And I would hear people in my family run him down, calling him uppity, and other two-syllable words that never have marked us very well,' said Will. 'It wasn't right. But it was the South, and that was the prevailing attitude. And for a long while I was part of that, and I was part of the problem.'

We journeyed in silence for a while, both of us looking out of the window at the forest, and its myriad greens that, when you took them in collectively, became a whole new colour altogether. And then Will sighed, and spoke again. 'When my father died, she came to the funeral. And I will kick myself to the end of my days that I didn't have her sit up front with us.'

He looked away, his voice cracking. 'Regrets. Yeah, I got 'em.'

CHAPTER 22

Full-blown summer had landed a sucker punch. The air was pregnant with water. Some days it was so humid you could see the warm fog waiting for you outside your window. In Boone, the temperature was still bearable, but when you came off the mountain, the heat gave the outdoors the oppressive tinge of a nightmare. One day I travelled with Zeb and Julie to a county fair not far from Taylorsville, and the shelves of produce took on a hallucinatory quality. Giant pears bulged. Cabbage heads sported jaunty ribbons. Muffins in cellophane bided their time, like DNA samples ready to solve a murder.

The South was revealing itself in increasingly surreal ways. At a Bojangles – the fried-chicken-and-biscuit fast-food franchise that Andrew's dad had got me hooked on – I waited in line next to a friendly and perfectly ordinary middle-aged man wearing an AC/DC T-shirt, who told me how the government was poisoning its citizens by putting fluoride in their water, and spreading aluminium through the atmosphere via chemtrails. 'I know about this stuff because I'm a conspiracy theorist,' he told me confidently, as if the term were interchangeable with 'molecular biologist'.

I was entrusted with other local secrets, now that I was a regular on the jamming scene. I learned that one of the men I picked with still had a bullet lodged in his head from an angry encounter over a woman. A local reporter who seemed as gentle as a lamb had brought down a crooked sheriff in a nearby county, where a Hatfield-and-McCoy-style family feud continued to rage. There was meth being cooked near some of the nicest houses west of town; they were close to the state line, where sketchy figures tended to congregate.

And, of course, there was the moonshine. *Everyone* knew where to get this illicit and supposedly secretive liquor, even the Baptists. And everyone swore that *they* had the best supplier. Each time I was offered a sip, it came with the reassurance that this stuff was the sweetest, smoothest corn whiskey in both Carolinas, guaranteed to leave you with a warm feeling and a complete absence of hangover. I only ever heard one person admit to drinking a bad batch, and that was Trevor, who had become convinced that it was distilled through a car radiator, and also that his eyes were going to fall out of the back of his head.

As for the music, I was finally locating its hidden heroes. Every mountain town I visited, however small, laid claim to its own great bluegrass musician, either living or dead. Some had become icons; some wouldn't have been recognised in the next county over. Many were so elusive they were rarely even seen to perform. In Todd, a tiny community fifteen miles from Boone, there was a painter-decorator called Steve who was a national guitar champion but whose blistering picking you could only witness by sidling up to him at a campfire.

My part of western North Carolina boasted any number of these local legends. Trevor and Zeb used to speak reverentially of Billy Constable, who had lived in Spruce Pine, a town hidden in the hills halfway to Asheville. Billy was the greatest picker they had known. He had played out in California for a while, then moved back and spent the remainder of his years perfecting his craft in his mother's two-bedroom home, bringing a perfectionist zeal to whatever jam he joined. He never made a record of his own – he didn't believe he'd be satisfied with the result – and when he died, his legacy existed purely in the minds of those who had heard him.

Sitting on a bench not far from Murphy's, there was a bronze statue of Doc Watson playing guitar. He had been born in Deep Gap, just a short way down the mountain, in 1929, and buried there almost ninety years later. I'd known nothing of him when I arrived, but it was impossible to stay ignorant about Doc for long in this town. He had busked on Boone's streets, been discovered during the sixties folk revival, and become world-famous for his unique blend of old-time, blues and bluegrass. But he'd carried on leading a modest life, and even before his death had become a sort of secular patron saint.

Doc's dextrous guitar picking was easily the most important musical influence in the area. Blind since infancy, he had learned by listening to records, and replicated both the rhythm *and* lead guitar lines, not knowing they were played on two separate instruments. He was the first to master complex fiddle tunes on guitar and there wasn't a flat-picker who grew up within a hundred miles of Deep Gap without emulating Doc's style.

Doc had influenced many lives of those I'd met; I'd even befriended a produce-supplier called Owen, who had moved from New York in the seventies to be close to the source of his favourite music. But nowhere was there a more dramatic case of Doc's impact than that of the two brothers who lived just off the mountain, in a place not far from Taylorsville. I had known their names for years, ever since my original visit to North Carolina. Jens and Uwe. The Kruger Brothers.

Everyone had told me about the Kruger Brothers. Trevor. Julie. Pete. The Taylorsville waitress. Fred and Doris had cooed about them when we first met. I understood why, once I knew their story. The Krugers had fallen in love with the music of Doc Watson when they were growing up in Switzerland. Decades later, as professional musicians, they had brought their own unconventional take on bluegrass to North Carolina, fallen in love with the place, and stayed. People wanted to tell me about them, because they wanted me to feel welcome. I *wasn't* the only European here, after all.

Kindly Southerners who knew the Krugers well often offered to effect an introduction for me, convinced that we would have 'lots in common' and 'plenty to talk about'. (I had heard these phrases before in regard to people's Italian, French, Swedish, Estonian and even Australian acquaintances – sometimes, I wondered if the rest of the world appeared to my American friends like a house party they hadn't yet received an invite to.) I fought shy of this well-meaning attempt at forced companionship; having crossed the Atlantic, it seemed counter-intuitive to seek out a pair of fellow out-siders for advice.

But then I saw the brothers perform at a festival: a jolly pair of fifty-somethings, their Swiss accents none the weaker for the past fifteen years of family life in the South. They were not your average bluegrass band. Jens was a prodigious banjo player, and Uwe a flat-picking guitarist; they played in a trio with their friend and bass-player Joel. They also had a string quartet in tow. Because when they weren't singing the standards, or paying tribute to their beloved Doc, they were staging the world's first bluegrass chamber music.

Jens, the composer, had written numerous concertos, suites and symphonies in a style that was far more Mozart than Monroe. But the usually fussy bluegrass crowds ate it up, and I suspected that the chief reason was the brothers them-selves. Wearing easy-going smiles and dad-casual clothes, the

Krugers sat on stage looking like they'd just been plucked out of the audience, and chatted away to the crowd in an unaffected, conversational style.

'They'll pick with anyone, you know,' murmured the man sitting next to me. 'Just the *nicest* guys.' I was suddenly keen to know these beloved, paternal characters. I wasn't sure what I hoped to learn from them, but I felt convinced that if anyone could help me navigate my sticky journey through bluegrass territory, it was them. After all, they were Europeans too.

They were nothing if not approachable. After a single tentative email, I received an invite to their home in Wilkesboro, a forty-minute drive east of Boone. Their directions deposited me in front of a large red barn on a remote plot of land. There was no bell or knocker that I could see, and the door was open; I shuffled nervously over the threshold, calling out a greeting and hoping I wasn't about to run into the muzzle of a shotgun. Trespassing did not tend to end well in the South.

The barn was actually a state-of-the-art recording studio, with offices, a kitchen and a spacious, sky-lit lounge, where I found Jens and Uwe sitting on sofas, speaking Swiss-German. They looked delighted at my arrival. 'Emma! So great to see you!' cried Uwe. 'Have you had your breakfast? Can we make you some snacks?'

They took me to the kitchen and plied me with coffee. Uwe pointed out his house, visible from the window; Jens lived on the adjacent plot. They had built the studio in order to produce their own albums. 'That way we don't have anybody to tell us what to do,' said Jens, who was taller than his older brother, and not quite as round. 'And we can make our own mistakes! We do a lot of things that maybe aren't the wisest business decisions. But we have tremendous fun!'

Uwe offered me a cookie and asked how I was finding the South. I admitted that the longer I'd been here, the less

I understood what was going on, and he gave a comforting smile in return. 'Even after twenty years here we have no idea,' he said. 'In Europe you feel like you're in a millpond, a perfectly contained little world. In America you're actually in the ocean.'

'Everything is here in abundance!' cried Jens. 'Did you know there are more people who believe in UFOs than there are in the entire country-music scene? There are more sleeping bags sold in America annually than musical instruments worldwide!'

'California is the seventh-largest economy in the world,' said Uwe.

'This place is so big we will never understand it,' said Jens. 'Since we moved here, we learned that our judgement of the country is and will probably always be wrong . . .'

'. . . so you stop judging,' Uwe concluded. 'You stop trying to put it into a compartment and start enjoying it.'

Their enthusiasm was infectious. The siblings seemed cosmically energised by each other, chasing each other's thoughts, finishing each other's sentences. Listening to them was like hearing a fugue where themes recurred and reinforced themselves in contrapuntal harmony. Jens, with his slightly curly hair and his rimless glasses, had a professorial air, his mind rampant with information and ideas. His older brother was the more pastoral of the two. Uwe's deep bass voice underpinned our conversation with a reassuring corroboration.

After they had satisfied their curiosity about how I came to be in North Carolina, the brothers told me their own story – children of post-war German immigrants who had sung them folk music each night to keep a link to their homeland. When Uwe was eight, his father had given him his guitar, the prized possession he had brought with him from Germany, and the boys would wander the neighbourhood, singing for treats.

'We figured quickly we could make people happy,' said Uwe. 'Remember "Lili Marlene"?' Jens asked him. 'It reminded all of the farmers of their wartime at the border and they would cry and give us hugs and love us to death for it...'

After the brothers discovered country, folk and bluegrass, including their beloved Doc, they started their own skiffle band (Uwe turned the family washtub into a bass – 'and got a whupping for it'). And when their mother died – Jens was only eleven – music became their refuge: 'We played ourselves into a trance,' said Uwe.

The boys were still only teenagers when they left home. Their father was drinking heavily and the family home was under constant threat from his volatile behaviour, like the times he'd shoot out the windows. Owning nothing but their instruments, Jens and Uwe busked their way around Europe for years.

Bill Monroe himself had sown the seed of their bluegrass-classical crossover music. At nineteen, Jens had made a pilgrimage to the Bean Blossom Festival not unlike my own. The difference was that Bill was still alive, and Jens had run into him on his very first day there.

'He asked, where are you from?' said Jens. 'I said, I'm from Switzerland. And he said, well, tomorrow you play on stage with me.' Bill had taken his new discovery to Nashville a few weeks later, and Jens performed with him on the *Grand Ole Opry* (their co-stars that night were Dolly Parton and Chet Atkins). For all his ornery ways, Bill had a knack for recognising and promoting young talent and, like many musicians before him, Jens was invited to stay on the Monroe farm.

'He was a visionary, different to anyone I'd met,' said Jens. 'He was a man who brought to light ancient tones – the sounds of these miners and this hauntingness - the mystery of a lost world, a bluegrass Atlantis. He had a mysticism of some kind, and I realised I have that too. The same that my dad had when he would tear up and sing. The same longing for a world that maybe never even existed. A search for a utopia in yourself.'

Still, Bill didn't exactly encourage Jens to follow in his footsteps. 'He told me, if you want a career in America, don't play bluegrass. You're not from Kentucky - you have your own music.' Jens raised his eyebrows. 'Of course, I was young, so I didn't really like him telling me that.'

I thought it sounded rather protectionist, like the old man was trying to keep out the younger competition. Jens shook his head. 'I played him something of mine, and he said, well, *this* is you, whether you like it or not. When I went back to Switzerland I realised I was a wannabe. Like somebody who learns fifty poems in English, thinking that makes them an English poet. It was a shock to realise how difficult it is to actually understand someone else's culture.'

Tell me about it, I said. Sometimes it feels like my classical background is as much use in becoming a bluegrass musician as a suit of armour to a jump jockey.

'Ah, but you're wrong,' said Uwe. 'You can see how intricately these tunes were composed, just like classical.'

'How does that help me, when it's all improvised?' I asked. 'Flatt and Scruggs never knew what they were going to play before they turned up to record.'

Jens exploded with laughter. 'That's *exactly* not true!'

'It's a myth!' chimed Uwe.

'Listen to their live recordings,' said Jens. 'Every break is almost the same, every show. They didn't want to screw up, the stakes were too high.'

'Improvisation came in mostly when they lost what they

were going to play and wanted to come back in to what they had rehearsed,' said Uwe. 'If you have to make up the music as you go you can't concentrate on your tone and timing.'

I looked at them both in shock. Improvisation was the basis of bluegrass. It was considered cheating to play the same thing twice. I'd been told that. By bluegrassers.

But the Krugers were about to drop an even bigger bombshell.

'Do you know how many musical notes your conscious brain can process per second?' asked Jens. 'Between three and five. That's the capacity of the human brain. It can't go faster. A song like "Blue Ridge Cabin Home" is already eight notes per second. So there's no way each player is actually making up every one. What they're doing is stringing together phrases they've already learned or invented.'

My own conscious brain struggled to process this new information. Jens, seeing my pained expression, spoke slowly and soothingly. 'When we improvise, we link together licks. But we are creative in the way we link them together.'

'It's like a language,' explained Uwe. 'Each of those licks covers a certain emotional or melodic ground. They're your vocabulary, your words and phrases, and like speaking, you have to know how to put them together in an order that makes sense. Then you interpret them the way you want to.'

'And the great players... well, they developed vast vocabularies,' said Jens. 'Which the rest of us still copy.'

And I realised that until this moment I hadn't understood improvisation at all. The discovery that bluegrassers *weren't* making up every measure they played was almost as mindbending as the combination of Benadryl and hot sun had been in Colorado. I felt like I'd been trying to reach the North Pole by walking there, and only just discovered that I could have had a plane drop me off in the Arctic Circle.

It was such a simple lesson, yet it had come so late. How had I failed to grasp the very principles of the music I was playing until now? I could only imagine how my face might look to the Kruger brothers: the face of Dorothy when Toto pulls back the curtain and reveals the true secret to the Wizard of Oz.

CHAPTER 23

Jens and Uwe had redrawn everything I thought I knew
about bluegrass. It was ironic, I supposed, that it took a pair
of Swiss brothers to open my eyes to how this music really
worked. But now, like a marble clunking its way down a
Heath Robinson mousetrap, the disparate elements of a music
that had seemed so impossibly confusing and alien were falling into place.

Our encounter changed the way I approached my practice
regime. I had been clinging to the vestiges of my classical
education with a daily self-flagellation of scales and arpeggios.
'You don't need scales,' Jens had told me. 'You need *words.*'
When I came across fiddle licks I liked, I played them over
until they were so lodged in my brain I couldn't get rid of
them if I tried. Until they were as familiar as a part of speech.

As for my lessons with Matt Glaser - whose face was still
beaming through my computer screen on a weekly basis -
they acquired a new and pleasing purpose. Before I met the
Krugers, I had chafed at the basic diet of fiddle tunes Matt
had me learning. They seemed too simple - the kind of thing
I could have sight-read when I was ten - and never sounded
half as impressive as the flashy stuff my friends were playing.
Now I understood the idea of music as a literal language, I
finally recognised what Matt had been doing - introducing me

to sentence structure, like working our way through a Janet and John book.

The scatting began to make more sense too. Previously I'd never understood how *singing* the notes was supposed to improve my fiddling. 'If you can't sing it,' Matt would say, 'you can't play it.' This seemed to me patently untrue. I was a much better violinist than vocalist.

But now I noticed what Matt had been trying to show me all along. When I sang, I wasn't thinking about what key we were in, or what note I should play next, or where to pitch it. I wasn't strictly *thinking* about anything: I was just listening and copying, hardwiring the notes into my cerebral cortex. 'You have to develop this stuff in your brain, so that your fingers can take dictation,' said Matt. He told me wanted me to be singing all the time. 'Out loud, in your head, it doesn't matter. When you're walking, when you're driving, when you're on the bus ... whatever you're doing, you should be *singing.*'

The effect of my homework was to turn my brain into a washing machine. Music sloshed about in there on a continuous cycle, its spinning drum churning over scraps of melody. I sang to myself in the car, in the street, in the supermarket aisle, and the tunes seeped deeper each day; before long they were self-playing tracks that ran on auto while I got on with the rest of my life. Sometimes I only noticed them when I climbed into bed and found, in the silence before sleep, that the tune was still there.

The last time my mind had been this noisily busy was in my teens, when I'd carried around constant earworms. Whatever pieces I happened to be working on at the time would set up camp between my ears and accompany me from home to school and back again. They embedded themselves in my subconscious so profoundly that I could still give you

Eine Kleine Nachtmusik from start to finish two decades after I last listened to it.

The difference was, those melodies required nothing from me but to let them in. They never changed or grew or asked me what came next: their invention belonged to the composer, not me. The bluegrass tunes, however, begged to be played with. They nudged me to add variations. They dared me to experiment. This, said Matt, was the next phase of the process: to mess with the order, use the phrases I had been collecting, construct my *own* sentences. 'But don't pick up your fiddle until you've sung the line to yourself first.'

My new routine was far more relaxing than the mechanical battle I'd been fighting with my fiddle before. In the kitchen, or the bath, or the car, I just switched my phone to record, and doodled my way around a tune until my throat got sore. According to jazz-cat Matt, there was no right or wrong when it came to improvising, only 'tasty' and 'not so tasty'. Most of the sounds I captured on voice memo weren't anything I'd want to share with the rest of the world, but it was the process that counted, not the result. Creativity was a mental muscle, and the more I used it, the stronger it was growing.

I was at the Murphy's jam when it happened. Something I'd never experienced. Something I didn't know was even possible. We had finished the free pizza, and Zeb was singing a song about a kid with obesity issues.

Roly Poly, Daddy's little fatty,
Hungry every minute of the day . . .

It was an old Western swing tune I adored - the outdated and wildly silly lyrics made me smile, and its catchy melody was just arch enough to match them. I had a recording I'd sung

247

along to a hundred times; even when I hadn't listened to it in months I would still catch myself humming it out loud. But it almost never came up at bluegrass jams, so I had never played it on the fiddle before. Then Zeb threw me a solo unexpectedly, out of turn.

Maybe it was because I was enjoying the song so much, maybe just that I knew it so well. It was as if a fuse tripped in my mind, and the conscious parts that usually took over the moment I was put on the spot - the ones that hunted so desperately for the chords and tried frantically to remember where the melody was headed - switched themselves off. My fingers took off before the rest of me could catch up, and my laggard brain, sensing it was already too far behind to offer assistance, decided to sit this one out.

Without its help - without any guidance at all - the hands that held my violin and bow worked together to replicate the melody, embellishing it here and there with little riffs and runs. Notes issued from the instrument like a ticker-tape machine printing stock prices. My ear, hearing them for the first time, found it all rather tasty, to borrow Matt's phrase. I let go and enjoyed the ride.

The solo unfurled with a casual poise that was utterly unlike me. Usually, even my better breaks were in danger of derailment by the time they neared their climax. Panicked by their own impetus, my fingers would become like misfiring pistons on a runaway train. Out of ideas and out of control, I tended to jump the track and crash in an ugly wreck some way short of home.

This time was different. The melodic line flew me up to the highest string, where I found my third finger holding it down, my bow carving up the sound into a rat-a-tat of repeated notes. Then, before I was aware what was happening, my fingers spilled down the remaining strings in predestined movement, a cascade of quavers and triplets in double-stop formation, one of the flashiest things I'd ever heard.

I recognised it *after* I'd played it: one of Benny Martin's showstoppers, a lick from an old Flatt and Scruggs song that Matt had encouraged to me learn. And here it was, emerging unbidden from my instrument, as if someone had programmed it into the wood. I looked at my left arm. I didn't feel responsible for anything it had just done. Like one of those cases of alien hand syndrome, when people have brain surgery and suddenly find their limbs moving autonomously and slapping them round the face.

The sensation was so magical, I barely dared to dwell on it: whatever had just happened lived in the realm of fairy breath and unicorn rides. I knew for certain that any attempt to recreate it in a conscious fashion was doomed; just the thought would be enough to jinx it. And yet . . . I couldn't bear the thought that this was a fluke. The following day I jumped in my car and drove to a jam in the next county, eager to play again and to find out what would happen when I did.

I played even better. More riffs and fills - some that I had no idea were in me - kept presenting themselves at the moment they were most needed. The bluegrass sound I had once struggled with exhaustion to reproduce was now flowing directly to my fingertips. Something had loosened, given way: it was like a roadblock in my mind had been cleared, and I could suddenly reach the music by a less circuitous route. Here was the release - and the relief - that I'd been wishing for. Every time I put my fiddle to my chin, I felt a small thrill of anticipation: who knew what might come out this time?

I sought out another jam the next day, and the next, worried that the enchantment would soon wear off, desperate to make the most of it. But no: my fiddling seemed to be permanently transformed. After months of getting nowhere, I'd been rebooted overnight with a major update, one that came with an extra gigabyte of bluegrass memory and upgraded improvisational power. Sure, I made mistakes, and still found myself running out of bow or out of ideas. But for the first time, I could trust myself to sound like I belonged.

I didn't pretend to understand what had happened. But I did start to trust that it had, especially when Matt noticed the difference. 'You fucking sound like Vassar Clements!' he shouted, on our next Skype call, with typical hyperbole. For once, I didn't try to shrug off a compliment. I just enjoyed it.

As I relaxed into the new reality, my playing rapidly grew in confidence. I sounded nothing like the timid apologist of just a few weeks past. Instead of finishing each jam in a state of self-loathing, I walked away with a swagger. Instead of watching with envy and longing as more talented friends and strangers picked in impromptu circles - be it at someone's house, or in a parking lot behind the bar - I strode straight up and asked to join in.

I even went back to the Isis jam in Asheville, where I'd come across Caleb and the terrifyingly hot-picking professionals. Those guys were still as intimidating as hell; one of them was wearing a T-shirt that said 'I play bluegrass because I love Satan'. But while their playing remained in a different league to mine, it didn't seem so impossibly fast any more. Now that I didn't *have* to think about what I was playing, I seemed to have *more* time to think about it. Weird.

In Boone, I was suddenly in demand for gigs. Bands had, occasionally, asked me to sit in before now, but I'd been disinclined to accept since my disastrous showing at the West Jefferson event. My sham routine of thumbing through my phone and looking up with a disappointed, oh-what-a-shame-I'm-busy-that-day face had acquired, I esti-mated, up to 95 per cent believability.

Now I jumped at the chance. There were offers to play at bars and birthday parties and hog roasts and holiday weekend festivals. Often they came from people I'd never met before. Sometimes I had barely got off-stage before someone in the audience wanted to book me for something else.

Any time I got to play with JM, Tim and Isaac was my favourite. On Sunday afternoons, they entertained the tourists who came to the Mast General Store, where you'd once been able to buy dynamite, and which was now crowded with barrels of penny candy, Gore-tex windbreakers, hammocks, knives, baby supplies, furniture, crockery, rubber chickens, expensive running shoes, and shelves of apple butter and sweet pickles. They often asked me to join them, and on the porch out back, Isaac swapped his fiddle for a guitar, and we performed to visiting retirees, resting their ample behinds in capacious rocking chairs.

Boone relied heavily on the seasonal business of these 'silver surfers', whose summer influx was a point of irritation to many in town. (There was even a nickname for those who came up from their winter homes in Florida and annoyed residents by driving 10 mph under the speed limit – 'Florons'.) I always enjoyed playing to the retirement crowd, having learned that almost anything would please them, especially when it took place on a deck, in a chair, where they could 'rest their eyes'.

But the aged audience were only a small part of the appeal; the real pleasure came from picking with my three friends. Each an expert musician, they had been in each other's lives so long that these songs were the weft of their friendship. Joining in was like being enfolded in a warm embrace. They felt a responsibility to entertain their listeners, but never doubted that they would. I never saw them stressed about a set list or worried about a mistake.

In fact, I'm not sure I ever encountered them in any state other than content: Tim placidly ruminating over his tobacco, Isaac with a cartoon grin that rarely left his face, JM prayerfully removing his ball cap whenever he played a gospel tune. Their easy rhythm carried me along as we played: like tubing, but actually fun. When I was with them, I noticed that my more painful mental habits – the exhausting perfectionism and self-criticism – melted away.

Perhaps the reason I felt so relaxed in their company was that bluegrass was so ingrained in them it felt less like a hobby than a way of life. They could certainly be as nerdy as any of the devotees I had met: string tensile strength, their collections of bootleg recordings, and the correct interpretation of the lyrics to 'Footprints in the Snow' were all considered fascinating topics of conversation. But they hadn't chosen this music because they were bored or challenging themselves, because they wanted to impress the heck out of people or to make it big. They chose it because it made them happy – and because it expressed some fundamental truth about themselves.

One of the songs Isaac liked to throw into a set was about a man recalling his youth, thirty years on.

Ohhhhhh how I'd like to be
Back in the hills of Tennessee
Ohhhhhh it would be so fine
If I could just go back to 1949 . . .

Isaac hadn't been alive when it was written. He was singing about a life he couldn't have known, remembered by a man several decades his senior. Yet the song always seemed a part of him.

252

Does life still go to sleep just after sunset
Are the berries still as big on the vine
Do old men sit and talk about the old days
The way they did in 1949...

Where did all that wistfulness come from? I wondered. And what was it doing in a man who hadn't turned thirty? I had got a few glimpses into the lives of my friends, through pragmatic conversations about Isaac's hiking trips or Tim's new truck or JM's kids. All three would have liked to be full-time professionals, playing this music all day every day. As it was, they had wives they loved, jobs that paid the bills, and a side-hustle that earned them a little extra.

Compared to the protagonists of most bluegrass songs, they had it pretty good. Sure, JM might feel overtaxed, but he wasn't working on a chain gang or riding the railroad. They lived in a college town where the only fields they had to tend were the lawns in front of their houses – and Tim had someone else do his mowing.

And yet that world of John Deere tractors and corn liquor was one my friends still identified with: Isaac told me that he liked the old songs because the people who played them were what he knew. 'They had it a whole lot harder than I did, but they still remind me of the folk I grew up around.' The bluegrass universe had been passed down to them with the power of a foundational myth.

I thought of what Jens Kruger had said about Monroe's utopian vision, his creation of a new world that idolised an old one. Nostalgia was baked into bluegrass. It was there in its themes, of mothers and children, and leaving home, and lost love, and it was there in the modal tones that harked back to the mountains, and even further back, to a life on the other side of the Atlantic Ocean.

Three generations on, it could still pull the same conjuring trick. To play this music was to indulge a belief in a brighter past: a golden age when life was simpler, and more honest, and people really cared about their mammas. Here in the Southern heartland, bluegrass wasn't what you did; it was who you were.

CHAPTER 24

I had not forgotten the white-haired guru from Galax. Since our mysterious encounter, I had discovered that his name was well known to older musicians in North Carolina. John Hofmann had played with numerous popular outfits in the seventies, but more importantly, over the course of his long career he'd scooped every fiddle prize in the tri-state area multiple times. For several years he'd gone unbeaten, seriously endangering the health of the scene.

'I'm not looking to get into your pants,' he said, in a blunt disclaimer, when I got in touch to see if his offer of help still stood. Nor was he suggesting I take lessons – John had plenty of pupils; more, his demeanour suggested, than he really wanted. But he was still insistent that I visit. Why this local legend had abruptly decided that I was worth his attention was never clear. 'I've got a good feeling about you,' was all he would say.

I had never been anyone's protégée. When I was a teenager, The Serb had always made it clear how low I came on his list of pupils with a future. And while I thoroughly enjoyed my Skype sessions with Matt, I noticed that he rarely made it through an entire hour before finding a reason to sign off.

Still, from my very first week at Pete's music camp, I'd listened to stories of reclusive geniuses passing down their musical secrets, knee to knee, and I'd hoped, all summer, it would happen to me. Bluegrass operated a sort of patrimony: all the stars of this music had learned from and performed with the legends who came before them. Sonny Osborne became one of Bill Monroe's Blue Grass Boys at fourteen. A teenage Ricky Skaggs toured with Ralph Stanley. The young J.D. Crowe played banjo for Jimmy Martin.

This was a genre small enough that its entire history could be enclosed in a single, biblical-style genealogy: *Bill begat Earl, and Earl begat J.D., and J.D. begat Béla, and Béla begat Nickel Creek.* And lo, there were other players who also learned from the greats, and they did pass down their learning on the distaff side, to those blessed with lesser talent than they. And from their offshoots could every picker in history trace their lineage.

Here was my opportunity to be part of that family tree. The thought that someone might even want to *audition* me as their disciple was thrilling.

John lived in Thomasville, North Carolina – less than two hours from Boone, which by American standards was barely a commute – and he repaired and sold violins from a workshop in his yard. He seemed well prepared for the role of eccentric mentor. When I showed up at his door, he greeted me with an anxious frown and the sentence: 'I don't know what y'all are gonna eat.'

It transpired that he and his wife, Mary, were vegans who were no longer bound by the earthly routine of regular meals. 'There's nothing in the kitchen but fruit and zoodles,' said John. I had no idea what zoodles were, but they sounded exactly what a Mr Miyagi-type *should* exist on.

He led me through to his shop: half-office, half-shed. Fiddles hung from the rafters like deli hams. A workbench in the back mimicked an operating table, with vulnerable instruments lying in half-naked states. John indicated a couple of chairs in the more comfortable half of the room, nesting beside a computer desk and some bookshelves. 'Do as you please,' he said. 'I've got bows to rehair.' And with that, he retreated behind the shelves and took up his tools.

I stood holding my fiddle case, feeling self-conscious. Did my new mentor expect me to sit down with a book or hit up the internet? Surely not: he'd invited me here to play. But I'd never practised in front of anyone else before. Learning new tunes, rehearsing the ones you already knew - it was an ugly business. The idea of doing that in company, exposing all my worst mistakes and inadequacies, was as appealing as doing squat jumps in my underwear.

Shyness was neither a welcome nor common trait in the bluegrass sphere. I thought of Zeb, who couldn't stand to be in the same room as an instrument without picking it up and noodling on it. Practising in public was his default state, although he'd never have called it that - he'd have just said he was 'messing about', which sounded much more like fun. Maybe this was the first truth I needed to learn. Maybe my path to enlightenment began with this simple step. Or maybe John was just really busy.

Either way, I took out my instrument and ran my fingers over some simple melodies. John kept his stock of fiddles tuned perfectly, and the air vibrated in sympathy with every stroke of my bow. The resonance gave my playing an unearned nobility; its richness flattered even my grisliest mistakes. Even stopping to play the same phrase over and over didn't feel a chore in a room like this.

I loved the way I sounded, and if this was a magic cave then John was my white-bearded genie. Invisible but ever vigilant, he began to transmit disembodied advice from the back of the shop. 'More down-bow on that phrase!' 'That's not an A chord, it's a D!' 'Stop using so much vibrato!' I did as he said. He was always right.

Hearing me struggle to land a particular phrase, he emerged suddenly from his concealment, unhooked a fiddle from a beam, and offered a solution: 'Not like that, like *this*...' Under his fingers, the notes suddenly made sense. I begged him to show me more.

'Well, what do you wanna know?'

'I want to know how to sound like you!' I said. 'I want to learn to play the way you did on stage at Galax.'

John shook his head. 'You don't wanna play like me,' he said. 'I'm no one. You could go less than five miles into the mountains and find a dozen fiddlers better than me. Even I don't wanna play like me.' He chuckled. 'I wanna play like Kenny Baker.'

He took up his fiddle and rattled out a tune. I couldn't identify it, but I did recognise the same jazzy, devil-may-care elan I'd heard at the contest. When he was done, he put in a CD and played me Kenny Baker's recording of the same tune. It was called 'Washington County', and from the opening bars it was clear where John had got that sound I enjoyed so much. The bowing was smooth, the tone was clear and clean, and the beat was so jaunty you could have stuck a sailor's cap on it and called it captain.

As soon as the track was finished, I grabbed for my fiddle, eager to reproduce its sauntering insouciance. It sounded like a relatively simple ditty until you tried to replicate it, and realised that its cocksure attitude disguised some seriously technical playing. But with John there to reveal its secrets – how to hit that tricky double-stop, or create that cross-string shuffle – the notes quickly implanted themselves. Within a half hour, I had it nearly up to speed, and John was impressed. 'Girl, if I had your ear, I wouldn't be wasting my time on bluegrass. I'd be playing *jazz!*'

The notes were only half the battle, however. Attitude was just as important. And capturing Kenny Baker's laid-back swagger, John said, meant appreciating one key part of his personality. 'Kenny liked his moonshine.' John patted his slender vegan frame. "Course, I don't take much alcohol now. But I can recall the sensation. And that's what you have to remember when you play. These guys were having a good time! They knew how to *drink*, y'know?'

I worked on the piece all afternoon, while John went back to his repairs. Except now it didn't feel like work. Chasing a spirit of inebriation rather than, say, perfection, turned out to be a great way to approach fiddling. I'd never played with such a persistent smile on my face, and sometimes I even found myself giggling at the tune's cheeky charm. When it was time to finish for the day, John made me promise I'd be back soon. 'Next time,' he said, 'y'all should stay.'

My long-awaited fiddling breakthrough had convinced me that I could now enter my first fiddle contest as a serious contender. John had recommended an upcoming fiddlers' convention in the tiny Virginia town of Fries. It was pronounced, for reasons I never discovered, *freeze*, and it was, he promised, a suitably low-profile event to make my debut. He wasn't even going himself – the prize money was too small to cover his travel costs.

Trevor's pupil Asa, still on a hot streak, *was* planning to go, however, and Asa's parents offered to take me with them and save me the two-hour drive through the mountains. I worked on my best tune – 'Road to Columbus' – all week, constructing variations and adding in licks I thought would impress the judges. Concerned that adrenaline and nerves might ruin all my effort on the day, I even tried drinking multiple cups of coffee before I rehearsed, just to recreate the heart palpitations and palm sweats I was sure to get.

On contest day Asa and I bundled into the back of the family's pick-up along with an assortment of chairs, coolers and two of the family dogs. There was a stop on the way at a gas station famed locally for its fried chicken – we bought their remaining dozen pieces – and an improvised game of guess-the-meaning in which Asa quizzed me on Southern phrases.

' "He wouldn't take a lick at a snake"?'

'I know this one! It means lazy!'

'What about, "If it was a snake it would have bit ya"?'

'I know this one too! It means something's close by.'

'I'll give it you. It's supposed to mean that something's obvious, but you've missed it. What about – "It makes you wanna slap your granny"?'

'Asa, I have no idea, but I don't think anything should make you slap your granny.'

'Go on! Have a guess.'

'It means you're a violent sociopath?'

'No! It means you've eaten something delicious.'

'Right. Well, that's ridiculous. That makes *no* sense.'

'Uh-oh, Mom, sounds like it's Katy-bar-the-door . . .'

We arrived late afternoon to a lonesome sight. Aside from the stage, the schoolground hosting the convention was almost abandoned. The large white tent canopy sheltered precisely no one; a set of rickety wooden bleachers were comically redundant. The woman who had taken our money at the gate pointed Asa and me towards a desk set up to register entrants; we were the first and only names on the list.

We sat in the shade and waited for something to happen. Beyond a fence, a dirt arena littered with upturned oil drums added to the sense that this was the OK Corral at noon, and we were the only ones who'd forgotten to lock ourselves indoors.

'It's for barrel racing,' Asa explained, as I looked quizzically across the fence.

'People . . . roll barrels around the course?' I asked.

'No, dummy. They ride past the barrels on *horses*.' I didn't think his explanation made much more sense than mine.

By the time the youth categories were due to start, a handful more families had arrived. There were few enough contestants that every child was going to win a ribbon just by being there. Unfortunately, Asa's nemesis had also shown up – a boy, two years older, who had beaten him out of first place at Galax. Asa went up, played his piece with typical aplomb, then came down off the stage and wept. It turned out he'd confused the A-part with the B-part. None of us had even noticed.

A few of the parents were loudly lamenting the lack of attendance, and wondering what was to blame – the poor amenities, the lack of prize money, or the new fire chief's failure to get behind the event. Personally, I was enjoying the thought of making my debut to no one but the judges, and possibly going home with an undisputed title. But as the youth contests proceeded, and the sun sank lower, more cars began to pull up, unloading fresh meat. I watched the new arrivals carefully, jealously counting the fiddle cases. I was going to have competition after all.

Since I had no one to back me up on guitar, Asa had introduced me to his friend Steve, who had partnered him in the youth contest. It turned out that Steve was already the unofficial accompanist to the majority of the bluegrass fiddlers in the competition.

'Whadday'all playin'?' he asked.

261

' "Road to Columbus", I said. He sucked his teeth and made a sighing noise.

'It's been a minute since I've done that one,' he said.

'That doesn't mean he played it a minute ago,' Asa helpfully translated.

'No, I cain't even think whenever I played it last,' said Steve. 'Hope I can remember it.'

When the announcer called for the contestants in bluegrass fiddle, I headed to the side of the stage, fussing over my strings. Even at 6 p.m. the sun was still hot enough to warp a violin out of tune. Steve was already at the front of the line, with his first client - there was no question of getting a run-through. Asa ran up to give me a pep-talk. 'Don't think about being nervous,' he told me. 'And don't think about forgetting your piece. ''Cos if you think about forgetting it, you will.'

Despite these inadvertent attempts to psych me out, I felt better the moment I heard the other fiddlers. There were only eight of us in total, and I found myself critiquing - and dismissing - each as they played. One had poor intonation; another was constantly a fraction behind the beat. None, I decided, could compete with me for tone. The standard was OK, but it wasn't spectacular. By the time there were only two of us left, I'd convinced myself I could win.

The remaining contender stood beside me, a fiddle tattoo on the inside of her left arm, and musical notes inked round the right. Her hair was pulled back in a tight ponytail that obscured her age; she could have been anything from eighteen to thirty-five. A woman with a clipboard approached and asked us who was going next. Fiddle Tattoo turned to me with a modest smile. 'You first,' she said. 'I'd love to hear you play.' I decided she was either very generous or very nervous.

The stage operated a one-way system - enter from the left, depart to the right - and Steve, who had been playing for the previous contestant, had to pant his way around the back before he could join me in front of the microphone. I only stood alone for a few seconds, but they were enough to remind me of Asa's words, and set off a chain of dark worry. How did the opening phrase go? I searched for it fruitlessly. Panic grabbed me.

What the heck was the first *note*?

I riffled through my mind like a burglar who hears a car pulling up the drive. The announcer was giving my name, and Steve had appeared by my side. But I couldn't even see my surroundings any more – my eyes were focused on the empty black box in my head where 'Road to Columbus' should have been.

Steve leaned in confidentially, his head angled away from the mic. 'Just gotta check – y'all are playing that intro before I come in?' And he hummed the first few notes in my ear.

Relief hit me like a sandbag. I could have kissed Steve right there, in front of Asa, Asa's parents, and, in all probability, Steve's wife. Instead I just nodded and flipped my fiddle under my chin. That rush of fear had, somehow, spiked the rest of my store, and as the first flurry of notes left my fingers, I knew things were going to go well.

Playing my violin when I knew I was being judged on the results had been, in the past, a waking nightmare. Other people may be able to 'lose themselves' in the music, but for me the sensation was usually one of being locked inside a fast-moving vehicle with only a hazy memory of the controls. The road in front of me was always a dangerous downhill, with chicanes and hairpin turns that required expert hand-ling. As soon as I overcame one obstacle, I could see the next approaching at speed.

Trapped in the tension – between what my brain knew the music was about to demand of me, and what the rest of me was going to have to do to accomplish it – it was generally a hellish ride. This time, however, I was a passenger. The music was still full of stomach-turning drops and bends, but now my fiddle and I were sat next to each other in the back of the car, squealing with pleasure as it threw us around.

In fact, when I stepped off the stage three minutes later, hearing whoops and hollers from the audience, it felt much like climbing down from a carnival ride. My wobbly legs got me only as far as the rear of the local radio van, where, out of sight of the judges, I doubled over, unsure if I was about to throw up or pass out. When I stopped seeing nauseating grey spots, I noticed Lynne, the bassist from Gaining Ground. I was thrilled – as she was the woman who had introduced me to my new mentor at Galax, I considered Lynne largely responsible for the fact I was competing at all. 'You did good, girl!' she said, clapping her arm round my shoulder and giving it a squeeze. 'They loved ya!'

We watched together as Fiddle Tattoo, the final contestant, stood up to the mic. It took me less than ten seconds to realise that I'd been played. She was the best musician I had heard all day. Her style was less showy than mine, but undeniably more authentic: a delicious, satisfying home-cooked meal that made my performance look like so much fancy garnish.

Still, it was clear I was a crowd favourite. Asa whispered to me that I'd got the biggest ovation of the night, and if this was a popular vote, I'd have it in the bag. Every time I stretched my legs, or joined the line for the portapotty, people came up to tell me how much they'd enjoyed my playing, and that they hoped I'd win. I jammed my face into the most modest expression I could muster, while behind it, miniature versions of myself threw streamers and danced on tables.

We had to wait another two hours until they announced the results, by which time I had eaten three hot dogs and drunk a number of semi-disguised beers (no-public-display) in premature celebration. I sat with Lynne and Asa as the announcer began to hand out the ribbons. Asa had won the youth contest, in spite of his alleged mess-up, and I was wrestling with how to look gracious if I came in second to Fiddle Tattoo. I didn't deserve to win first place, but deep down I couldn't help but hope that I'd managed to fool the judges along with everyone else.

There were ribbons for first to fifth place in every category, announced in reverse order, which I figured would build up the tension nicely, and give me a chance to practise my fake smile. I tensed my hands, ready to applaud the fifth-place winner.

It was me.

I returned to John's house a humbled woman. 'Losing don't mean nothing,' said John. 'You never know who's there who doesn't like you, or who you pissed off last year.' But I wasn't even *here* last year, I said, and *nobody* there knew me. 'Well, that'll do it too. A lot of these judges prefer the faces they already know. They think you've gotta earn it. Let's hear what you played.'

I performed my piece to John, who sat and listened with an inscrutable expression. When I was done, he leaned back against his chair. 'Well, girl, you've got a lot there,' he said. I felt vindicated. 'But you've overcooked it,' John continued. 'Too much fancy stuff. The judges'll think you're trick fid-dling. And they don't care for that.'

What the heck was trick fiddling? I asked. He reached for a CD: 'Ever heard of Scotty Stoneman?' Matt had mentioned him once - a showman from the fifties who had wowed crowds by making his fiddle sound like a train, a dog or a bird, or by playing it upside down and behind his back. He had also, according to Matt, drunk anything he could lay his hands on from lighter fluid to shoe polish, and died at forty-one of alcohol poisoning.

John pressed play and the workshop filled with the aural equivalent of an explosion at a clock factory – a lot of precisely crafted cogs and springs sailing through the air to no discernible purpose. The playing was technically brilliant but not something I'd ever have chosen to listen to for pleasure. 'It sounds like a reference library,' I said to John. 'A multi-volume dictionary of licks.'

He chuckled approvingly. 'Scotty's got his uses,' he said. 'If you can learn all those licks you can find a way to put 'em together tastefully, 'cos he sure as shit didn't.' He shook his head. 'Rolling around on the floor playing "Orange Blossom Special" is cool but it's not who I wanna be.'

Those kind of stunts and fireworks might impress the crowds, said John, but not the judges at a fiddlers' convention. They had an abhorrence of anything too flash; pieces that involved a lot of shuffle or pizzicato or sliding around, like 'Orange Blossom Special' and 'The Mockingbird', were sometimes outright banned. Judges saw themselves as the gatekeepers of tradition and if you wanted to win, you had to play by their rules.

'Like Olympic figure skating in the eighties!' I said.

'If you say so.'

Winning was less about the art of performance than it was about the science of giving the judges what they wanted – while avoiding boring them with something they'd heard too often. John reckoned the biggest secret to his success was his ability to pick the right tune. 'Last year I won all over with "Cattle in the Cane", which no one was playing,' he said, matter-of-factly. 'Now I hear it everywhere. They ain't winning with it, though.'

'Road to Columbus' wasn't particularly common, apparently, so that was a good start. But now I needed to learn to maximise my three-minute time limit. In that brief window, the judges wanted to hear orthodoxy and originality; they wanted to hear good tone and fast licks; they wanted to hear something that sounded perfectly authentic, yet somehow stood out from the reams of contestants they had to listen to. But most important was letting the judges hear the melody. Judges were *obsessed*, John said, with the melody.

His answer was simple: work your tune up into an arrangement that kept impressing, the longer it went on. First he played the tune in its most original form - a palate cleanser that showcased his rich, deep tone. He followed this no-frills version with some tasteful variation that didn't stray too far from the original. Harmonies worked well, because they enhanced the melody rather than obscuring it. The third time round, though, all bets were off. '*That's* when you bring out all your best licks. Really smoke it up.'

There was one other trick to competing, said John. Play last. 'You go on stage first, you can play as pretty as all get out, and the judges'll still forget y'all,' he said. 'You play at the end, y'all are the last best thing they heard.' Fiddle Tattoo had known what she was doing.

I moved into John and Mary's spare room and, over the course of the next few days, began to rework my piece. John lent an attentive and encouraging ear, as well as the occasional Yoda-like pronouncement. 'The best judge of what's right is on either side of your head.' 'Your bow isn't a stick! It's your *breath*!' Sometimes, he switched roles and appointed me the teacher. 'What are you doing there?' he'd ask suddenly, as I played through one of my own arrangements. 'I like it! Show me!'

Since there were no such things as mealtimes at John's

house – I survived by memorising the locations of the nearest breakfast diners and late-night burger bars – lunch and dinner breaks were when John put away whatever injured instrument he had been tending and sat down to play with me.

'Know any twin fiddle?' he asked, the second day of my stay. I told him to pick a tune and I'd find a harmony. John was impressed – he had always had to teach his pupils harmonies from scratch, he said.

He started playing a waltz he loved, an elegant piece I hadn't heard before. Tentative flights of notes swelled with romance, held in check at the last moment. It sounded like a chaste novella of the antebellum era, all yearning glances and unconsummated desire. I listened through once; I could already imagine the notes beneath the melody adding a silky warmth, like the satin lining of a coat.

I picked up my bow and shadowed John's lead, moving in tight formation a third below the tune. Some notes weren't exactly right, and a couple of times I lost the thread altogether. But it didn't matter. Our fiddles blended as if they had been created for each other, setting free all the latent emotion held in the music's undulations and sweet grace notes. The rich, clear sound wove through the instruments that hung above our heads, in and out of their bellies, adding endless layers of frequency. The little shed resounded like Carnegie Hall.

When the waltz ended, neither of us moved. The double echo of the final note, impregnated with emotion, still hung about us, and I listened to it drift slowly out of hearing. Eventually, John spoke. 'I've been waiting my whole life to find someone I could play with like that.'

From that instant, he had a plan. The Happy Valley fiddle contest had a category for twin fiddles; it was one of the few honours John had never claimed. 'We're going to enter,' he said. 'And they'd better get ready. 'Cos if we play like that, there ain't no one can touch us.'

Then came the strategy. Happy Valley was a bigger event than Fries: it had two rounds per category. Assuming we made the final – which John did – we'd have to play at least three pieces. The decorous symmetry of waltzes was only going to get us so far. The judges would want a little spectacle, something with drive.

The breakdowns he wanted us to play were some of the toughest I knew: 'Big Mon', 'Wheel Hoss', tunes with added kick. Getting my fingers round them was hard enough when I was playing alone. Doing it while attempting to stay in perfect time with someone else was like motorcycle ballet. I was convinced that something was going to get broken: either my bow, my ego, or John's reputation. Possibly all three.

We worked every day: trying out tunes, searching out harmonies. John may have had bottomless wells of skill and experience, but he also had limited amounts of energy and patience. If we practised too long, he would complain that his brain was hurting, and that *I* was working *him* too hard.

John had never been anything but generous to me. When it came to interacting with the rest of the world, he could be more irascible. I once heard him tear into a possible customer on the phone because the guy had mistaken him for someone else. He warned me that when we went to Happy Valley, I shouldn't expect small talk. 'When I play I don't have any friends. I play to win.'

So no, he wasn't a Robin-Williams-in-*Dead-Poets-Society* persona. To be fair, he had given up meat, dairy and alcohol for the past two years, and while his new diet had had a great effect on his waistline (I saw the 'before' pictures), it would be understandable if it also left him a little irritable. I suspected, however, it had something to do with his musical career. John told me often how he had never been one of the 'good ol' boys'. His father, a German immigrant, was from New York, and even with a North Carolinian mother, he'd always been considered an outsider in the South.

In the seventies, John had won fame without fortune. 'You heard of Mickey Gilley and the Urban Cowboy Band?' I shook my head. 'Too young,' he said. 'Too British,' I replied. He told me they'd been the most popular country act in America for a couple of years. 'I got to do it all. *Dukes of Hazzard*. Radio City Music Hall. But it was gruelling, grinding, and whenever you showed up to work, there wasn't so much as a hello, kiss my ass or a go to hell.

'They didn't ask me what I thought about the music. I just had to be sober enough to play the gig and be at the bus on time, so's someone else could make all the money. The last year I was out on the road for three hundred and three days. It sucked. And I decided if that's what playing music was I didn't want any part of it. I quit for ten years after.'

Now John was in his seventies, and he was supplementing his income as a luthier by making art lamps for local fairs. I could understand why winning at the fiddle contests meant so much to him. And I felt, too, the strange, proxy power of his trust in me. My confidence was growing daily; knowing that he thought highly of my playing made me believe in myself too. And I didn't want to let him down.

CHAPTER 25

I was not a fan of Nashville, Tennessee. I had travelled there once before, in years gone by, and found it rather depressing. When I thought of Music City, I pictured Broadway, the garish strip of mediocrity that passed for entertainment. I shuddered at the memory of the Opryland resort, whose obscenely vast hotel was to good taste what Versailles, Kentucky, was to Versailles, Paris.

I might never have felt the need to go back, if I hadn't spent so much time listening to those classic bluegrass recordings in the library at Boone. Bill Monroe's legendary Decca sessions, the Stanley Brothers' Mercury recordings, Flatt and Scruggs at Columbia, Kenny Baker's albums for County Records - so many were made in Tennessee's capital, the epicentre of country music and home of the Grand Ole Opry. Bluegrass may have been conceived in the mountains - and born, with Bill, in Kentucky. But there was no denying where it had thrown its coming-of-age party.

John was the one who nudged me on my way. He told me that Nashville was where I would find the greatest Kenny Baker-style fiddler on the planet. I had missed my chance to see the original - he died in 2011 - but if Kenny's spirit had slipped into anyone, said John, it was a man called Aubrey Haynie. Aubrey had been Nashville's most in-demand session musician for two decades; his work graced literally hundreds of albums. And once a week you could hear him play live at a somewhat grimy bar called the Station Inn.

Aubrey's regular gig was on a Monday. And so, as it happened, was the day that Nashville would witness the first solar eclipse to cross the American continent in ninety-nine years. As I began the six-hour trip, my radio played a selection of themed rock and pop: Bruce Springsteen's 'Dancing in the Dark', Bonnie Tyler's 'Total Eclipse of the Heart'. A couple of hours in, I pulled over at a rest stop on Interstate 40 and found a father and son passing a cereal box between them, and staring at its empty contents through a hole they had cut for the purpose.

They offered me a look, and I peered into the box: it contained nothing but a small dot of light, which someone had taken a tiny bite out of. The men had left Washington DC nine hours ago on their journey towards the 'path of totality', which made them sound like redshirts in a next-generation *Star Trek* film. Except that their car had broken down on the drive, and they'd had to leave it behind and pick up a rental. The eclipse was due in an hour, and the path of totality was still two hundred miles away. They were coming to terms with their disappointment. 'It'll be 98 per cent here,' shrugged the son. 'It'll still get dark...'

By the time I reached the outskirts of Knoxville, the light had turned unnerving. How could it be both too dim *and* too bright at once? I pulled over as the radio DJ began his ten-minute countdown, and got out to the blinking of a confused street lamp. Donning my special-issue glasses, I leaned on the car door and stared gormlessly upwards as Bill Withers sang 'Ain't No Sunshine When She's Gone'. I began to wish I'd made an effort to find somewhere more atmospheric than an empty parking lot opposite a construction site.

The moon's shadow nosed out all but a tiny remaining sliver of sun. A minute later, a klaxon sounded to tell the construction workers to get back to their jobs. Trees erupted with twitter from birds who'd accidentally reset their body clocks. I drove only a couple of blocks further before I found myself alongside a market square, where a crowd of smiling strangers had just bonded over their once-in-a-lifetime experience. If I'd stayed in the car a minute longer, I could have shared the moment with them too, instead of being alone with Bill.

When twilight came for the second time that day, I headed for an area of Nashville known as The Gulch, which sounded like the abandoned district the oppressed masses would be assigned to in a dystopian YA novel. Parts of it turned out to be highly gentrified; a run of empty lots and chicken-wire fences suddenly exchanged itself for blocks of shiny development and mid-range retail and chain bistros. The only blot was the Station Inn itself, a flat-roofed stone-clad single-storey that resembled a nineteenth-century town jail. It lurked in the middle of high-rise condos, its boarded-up windows leering at the Urban Outfitters opposite.

The bill promised 'Val Storey and Friends', and the cover charge was twelve dollars, which was a pretty good deal when you discovered that Val's friends included the Grammy award-winning Carl Jackson and Larry Cordle. A man sitting at a card table by the door tucked my dollars into an old cigar box and waved me into the gloom. The Station Inn's interior was no more prepossessing than the outside: if it had ever known a decorator, their knowledge of the colour palette had ended at brown.

Wobbly-legged chairs fought each other for space under aluminium tables. The backdrop to the stage was adorned with ugly soundproofing and a small wooden lozenge, which announced the venue's name in medieval gilt lettering. I looked

273

up at the unfinished ceiling, and noticed that it buckled alarmingly halfway across the room. The best things the owners had done for the place were to cover the walls in old posters – and to keep the lighting at submariner levels.

The bar was little more than a hatch; it sold cheap beer and cheap whiskey and cheap pizzas, which emerged somewhat magically from a kitchen that looked suspiciously short on cooking equipment. I chatted to the bartender, Justin; he was a bluegrass musician himself. 'Almost everyone who works here is,' he said. 'Most of the customers too.' It was how the place had survived so long – as a second home for the town's indigent bluegrassers. It was also why it could attract some of the biggest names in town, who came to play low-key sets with their buddies, for the camaraderie as much as the pay.

Tonight's gig was a mash-up of bluegrass and country. A banjo, guitar, pedal steel and keyboard all waited on-stage until their owners emerged from a door near the bathrooms to join them. Aubrey Haynie carried his fiddle to a stool at the far left of the stage; he was far taller than I'd imagined, and, I estimated, no more than a few years older than me. His hands were huge, so large that they somehow foreshortened his arms. When he took up his bow I thought that this was how a T. rex might look, if dinosaurs had ever engaged in a little night music.

The sound Aubrey made was soft and smooth as whipped butter – spread creamily on Larry's ballads, adding dollops of salty swing to Val's sexy alto. He seemed to be performing some kind of illusion: when Carl ratcheted the band up to full tempo with his banjo breakdowns, Aubrey didn't speed up his movements in the slightest, yet hundreds more notes flew out of his fiddle, in fantastic concoctions the world had never heard before.

I felt like I was losing my mind. The impossibility of what

he was doing made me dizzy, light-headed; one break was so implausible I almost laughed out loud. The only person I'd seen who could compare to him in skill was Michael Cleveland, but their styles couldn't have been more different. I had never seen anyone look so utterly relaxed as they played.

The room was clearing out by the time the set ended. Justin had left his hatch to clean tables; there was a late-night act to come, but he didn't expect much of a crowd for it. He had moved here from Ohio six years ago, he told me. He'd grown up obsessed with bluegrass, playing banjo in a family band with his teenage brothers. When his parents discovered he was gay, they sent him to conversion camp. As soon as he'd got out of college, he'd moved to Nashville and found friends and allies.

'I started out feeling like an outsider,' said Justin, 'but once I got to know the people here' – he gestured around – 'I realised they knew I was gay and they didn't care.' He often played gigs with Roland White, one of the bluegrass stars of the sixties who still performed regularly at the Inn. 'I thought it was a don't-ask-don't-tell thing, but no, he was just totally supportive of me.' Justin said he was lucky; he knew people who had lost gigs and friends in bluegrass for being gay.

There was some movement towards inclusivity, he explained. That year the California Bluegrass Association, which had a traditionally conservative membership, had voted to enter a float in San Francisco's Pride parade. That single act had won them so many new members that it was now the fastest-growing bluegrass association in the country.

I found myself rather inspired by Justin. He was so clear-eyed about the divided community he occupied, yet optimistic for it too. 'You still have two really different sets of people who think that bluegrass "represents" their side,' said

Justin. 'But the positive thing is that you can sit down next to each other and play music and just be humans together. I've been *so* many people's first gay friend.'

I thought about the struggles I'd been having with my faith, and my own identity. They were nothing compared to what Justin had faced. If he could be himself in this place, without compromising, then I really had no excuse.

Justin also helped me uncover something about Nashville I actually liked: the undercard. Behind the big brash show the town put on for the tourists and the record executives, its micro-economy of musicians were living a very different life. It turned out there was an entire community of bluegrassers clustered around the same few streets in East Nashville, the cheaper end of town. Several were people whose names I recognised from festival line-ups, musicians I had pictured crossing the country in tour buses with managers and personal assistants.

In reality, they travelled in transit vans and lived in house-shares. Having profile in bluegrass didn't mean you were making any money. The ones I met slept till noon, and spent their afternoons trying out instruments they couldn't afford at Carter's Vintage Guitars or Fred's Violin Shop. They knew the nicest places for an afternoon walk (Nashville was a lot greener once you got out of the centre). And they could show you the joints where $4.75 would buy you hot chicken so spicy that there were warnings taped to the walls on A4: 'PLEASE DO NOT RUB EYES OR USE RESTROOM UNTIL YOUR HANDS HAVE BEEN WASHED'.

In the evenings, they clustered at gigs in out-of-the-way bars where the audience was half-populated with their friends and the atmosphere was far more collegiate and caring than I had imagined the music business to feel. But then, my previous source of information had been the eponymous TV drama *Nashville*, where the characters were mostly alcoholics, pill-poppers or nymphomaniacal narcissists. No one here bore any resemblance to Juliette Barnes, or seemed about to sabotage their rivals by spreading rumours about them in the media.

Justin's first position in town had been an internship at Compass Records, whose artists included Michael Cleveland as well as the Samwell Tarley-Kurt Russell duo I had blissed out to in Colorado. Within twenty-four hours I'd been invited to the studio myself – to look around, admittedly, not to make my own record. The drive to their offices took me through downtown, past the oversized corporate edifices with which Nashville liked to assert its importance – the Bridgestone Arena, the Music City Center, the Country Music Hall of Fame.

I liked the Hall of Fame, the one part of the city's Disneyfication that I admired, with walls of video screens playing out country music's history, from the moment the 1927 Bristol Sessions turned the Carter Family into its first stars. I'd never appreciated how many distinct strains of it even existed – the only stuff I'd been exposed to in England were the Shania Twain number ones that got sung at karaoke. Here were honky-tonk, cowboy songs, Western swing, the outlaw movement, 'hard country' – a litany of styles that dazzled like the rhinestone jackets. No wonder bluegrass struggled to be heard.

Where Bill Monroe and his legacy belonged in the history of country music was an unresolved question. Was it a vestigial structure from the music's early evolution, which had diverged only when everyone else went electric? Or had it always been an outlier? Bluegrass's moment in the limelight had been brief, and even in its heyday was derided as 'hillbilly music'. Yet it wielded a disproportionate influence on what

277

followed, and inspired country legends from Johnny Cash to Waylon Jennings.

What relevance bluegrass had to the current inhabitants of Music Row was debatable. On my way to Compass, I passed the headquarters of a major record company, whose offices looked like concrete poured into a jelly-mould. Giant billboards lurched from their driveway into the sidewalk, congratulating their artists on 'Another #1 hit!' They were all men whose faces and cowboy hats were airbrushed smooth, purveyors of the so-called bro-country that ruled the radio waves with its lyrics about beers and pick-up trucks.

Turning off the main road and on to a residential side street, I stopped to check I hadn't made a mistake. The building I had arrived at looked nothing like the one I had just cruised by. It was a two-storey clapboard house that might, if anything, have housed a dentist's surgery or a small family accountancy practice. It even had a doorbell. But it was the right address, and inside I was ushered up the steep wooden stairs to meet the woman who had founded Compass Records. Alison Brown also happened to be one of the most accomplished banjo players in the business.

She showed me through a sequence of recording rooms which, despite being quite small, managed to contain a panoply of equipment and instruments - including, by sheer act of will, a grand piano. The place had a tidy yet familial air which was, perhaps, a reflection of its owner. Alison was petite and casually stylish and exuded an instant warmth. She was also a Harvard graduate with an MBA and a mind capable of divining a path through the most complex of issues.

Her company had taken over this studio thirteen years ago. In the seventies, it had been known as 'Hillbilly Central', a hippie hangout where Waylon Jennings and Willie Nelson fashioned their outlaw music, and where John Hartford recorded *Aereo-Plain*. 'When we renovated we had to patch up the holes in the wall where Waylon used to throw knives,' said Alison. 'We found drugs when we rolled up the carpets. They'd boarded up the windows and people could come any time of night or day and just create.' She patted a wall. 'And these have absorbed all that. Here was this bunch of greasy hippies and they blew the doors off the music industry!'

I knew that, in her own way, Alison had been just as pioneering. The banjo remained the most macho instrument in bluegrass - 'Southern guys still say you don't pick the banjo, you lay the thumb to the five,' she smiled. She had made her name in Alison Krauss's band in the late eighties, at a time when there weren't many women in the industry at all. Krauss was one of the few bluegrassers to make it big on the country scene, singing about bad break-ups and sad goodbyes with the voice of a wounded angel. But her banjo player, Alison Brown, was regularly told that she was 'pretty good for a girl'.

Today, the Compass Records roster of artists included women who had won major industry awards, including Missy Raines, Claire Lynch and Molly Tuttle. Change was happening, said Alison, but it took generations; there were still bluegrass bands that wouldn't employ a woman, however good she was. 'We're all at different stages of enlightenment, and how inclusive we think society should or shouldn't be,' she added, thoughtfully. 'And yet we can sit there and play "Uncle Pen". People who don't speak English, people of different races and genders - you can welcome them all into the circle.'

Justin had said the same. I was reminded of bluegrass's own background, of a recipe cooked up in America's melting pot of influences, seasoned and perfected by hillbillies and hippies. 'There's some beautiful grain of hope in the whole thing,' said Alison. 'I feel like some of the answers that we're seeking today are to be found in this community because it's such a fascinating microcosm of what this country is. If we can coexist in this music, understanding can grow from there.'

The doorbell rang, announcing one of her most venerable clients: Bobby Osborne, the mandolin-playing half of the famous Osborne Brothers. Bobby was eighty-six years old; his younger brother, Sonny, had retired more than a decade ago. But Bobby's combed-back hair still mixed plenty of black with the grey. It took him a while to get up the stairs, though.

He was a square man - or maybe his jacket's gangster shoulders just made him look so. The shirt beneath was a colour that could only be described as dun; his left sleeve ended in a gold watch. His long earlobes extended almost past his sideburns. Bobby hadn't made a solo album in years when Alison offered to champion him; even then, they had to crowdsource the project. 'A lifesaver,' was how he described it. 'I've learned the hard way that if you don't keep your name out there, they forget all about you. If you want to be in this music, Nashville is the place you've got to be.'

We all sat down to a cup of tea and I asked Bobby what the city had been like when he'd first moved here in 1964. 'It was just a plain Tennessee country town,' he said, 'maybe five or six hotels. It didn't have any of what it has now. But I was just happy to be where the Grand Ole Opry was.' He'd been born in eastern Kentucky, in a house with no electricity or running water. 'So on the weekend there wasn't nothing to do but visit with somebody who had a bigger house than you.' More specifically: someone who had a radio. It was listening to the *Opry* on Saturday nights that had fuelled the Osborne Brothers' ambition.

Bobby was a good talker, his ego held in check by his

evident eagerness to remain involved in the music. His opinions of modern bluegrass were far more generous and open-minded than I might have imagined from one of the last living bluegrass legends. He even liked some of the progressive stuff. 'But then, music's always progressing,' he said. 'In the sixties, Sonny and me used drums and electric guitars. If you don't move forward, you die.'

When Bobby played the Grand Ole Opry that weekend I went along to watch. The WSM radio show that had started it all back in 1925 was one of the city's biggest attractions, bringing busloads of out-of-towners like me to its Tuesday-, Friday- and Saturday-night broadcasts. When the audiences had grown too large for the Ryman auditorium – the converted Methodist tabernacle downtown that had housed it for thirty-one years – the Opry had moved into a purpose-built entertainment complex on the outskirts. At the time, John Hartford penned a mournful rebuke. 'They're going to tear down the Grand Ole Opry,' he sang. 'Another good thing is done gone on.'

Maybe he had a point. The vast theatre could certainly entertain thousands of punters at a time. It could also sell them rhinestone jewellery and Hatch Show Print posters and snow globes and a whole host of other merch out of its on-site store. But the stage was so deep and wide that the acts seemed remote, and there was an ersatz quality to the whole thing. When Bobby shuffled out in a boxy red suit and sang his three songs – ending as he always did with his most popular hit, 'Rocky Top' – it felt like watching the dramatic recreation of an event, rather than the event itself.

Bobby wasn't the only bluegrass legend in town. An eighty-eight-year-old Jesse McReynolds, the surviving member of Jim and Jesse, was in his fifty-third year as an Opry member; he had been promoting his Grateful Dead tribute album before a recent aneurysm put him in hospital. Mac Wiseman, an original member of Flatt and Scruggs's Foggy Mountain Boys, whose solo career earned him the moniker 'the voice with a heart', was barely mobile. The ninety-two-year-old held court, looking like a jolly Henry VIII, from under a blanket in the armchair in his living room, which was decorated for Christmas all year round. But he, too, had released an album within the past year: a collaborative effort that told the story of his own life.

I tracked down Roland White in a newly opened tap-room, at a suburban strip mall north of the airport. Roland and his brother Clarence had been trailblazers on the California bluegrass scene with their band the Kentucky Colonels; Clarence had died young, hit by a car. At seventy-nine, Roland was about to be inducted into the International Bluegrass Hall of Fame. But until then, he was playing under an exposed ceiling to a guy working on a laptop, a family playing Yahtzee, and a couple dining on mac'n'cheese and something called General Lee's meatloaf.

The band sat by the wall; Roland wore a straw fedora with a brown hatband, and an expression that belonged on a long-eared hound. He looked frail under his two shirts – blue pyjama beneath plaid flannel – and sang so quietly that I didn't recognise the song until the second verse. But there was nothing decrepit about the music. When he took a break on his mandolin, which he held close to his chest, his fingers still retained some old magic. He nodded his head to the beat, only a little detached.

His bandmates included a bass player who might have been a teenager and a banjo player who turned out to be his wife, Diane. After their set, I wandered over and said hello. This was just a small scratch gig they played with friends once a

282

week, Diane explained. Roland's regular band played at the Station Inn. He had, in fact, helped start the Station Inn back in the seventies, after Clarence had died; Roland had moved to Nashville to play first for Bill Monroe and then for Lester Flatt. He'd helped sweep the floor and keep the place going so that he and his buddies would have a place to play.

Diane could recall more of Roland's stories than he could. How as kids, Roland and Clarence had gone to a Bill Monroe gig in Los Angeles, and their father had invited the great man for lunch, sparking a lifelong relationship ('If you offered a bluegrass musician a meal, chances were they'd turn up,' said Diane). How Roland only ever scraped a living until he was in his fifties, and how the *O Brother, Where Art Thou?* film had given him a new lease of life. 'He had lots of people coming to him wanting to learn mandolin after that.'

It didn't seem to matter which stage of the curve you were at – whether you were working the bar like Justin, or playing the Opry like Bobby. If you were a bluegrasser in Nashville, there wasn't a whole lot of money or prestige; you just kept working, and you got by. It was the same reason that even the big-name artists were so approachable at festivals, and so quick to pick with their fans, or share credit and stage time with each other. Because if you chose to pursue this music, you really didn't care much about fame or fortune.

I stayed in Nashville till the following Monday evening, so I could go and see Aubrey one more time. Someone had introduced me to Carl Jackson during the week and I'd told him how much I admired Aubrey's playing. Carl had asked how I came to be in the US, so I'd explained to him about my fiddle quest. When he spotted me again at the Station Inn, while the band was taking a break after their first set, he beckoned me over.

'Have you met Aubrey yet?' he asked.

No, I said.

'Have you got your fiddle with you?'

Er. Yes.

He walked me over to the tall, placid man who was drinking a beer with a friend.

'Aubrey, this is Emma, she's a big fan of yours and she plays fiddle. Do you think you guys could do a number together in the second half?'

Aubrey, who I could tell already was a man of few words, seemed unperturbed by this request. Certainly far less perturbed than me. 'What do you wanna play?' he asked.

Even as I struggled to contain my panic at what was unfolding, some part of me was grateful to Carl. It had all happened so fast that my default reaction, to shake my head and bow out of the situation, wasn't even a possibility. Not without looking ungrateful, cowardly and an utter wimp.

I silently thanked John for all our twinning practice. 'I can do harmonies to "Wheel Hoss",' I said. 'Sure,' said Aubrey. And that was it. There was no further discussion, no practice. I just had to get out my fiddle, and sit in the audience until they called me up.

They didn't leave it long. I tried to convince myself, as I walked up to the stage, that this was all completely normal. The band had found me another stool like Aubrey's, which was kind of them, because my fear of falling off it soon outweighed my fear of messing up the music.

'Tell 'em all about yourself!' said Carl. Peering into the murky vacancy in front of me, I explained to the room where I was from. Just before we kicked off the tune, Aubrey leaned over and whispered into my right ear: 'Let's not do it too fast.' I loved him even more.

But I gave a professional nod, took a breath . . . and together we threw ourselves into the opening. My fingers were so well drilled from my days with John that I didn't need to think about what I was doing. That didn't mean my brain wasn't busy. It was becoming clogged with thoughts - like, 'Don't freak out!' and 'Don't over-think this!'

So instead, I focused all my concentration on the genius sitting next to me. I made it my mission to stay in perfect touch and time with him, and kept my eyes clamped on his fiddle. When I was brave enough to look into his face I saw something I hadn't expected: he seemed to be enjoying himself.

The notes rolled on beneath us. It felt like flying. When it was over, the audience cheered, Carl clapped me on the back, and I felt a sense of pride in my playing greater than any I'd experienced before. Aubrey leaned over and gave me a fist bump. 'That was *good*!' he said, with just the faintest hint of surprise.

After the set, I went back to the small green room, behind the kitchen, to thank Carl, and looked around to say goodbye to Aubrey. Somehow, he'd managed to leave the building within a couple of minutes of getting off-stage.

'That's session musicians for you,' said Carl. 'Always got another job to do.'

CHAPTER 26

Murphy's was closed. A sheet of paper pinned to the door announced in Arial that they were under new management. I peered through the windows to a mess of chipboard, stepladders and negative space where the booths used to be. It was even changing its name: Ransom. It didn't sound right. I'd been here half a year, and change already annoyed me.

No more jamming, then. I walked along the street, kicking my feet sulkily. I'd been looking forward to seeing my friends. It was late, and the sidewalks were empty, but the store that sold incense sticks to students and cat T-shirts to tourists was still open. I nosed around the racks for less than five minutes, but it was enough to make me feel even more lonely.

Maybe it was because I was walking at a slower pace than normal this time, that I paused at the nameless, narrow windowfront. I must have passed its blank glass a hundred times before without spotting it. No wonder: it was so gloomily illuminated you had to peer hard to see inside, to the cheap wooden fittings against the walls. The rest of the room was unfurnished and barely decorated; the two figures inside might have been squatters. But they faced away from each other, to the walls, and the way their fingers worked over something in front of them, like librarians at a drawer of filing cards, betrayed them. Boone had a record shop, and I'd never noticed.

The wash of electronica that greeted me on the other side of the door would normally have seen me off the premises pretty quickly, the way piped Bach was used to keep teenagers out of bus stations after dark. A glance along the shelves revealed that not only did I not recognise the names of the artists, I'd never heard of most of the categories, either. I saw a section marked 'ambient sound', and wondered when the music industry had started commissioning albums of background restaurant chatter and pre-theatre audience mumbles.

Standing in front of the alien vinyls, their gleaming metallic covers suggesting a future in which humans played little part, I let the noise cloud settle around me, and infiltrate my brain. Once, I would have resisted or, more likely, ignored it. Now I invited it in, felt for the underlying groove, tried to parse its dissonance. All the work I'd been doing on my fiddle - every lesson with Matt, every conversation with John - had been reconstructing the way I approached music. It was as if I'd been given a new set of ears.

Long, solo drives through the country were where I'd first noticed the change. It used to be a tortured process to find a song I could settle on at any given moment. Left to my own company, I was far more likely to put on a podcast or travel in silence. Now I would set my phone to shuffle, or leave the radio tuned in to the nearest music station it could pick up. I found myself interested in all sorts of genres I had no knowledge of - blues, funk, heavy rock. And when I heard an old, familiar track, instead of singing along, I listened closer, making out instruments, harmonies and bass runs that I could have sworn weren't there before.

I was learning, too, to let music take me to places I didn't want to go. For most of my life I had only been interested in

287

tunes that brought me instant happiness; my thumb would hover, ready to skip to the next track if they threatened to make me feel anything else. I had rejected or rationed much of the music that moved me most. Creations that felt too tender or raw or agonisingly beautiful were dangerous, made me ache inside with feelings I couldn't put words to. Those anonymous emotions were frightening, and to be avoided. Best to keep it light and cheerful.

In the record store, the electronica was making me feel anxious, but I stuck it out. I came to a corner that contained a small half-stack of bluegrass, and flicked through the dozen or so vinyls, finding comfort in the now-familiar album covers. John Hartford's long-haired hippie face hidden behind a pair of steampunk goggles: *Aereo-Plain*. *J.D. Crowe and the New South*, an album known to true aficionados by its catalogue number, Rounder 44. The blue-jeaned band had posed for their photo in jackets that looked too hot for the day.

There were a variety of Flatt and Scruggs collections, too, their sleeves all illustrated by the same man, Thomas B. Allen. The dark tones and expressionist brushwork the painter used always left Earl and Lester rather sinister-looking to me; the co-stars leered out from their portraits with malign intent and suspiciously white teeth. But Allen's work had been voguish in the sixties. These covers had been considered as modern in their time as the minimalism that now marked out ambient sound.

It was getting dark on the sidewalks when I headed back outside. Boone didn't have much in the way of street lighting, but this wasn't the kind of place you worried about being out alone, whatever time of night. The electronic beat had lodged in my head, insistent and alienating. It pushed clinically forward, dragging the present with it. I passed the places

I usually ate and drank with my friends, feeling a little worse with every step. The summer was nearly over.

At the crossroads, Doc sat on his bench, hunched over his stringless instrument. In the daytime, tourists took selfies with him; maybe that's why I'd always been too self-conscious to stop at this spot. But there was no one around now, and the hood of my jersey was pulled tight around my face, warding off both recognition and reality.

Curling my legs up on the seat next to Doc I realised what a good statue it was. Side-on, in the dark, it was weird how real he looked. Natural. Sympathetic. Andrew's dad, John, had often told me what a remarkably modest and generous man Doc was. John had known him perhaps as well as anyone in Boone. He had been in business with his son, Merle, and, after Merle had died in a tractor accident, only thirty-five, John had become one of Doc's regular drivers, taking him to gigs and home again. Doc had a fiery stubbornness, said John, and liked things done his way. But he was unparalleled in his humanity.

Perhaps that's why everyone I knew had their own Doc story. He had spoken to everyone, played with everyone, never held himself aloof. Zeb remembered a time he was busking on the street when a car with dark windows had pulled up next to his piece of pavement and its windows had rolled down to reveal Doc nodding approvingly in the back seat. Doc never claimed to play bluegrass or old-time or made any distinction between the two. He had no time for feuds or divides. He just played good music, he said.

A plaque on the bench read 'just one of the people'. The man himself had insisted on it. John had heard Doc say, before the unveiling, that if the inscription wasn't there he would tear down the statue with his own hands.

I had started my confession before I even realised that I

was speaking aloud. 'It's just so *annoying*,' I murmured. Doc listened impassively. 'I mean, Murphy's is our *place*.' I could feel the lump rising in my throat. 'I don't want to go somewhere else.'

This was silly. Talking out loud to a statue. Getting choked up over a totally unremarkable pizza joint. And what did it matter whether Murphy's closed anyway? Everyone had told me that the picking ended when winter came. People stayed home, hunkered down between the snows. There wouldn't be anything to keep me here.

It did not appear that Happy Valley was going to live up to its name. By the weekend of the contest it had been raining for days. Hurricane Harvey, which had been tearing up Texas, had visited its outlying tantrums on us in the east. Thunder broke through the mountains in long-drawn-out rolls and sudden, dramatic crashes; like God was sending his bowling ball down the heavenly lanes, and every now and then coming good with a strike. Cloud clung to the ground and refused to move. I woke up feeling morose and ill.

The weather seemed to be affecting other people's mood. On the drive down the mountain I stopped at a Wal-Mart and saw two men leave the store together; they looked like buddies until they stopped abruptly for a pre-arranged duel in the parking lot. The shorter, slighter man had darted forward, his first punch sliding off the other's shoulder, and after a few more lunges and partially connecting hits, the bigger guy had trapped him in a headlock. There was no shouting or secondary panic. A security guard who wandered over stayed to watch, and eventually the combatants broke apart and left in separate directions – a little stiffly, but without any lingering animosity.

Trevor and Savannah had met at Happy Valley and they

often remarked how pretty it was, stretched alongside the Yadkin River, surrounded by the Appalachian foothills. As my car bumped boggily across the farm that hosted the fiddlers' convention, I had to take their word for it. The verdant, forest-covered hills had disappeared, and mist and mizzle had leached the remaining sights of all colour. Only a field's worth of grass remained, much of it so long and so wet that my boots and socks were saturated by the time I'd crossed from my parking space to the registration tent.

The constant drizzle and intermittent downpours kept everyone in the contest marquee, where a mixed parade of harmonicas, flutes, accordions and folk singers were traversing the stage in the open category. My fiddle partner, John, was nowhere to be seen, but Tray was there, just returned from Cane Mill Road's debut trip to New York City, where they had been booked to play a couple of gigs in Harlem, and Casey had had an emotionally charged first encounter with an escalator.

Tray agreed to back me up on guitar for the first round of individual bluegrass fiddle. Only the top three contestants in each category made it through to the evening finals and I grimly waited my turn, my hands cold and starting to numb, my feet essentially fishbowls. After a month of excitement and anticipation, this was not the climax to my summer that I had hoped for.

It wasn't the performance I had wanted either. Self-conscious, and rather convinced that nothing good could come of this day, I had kicked off my tune a little faster than normal, and spent the first minute clinging onto it as to a mechanical bull. By the time I finally found a settled rhythm, I could see the end approaching, with its complicated sign-off. Something it now seemed I had created geologic eras ago, back when the world still knew sunshine, and my fiddling was lithe and limber.

I have never been any kind of athlete but I felt, at that moment, like a gymnast facing the vault, having told the judges I'd be doing a double-twisting Yurchenko. It already seemed like a huge mistake, but there was no way out of it, no option but to sprint down the runway. In this case, I mistimed my handspring and found myself somersaulting through the air with no sense whatsoever where the mat might be.

My pre-prepared phrases were out of reach; instead I scrambled for any note I could land as my fingers tumbled chaotically down the strings. After the ugliest of flourishes, I somehow managed to finish on the right chord. Tray had been too concerned with getting his own part right to notice anything wrong, but I was miserably angry with myself.

All that work. All those lessons. Half a year of effort and struggle and driving thousands of miles between jams – they had all come down to this, my one last chance to prove myself. And I'd blown it. The past six months had been nothing but an epic waste of time. The thought dawned on me that I wasn't made for bluegrass. That bluegrass wasn't meant for me.

Trudging through the soggy field, I found John's camper by the edge of a swollen creek. I did my best to hide my disappointment, but perhaps he intuited it: either way, his brusqueness was not as marked as normal. The win-at-all-costs approach I had grown used to as we rehearsed was temporarily absent. 'Let's get up there and have fun,' he said, as we tuned our instruments to each other. 'Let's play the "Lovers' Waltz" real pretty, and give 'em a doggone good time.'

It was the kindest thing he could have said. And when our time to perform came round, I knew he was right; the only way to put my failure behind me was to care nothing about the outcome, and rinse all the pleasure I could from the music. We played our waltz slower than usual, not labouring our technical skills or drawing attention to our clever arrangement. But the emotion - the wistfulness, the shade of regret, the pang of something over too soon - those I couldn't have kept out if I'd tried.

The afternoon wore on, and the dense mist began to disperse. Zeb and Julie arrived from a wedding they had been playing, Trevor and Savannah from his parents' farm. Jams sprang up, as soon as it was dry enough to form a circle, and added some jollity to the atmosphere. Happy Valley had none of the historic prestige of Galax or Mount Airy - the event was only fifteen years old - but the prize money was considerably better, and so it attracted musicians from multiple counties to compete in the evening band contest.

I was munching down a hamburger from the Scouts tent when Lynne and Wendell discovered me. Wendell grinned and growled something friendly; Lynne, translating, explained that they wanted to commandeer my fiddle skills for the band competition.

'We only realised youse all was here when we saw your name up on the board,' she said.

'What board?'

'The one where they announce the finalists.'

'We made the twin fiddle final?' I said. A surge of joy: I'd get to play with John once more.

Wendell clapped me on the back, and said something else. I could just make out the word 'proud'.

'Honey,' said Lynne. 'You made *both* finals.'

Did the sun really come out? It seems unlikely. There was so much collected moisture in the ground and the air that a blast of Southern sunshine would have turned the place tropical.

If it brightened at all, the effect could only have been the soft whitening of an overcast sky, and outlines sharpening around us, like a photographic image emerging in the developing tray. I know my feet never got dry - when I got home, my toes looked like pickles.

And yet my mind gave the rest of that day a golden hue, and a warmth that defied meteorological analysis. It seemed that, for one special moment, all my various friends were in the same place at the same time, sharing the music they loved. Some had known each other for ever, some were just meeting for the first time. Young liberals and ageing conservatives, John the hippie and Lynn the Baptist, gathered in the damp middle of nowhere, engaging in an art that meant more to them than anything they disagreed upon. Out here, celebrating a music that barely registered outside these mountains, everyone was an outlier, and everyone was family.

Even I belonged. The afternoon and evening were stitched together less in a sequence of events than a quilt of feelings: the vicarious pride as I watched Zeb and Tray trade licks, the group delight as we witnessed each other perform. When Trevor offered to back me up in the fiddle final, I realised I was far less excited about competing for a title than the chance to share the experience with my friend.

The finals ran early. When the PA announced bluegrass fiddle, I found Trevor still wrestling with one of the Scouts' voluminous hot dogs. I told him we were about to go on and he looked at me in alarm - 'I haven't even got a guitar,' he said. I thought it was another Trevor joke, but he was serious; he hadn't brought one with him. I waited behind the stage as he raced off, still grasping half a hot-dog bun, to scour the campsite for something to borrow. The MC gave me a serious look. Rules were rules, she said. If I wasn't ready for my slot, I'd have to forfeit.

With seconds to spare, Trevor returned. And whatever nervous paroxysms I would normally have had walking out on stage were overwhelmed by the thought of my friend hurtling through a muddy field, determined to have my back. Later, I could remember nothing of how I played that night. Not a note that went through my fingers seemed to have made an impression on me. I could have been under hypnosis, for all I could recall.

The comforting, unshakeable rhythm of the guitar, however - that remained. And the artful runs that Trevor threw in, solely to make me sound better. The presence of my friend alongside me was the validation I'd been seeking all this time - the only endorsement my playing needed. I had fallen in love with bluegrass for its showmanship, but the past year had taught me that it was nothing without relationship.

So I didn't, strictly, require the red ribbon that I won for second place. I didn't even *need* the blue one I took with John, after we won the twin fiddle title. But it would have been churlish to turn them down, or the two hundred dollars in winnings that came with them. And I can't deny I sat in John's camper van that evening with a new appreciation of how it felt to be a state-sanctioned bluegrass musician.

I left him late that night, still clutching a bottle of vegan wine. We had thoroughly debriefed our performance - a daredevil ride of speed and skill that, we rather thought, rivalled a pair of Top Gun pilots. I had almost reached the fence when his voice followed me into the dark.

'I *told* you we'd do it!' he yelled. 'Y'all better come back now.'

A brief and incomplete history of bluegrass, part 7

Pierce Van Hoy ran his last fiddlers' convention at Union Grove in 1979. There were one hundred thousand people there, and every one of them came home with a story involving sex or drugs or alcohol. The Hell's Angels were rumoured to be running security. The State Police shut it down.

Harper's fiddlers' convention kept going until his death in 2013.

Bill Monroe made up with his brother Charlie. He made up with the Stanley Brothers, and for some time Carter Stanley played in his band as a Bluegrass Boy. Bill even started picking with Lester Flatt and Earl Scruggs again. These things weren't for ever.

Earl and Lester had their own falling-out. They recorded their last album together in 1969. The Bob Dylan and Leonard Cohen and Johnny Cash covers they were playing at the time were largely to blame for the split. Earl had embraced the next generation's music and wanted to push the boundaries of bluegrass. Lester wanted to keep it traditional.

So they went their separate ways. Earl started a rock 'n' roll band with his sons and became a national treasure. Lester kept playing the classics and faded from view. They didn't speak for a while.

In the early eighties, Sam Bush was diagnosed with cancer and had to undergo several surgeries. During one spell in hospital, the phone rang, and it was Bill Monroe, calling with sympathy and support, offering to help him out in any way he could. Sam and Bill played together on stage before Bill died. These things weren't for ever.

Pierce Van Hoy's son Casey took over his dad's farm. He said the family feud was always a bit overblown; it made a better story, he guessed. The brothers had made up long before they died, even if they still saw life differently. Even if they didn't always understand each other.

Casey had a photo from the fifties, of his grandfather HP holding a fiddle. Pierce was on one side of him, and Harper on the other. And when Casey looked at it, he thought, you know, everybody got what they wanted in the end. Grandpa got the legacy, Dad got the publicity, and Uncle Harper got the legitimacy.

There are still fiddlers' conventions at Union Grove.

CHAPTER 27

Everything was pumpkin, Julie told me, come September. Pumpkin candles, pumpkin candy, pumpkin ale, pumpkin soup, pumpkin lattes: its gourdy glory was suddenly expected to scent, flavour and colour every aspect of our lives. Julie wasn't exaggerating: I watched, bemused, as people went legitimately insane for what I had always considered an essentially low-ranking vegetable.

Roadside encampments sprouted overnight selling giant orange pyramids of the crop. The swollen bodies looked perky enough until you tried to lift one into the car, and realised it had the density of a neutron star. When you got it home, and broke it open, you noticed two more things. That everything you touched was now indelibly stained with pumpkin, and that you were going to have to eat the wretched stuff for a month.

The trees, too, began to turn pumpkin. It had taken me by surprise, the colour change - not that it was sudden, but that it happened at all. I'd come to think of the forest scenery as evergreen; its vast verdure had become the de facto backdrop to this act of my life, a presence more constant and intimate than man or God. The discovery that it would, within the next month or two, transform the hillsides into a fiery canvas - that this unfashionable hinterland would rival uppity New

England in its autumn spectacle – was just one more reason to love it.

The drive west back to Boone – from John's house, from Taylorsville, from any number of gigs, conventions and festivals – had become my favourite journey. I loved the way the farmland of the Piedmont rolled up and down in increasingly exaggerated fashion, a long, slow wink, teasing you with the prospect of home. A first, far-off glimpse of the Blue Ridge, at the crest of a particularly prodigious hill, disappeared almost immediately as you bowled down the other side. It would be half an hour before you got another peek. And then it would be gone again, the game repeated over and over, the prize a little larger each time.

I had approached the mountains in all kinds of weather, and all types of light. They never disappointed. Against a clear blue sky they were imperial, casting their own majestic shadows, projecting their blue and purple outlines in a panorama that laughed in the lens of your puny iPhone camera. Rafts of cumulus brought out their homelier side, and revealed the breadth of their palette, greens from avocado skin to bar-bottle chartreuse. The intermittent sunlight became a highlighter pen drawing attention to different parts of its folio.

In thicker cloud they turned mystic, artistic, even mischievous. Sometimes the vapour skirted their peaks in dark layers that created a mirror world above them. Sometimes it drew upwards like steam from a bath. Once I witnessed it in grey, low-floating wisps that made me think I was driving through a volcano. The mountains retained their beauty even when, on dark days, they faded to monochrome like Japanese prints, or disappeared behind fog to leave just a suggestion of themselves, as through tracing paper.

The best time to make the trip was sunset, when the clouds

seemed to embark on their most creative projects: giant confections of frosted icing, or waves that raced towards the horizon, first as surf, then as smoke, trailing licks of orange flame. For a time, the sky would outshine the mountains, its reds and pinks and yellows in violent combinations you would find distasteful anywhere but nature. But then, once the show was over, a quieter bronze backlit the ridge, and returned it to prominence.

Even in the dark, the journey could be beguiling. A couple of times I had set off too late to enjoy the view, driving home by headlight and autopilot, until a growing awareness of something large and silent had caused me to turn my head to find one of these ageless elders, robed in midnight blue. In silhouette, they always seemed more immediate than ever, protective, near.

Another night, I had found myself barrelling towards a storm. Two lightning strikes, one to the left, and then to the right, had momentarily revealed that I was trapped inside an enclosing ravine, before a huge orange flash lit up a thunder-cloud dead ahead, like a supervillain showing up for a date with the Avengers.

Right now, however, I was making the trip in daylight; it was warm, but not too warm, bright, but not too bright. I decided, once I reached the foothills, to turn off the main highway; there was something about the afternoon I wanted to eke out. Besides, the colours were coming on daily. Julie had told me they were still a couple of weeks from their full splendour. But I liked this stage, when you could be surprised by a single pink tree peeping shyly from among the green. At higher elevations, the russets and reds were gaining in quick, vibrant patterns like the embroidery on an Appalachian quilt.

It had happened enough that it no longer scared me: the heady combination of pain and pleasure that the sight of

300

the mountains evoked. I hadn't experienced such visceral emotion for a place before – not for the town I'd grown up in, or the houses I'd lived in. Not even for London, the city I considered the peak of civilisation, the defence of whose cultural life was the closest I'd ever come to patriotism.

Sure, I had felt wonder at my city. My chest still inflated with pride whenever I took the number 10 bus across the Waterloo Bridge, as I ritualistically turned my head left to right and took in the Shard, the Eye, the Houses of Parliament. But the effect of the mountains had been new to me, eliciting sensations I'd only ever heard in song and cliché.

There was a tug on my heart as I returned to them, as if some small child was trying to get my attention, and had by chance grabbed hold of the most tender part of me. The fibre of my insides pulled and stretched. Were they reaching out to the mountains themselves, trying hopelessly to touch them, to connect?

I would swallow down mixed emotions, a blend of love and pain. Sometimes they were so acute I wanted to cry out, and made do with a frustrated groan that I was glad no one else could hear. Sometimes tears fell, unexpected, for no discernible reason. It was like my soul was getting too big for my body, and trying to break out.

Today, the smaller roads took me along miles of winding hills, past the rough ephemera of rural life. Cars and vans rusted in overgrown drives and unmown fields. Their decomposing bodies were complemented by a number of derelict gas stations, slabs of concrete floor still intact, vestigial signage advertising 1990s prices.

When I had first arrived in the South, I'd found the preponderance of these abandoned fuelling places somewhat menacing, a borrowed vision from an apocalyptic, post-oil future. It didn't help that I'd seen one of them proclaim

'**DIE E**' in large black lettering. The prevalence of decrepit vehicles had been a bit too *Deliverance* for comfort. Now, however, these corroding edifices seemed to me at one with nature's own decomposition, as brown and rotting as nurse logs.

Of actual humans, there was no sign. A school noticeboard reminded invisible students that homecoming weekend was upon them. Thin green placards indicated sideroads that might yield family homes or farms, hidden out of sight. They bore names that sounded like *Dallas* characters: Misty Meadows, Cane River, Forest Fisher, Mitchell Prospect. I passed a number of Cemetery Lanes and Cemetery Avenues; sometimes I saw the tombstones themselves. Over the course of the drive, I reckoned I was averaging a memento mori every thirty minutes. Proof of death was far easier to come by, here, than proof of life.

Crossing a one-lane bridge, I followed the winding road next to a verge of long grass that my car set waving like a metronome. The windows were rolled down, an attempt to somehow suck in the loveliness outdoors. And then, travelling downhill, I saw in front of me a lime tree, still in full leaf. Its outline was that of a tubby ace of spades, and it seemed to radiate its bright harlequin green. It was the perfect facsimile of a tree, one more instantly tree-like than artist had ever managed to convey.

The lime tree seemed to embody all the beauty this countryside held: beauty real and imagined, remembered and never been. I thought of the doomed tale of the American chestnut, the majestic creature that had once populated these hills with its stunning corkscrewed trunk and its useful lumber. Progress, in the guise of imported wood from Japan, had been its executioner, spreading a formerly unknown blight through its community on the same helpful winds that used to scatter its seed. Trevor had told me how the same was now happening to the hemlocks, whose stark carcasses still stood, long after they had died, reaching above the treeline with stubs of arms, like lightning-blackened telegraph poles.

A sadness opened up somewhere inside me, not quite stomach, not quite heart. An ellipse of melancholy. I listened to the voice coming through my car stereo, singing about his childhood in the old Kentucky hills. The music felt like a companion, a familiar presence that held my hand and murmured: stay here a while.

I had spent the last few days in Raleigh. It was one of those North Carolina cities like Charlotte and Asheville that appeared, from the outside at least, as an antidote to the heavy conservatism of the rest of the state. Each year it hosted the climactic gathering of the bluegrass community in its concrete conference centre downtown. The music industry celebrated itself with a lavish awards do, and the Marriott opened its doors to a 24/7 pickathon, where three entire floors of hotel rooms and every square metre of public space were commandeered by live music.

It was a curious week. The fact that every bluegrass lover you had ever met was in attendance meant that you couldn't make a trip across the lobby without being greeted by three or four familiar faces. And yet the scale of the event made it nigh-on impossible to track down your picking friends, or get them together for a session. All day long, I'd bump into folk I wanted to jam with, and we'd chatter excitedly about hooking up in the evening, then go our separate ways and not see each other again for two days.

The Raleigh gathering did, however, offer a great observation platform – a chance to see bluegrass's extremely different constituencies all collected in one place. The week played like a highlights reel of my summer: a hug from Carl Jackson, pizza with Cane Mill Road, late-night chats with Ty, a bar gig with Never Too Late. My own playing had plateaued since the high of Happy Valley. I felt OK about that. It was the taking part that counted.

One of the purposes of the event was to showcase emerging artists: the second-, third- and even tenth-tier bands that bookers needed to fill the majority of their summer programming. Bars, churches and hotel suites became full-time music venues, and the streets crawled with musicians slinging their cases from one thirty-minute set to the next. They came from every part of the country, thick drawls contending with the tinny yabber of New York, West Coast ease meeting Midwest formality.

Come 1 a.m., when the showcases were mostly over, they joined the jams in hotel corridors and elevator lobbies, keen to see what else was out there, to source new licks and tricks. Each night was a fresh shuffle of the pack, and you never knew what you'd hear. Fast jams, slow jams, hardgrass, spacegrass, hybrid crossovers with drum kits and slide guitars and melodicas, deep dives into Jim and Jesse B-sides.

Everyone was exposed to everything. There were eye-opening experiences and unlikely collaborations. I overheard one of the Berklee graduates declaring her eagerness to join the mashers in the business centre. Another night I saw the fiddler Nicky Sanders – one of bluegrass's biggest superstars – playing a closed-circuit tour of the lobby escalators, as youngsters rushed to provide back-up. It was like watching the Pied Piper riding a magic carpet.

I had been picturing bluegrass as two worlds colliding, but here was an entire solar system. There were festival junkies and industry professionals and folk who picked in their garage. There were bands with light shows, bands in suits, bands in skirts; bands who made you shake your head at their brilliance, and bands who made you dance so hard your beer slopped over the floor.

There were academics who went to bed early and met at breakfast to analyse the discourse of self-expression in 1960s song choreography. There were teachers who complained that the kids today were *too* advanced. There were women, and people from different ethnic backgrounds, and a showcase hosted by Bluegrass Pride. There was a speech by Rhiannon Giddens that proclaimed, 'Music can bring us together in a way indoctrination can't.'

And still some argued that the focus on inclusivity and diversity was unnecessary – that the industry was trying to solve problems bluegrass didn't have. I listened to at least one person argue that the Southern white working-class male was as marginalised as anyone: 'This is already a minority's music!'

The awards told their own story; almost every winner came from the bluegrass heartland or played in the approved, straight-ahead style. The most popular act, voted Entertainer of the Year, was the Earls of Leicester – a supergroup of sorts, in which a number of already beloved bluegrass musicians had joined forces to meticulously recreate the sound of fifties Flatt and Scruggs.

And they were, indeed, hugely entertaining. They took to the stage in old-school hats and Kentucky gentleman ties and when someone yelled a request – 'Your Love Is Like a Flower!' – their band leader, Jerry Douglas, responded, 'Thanks! So's yours!' Lester Flatt's smooth radio voice and high-pitched singing was faultlessly channelled by Shawn Camp, in real life a big-time country singer. And the offhand manner in which he rendered 'I don't care what you do any more' made me understand, for the first time, how cool Flatt

305

and Scruggs's attitude might have been to their contemporary audience.

I admired Jerry, whose zesty Dobro playing had flavoured many an Alison Krauss album. And I got to meet him, when I managed to crash the VIP awards reception by wearing a smart dress and walking confidently along a red carpet through a door completely devoid of security. (I wish I felt some sense of shame about my behaviour, but I didn't then, and I still don't. I had become accustomed to my British accent endowing me with outrageous privilege, plus, bluegrass was just too damn friendly for its own good.)

Jerry, whose own back catalogue was as eclectic as they come, told me how the Earls had been his personal passion project. It was begun as a mark of respect to a style he himself had helped to dismantle in the seventies when he played with artists like J.D. Crowe and Ricky Skaggs and Tony Rice. 'I knew even then that was the end of the Flatt and Scruggs sound that I loved so much,' Jerry said. 'We did all these alternative versions of their songs, tearing it up and changing them. That sound was gone.'

He was glad that the Earls of Leicester could transport older folk back to a forgotten time. But Jerry was just as pleased that younger kids would ask him 'What the heck was that?' and he could direct them to a whole world of classic recordings. His early listening, he said, had been a mash-up – of his dad's rehearsals with a band of West Virginian migrants working in the Ohio steel mills, and his own obsession with whatever the Beatles and the Stones did next. 'If I can help someone else to bridge the divide, that's great.'

I met another of my idols in Raleigh: Matt Glaser, my fiddle teacher. He had come down from Boston to give a couple of presentations, first as part of a panel of academics, and then to the high-school kids (and parents) still wondering what college to apply for. I bumped into him after the first and before the second, perched on the edge of a colourless synthetic couch outside an equally colourless conference room.

Beside him were a bevy of current and former students, who were entertaining themselves with esoteric improvisation and bouts of irony. After all these months in the South I couldn't help noticing their comparative brashness. They spoke with a licence and a cutting humour I'd been used to in my old London life, but in these surroundings felt a little raw.

Matt himself had just managed to convince a room of educators that Berklee's required reading included a 1,500-page Cryptonomicon by Ralph Stanley's former fiddler, Curly Ray Cline. He had been giving a talk on bluegrass's radical beginnings, tracing the influence of Louis Armstrong, Charlie Christian and Benny Goodman in the music of Bill Monroe and his followers. I found it heartening to watch his enthusiasm on the topic boil over, as we sat surrounded by his protégés. I might never be able to play music the way they did, but I was proud to have the same teacher.

I knew there were people elsewhere in this building who were still suspicious of Matt's difference and who considered him, like me, an outsider. But his detachment gave him a rare and valuable perspective. I heard one of his pupils ask: 'Matt, do you *love* bluegrass?' and Matt paused before answering. He looked around the hotel corridor, with its passionate pickers creating a welter of sound that would have sent more than half of the world running for the check-out desk. 'I love humanity,' he said. 'And bluegrass is a part of that.'

Some of my Boone friends, like Julie, thought that walking in the mountains was the closest you could come to heaven on earth. Personally, I preferred to be in a car. Hikes were perfectly enjoyable. I could appreciate the soft rustle of the trails through the woods, and a certain claustrophilia from the enclosing bars of timber. I never grew bored of the utterly predictable yet always breathtaking moment when you reached a lookout: the splendour of Appalachia's solid vista, of nature so huge and immutable and unavoidable it practically punched you in the face.

But for me the majesty of the mountains intensified on the move. They were more characterful, more alive. Hurling my car up and down their backs and bellies, clinging tightly as I circled their midriff, I experienced their dramatic dimensions in high-definition 3-D. The slopes crowded so close they played tricks with perspective, layering the background at confusing angles. Sometimes they made the climbs seem steeper than they were. More than once they confused me into thinking I was heading downhill when I was actually going up, and I had wondered worriedly why my car was starting to wheeze before I caught on to their game.

Bill Monroe was still singing from my car speakers.

I'm on my way back to the old home
The road winds up round the hill...

I drove on towards Boone, past harmony and dissonance. The harvest bounty at a fruit-and-vegetable stall reflected the hills beyond; green and brown squashes, yellow gourds, peaches, oranges, the inevitable pumpkin. Ageing barns retreated into their surroundings, dark grey fibre returning to the earth; shimmering pick-up trucks pulled out of driveways, flickering light from their bright bodies. I passed a beaten-looking trailer, a low-ceilinged shipping-container of a home; on the very next plot was a manor house with fancy chimneys and a portico and a garden of immaculate bedding that must have taken a team of gardeners to keep primped.

Golden leaves fell in sudden squalls, raining paper. The higher I climbed, the more varied the colour spectrum became. Trees in startling reds stood out from their less fashion-forward tribe. The dirty grey webs were visible all over. Only recently had I learned that they weren't made by spiders at all. They were cocoons made by caterpillars. Not everything around here was as it seemed.

But there's no light in the window
That shined long ago where I live

I let myself feel it, the ache of sentiment. The lonesome, keening voice expressed the sadness of a life that can be lived no way but forward. To be human was to live under tensions that would never be resolved: between aloneness and togetherness; between understanding and misunderstanding; between what had been, and what was to come. The voice called out across the divide of past and present, all too aware that we could never relive what had come before. We could only mourn its passing.

I had made a confession to Matt, about the awards reception I so shamelessly busted into: I told him how I had found myself surrounded by the great and the good of bluegrass, and realised I still only recognised a fraction of the faces. It seemed to sum up my time in the States, I said: a little knowledge just served to highlight my vast reserves of ignorance. Matt had shrugged. 'If you learned one thing all year it's worth it,' he said. 'No one ever cracks this music.'

But I wasn't sure of even bluegrass's basic rudiments any more. I'd been taught that the music I loved had strict rules – and discovered that they were constantly broken. I'd been sold a history shaped by bitter feuds, only to discover that its joyously unlikely collaborations were just as defining. I *knew* that bluegrass was riven in two by diametrically opposing cultures. And I'd also seen that they mostly got on just fine.

Who the future of bluegrass belonged to remained a mystery. It was hard enough to judge who could claim its past. Maybe it was a mistake to think it belonged to anyone. After all, here I was, choked up on nostalgia for a past I never knew. Hearing the call of music and mountains I knew I couldn't leave, not yet. I may have arrived a stranger, but this place, and its people, hadn't allowed me to keep my status for long. Acquaintances had turned friends had turned family. Now my own memories were soaking into the landscape.

I listened again to the song, and looked once more at the mountains. They may not have been part of my history, but surely they were part of my future. The car took me forward, to a town I'd learned to call home.

SONGS CITED

'Black Dog', John Paul Jones, Jimmy Page, Robert Plant (1971)

'Coming Home', Forrest O'Connor (2016)

'A Far Cry from Lester and Earl', Junior Sisk, Tim Massey, Rick Pardue (2011)

'I Don't Care Anymore', Tompall Glaser (1958)

'Mother's Only Sleeping', Lance and Maynard Spencer (1941)

'Rain and Snow', traditional

'Roly Poly', Fred Rose (1946)

'Salty Dog Blues', traditional

'Tear Down the Grand Ole Opry', John Hartford (1971)

'Tennessee 1949', Leroy Drumm and Pete Goble (1987)

'Uncle Pen', Bill Monroe (1950)

'The Wayfaring Stranger', traditional

'White House Blues', traditional

'You Go to Your Church, and I'll Go to Mine', Phillips H. Lord (1930)

ACKNOWLEDGEMENTS

Southern hospitality is not a myth. And - unless I win the lottery - there is no way I can ever repay the kindness and generosity of the people I met on my travels. I can only hope that, when they read this, they will at least understand how special they are to me.

And, of course, how responsible they are for the story in the first place. There would have been nothing to write had Diane Merryman not made that fateful call to Fred Meekins, who sadly passed away in 2019, or had Fred and Doris not welcomed me into their home. The town of Boone wouldn't have felt half so magical if Andrew, Carrie, John, Pat and the rest of the Payne family hadn't adopted me on sight. Or if Trevor, Zeb, Julie and a host of others - like Brandon Holder, Cecil and Julie Gurganus, Steve Johnson, Wayne, Barbara and Annie Erbsen - hadn't decided that I was OK to have around. I love them dearly.

So many caring folk invited me into their houses, many when I was still a stranger. Owen and Pam Margolis, Amy and Kirby Nelson, Jack and Martha Betts, John and Susan Ritchhart, McRoy and Julia Gardner, Tom and Millie Cox, Judy Richtel, Rebecca Jones, Amy Jacobs, Michael Yuen, Bryan Armen Graham - your welcome and friendship have meant everything to me. And Geneva Masters, you remain my all-time favourite roommate.

The bluegrass world is so open and community-spirited that many of its best-known musicians happily gave up their time to talk to me, and their insight was invaluable. Thanks to Darin and Brooke Aldridge, Seth and Scott Avett, Alison Brown, Becky Buller, Sam Bush, Michael Cleveland, Lois Constable, Jerry Douglas, Béla Fleck, Bobby Hicks, David Holt, Sarah Jarosz, Jens and Uwe Kruger, Doyle Lawson, CJ Lewandowski, Tim O'Brien, Bobby Osborne, Carson Peters, Tim Surrett, Bryan Sutton, Sean Watkins, Pete Wernick, Roland White, the late Mac Wiseman; and bands Mandolin Orange, and the Steep Canyon Rangers. And my special appreciation to Chris Eldridge, who doesn't mind that I can't pronounce his nickname, or that our conversations have sometimes gone on for hours.

The Belk Library at Appalachian State University was my de facto office for nearly a year; I wouldn't have got this project finished half so quickly if Dean Williams hadn't been there, suggesting books, checking that I was *actually* working, and taking me out for lunch. Among the titles I researched, Richard D. Smith's biography of Bill Monroe, *Can't You Hear Me Callin'* (2000), has been invaluable, as has Ralph Stanley's *Man of Constant Sorrow* (2009), and Neil V. Rosenberg's comprehensive *Bluegrass: A History* (1985). I was also fortunate to speak to Gordon Castelnero and David L. Russell, authors of *Earl Scruggs: Banjo Icon* (2017), and to Ken Irwin and Marian Levy, founders of the Rounder record label. (And to be Facebook friends with Brett Bass for the banjo jokes.)

A few names have been changed in this story - some to avoid confusion, some to avoid awkwardness - and sometimes I have combined incidents that happened on different occasions. These include stories previously published in an article for *Afar* magazine which was the genesis of this book.

I'm very grateful to Fred Bartenstein and Alexandra Davison for reading my manuscript - this is a better book for their excellent interventions. Thanks, too, to my agent, Mark Stanton, at the North Literary Agency, my editor, Simon

Wright, and my publisher, Alan Samson, at Weidenfeld & Nicolson, for all their patience and wisdom. And thank you Rob Biddulph, for once again making a book I've written look so very pretty.

My friends in the UK have been very forbearing as I've bombarded them with pictures of places much warmer than London. Thanks to the Eagles for their long-range support, and to Nicola and Alastair Little for letting me crash so often. My deepest sympathies to my mum and dad, who have found themselves cooking for me, doing my washing and lending me their car on far too many occasions. And to Kate and Justin and Isabella - in whose house many of these words were written, with the help of bourbon and *Justified* - all my love.